THE PROBLEM OF YOUTH

Also by Paul Ryan

INTERNATIONAL COMPARISONS OF VOCATIONAL EDUCATION AND TRAINING

Also by Paolo Garonna

LA NATURA DELLA DISOCCUPAZIONE GIOVANILE ED I PROCESSI DI AGGIUSTAMENTO

IL MARGINE E LA VOCE

Also by Richard C. Edwards

CONTESTED TERRAIN, SEGMENTED WORK, DIVIDED WORKERS
(*with David Gordon and Michael Reich*)

UNIONS IN CRISIS AND BEYOND
(*with Paolo Garonna and Franz Tödtling*)

THE FORGOTTEN LINK: Labor's Stake in International Economic Cooperation
(*with Paolo Garonna*)

The Problem of Youth

The Regulation of Youth Employment and Training in Advanced Economies

Edited by

Paul Ryan
Lecturer, Faculty of Economics and Politics, and
Fellow, King's College, University of Cambridge

Paolo Garonna
Professor of Applied Economics, University of Padua

and

Richard C. Edwards
Professor and Chair, Department of Economics
University of Massachusetts, Amherst

First published 1991

Published by
MACMILLAN ACADEMIC AND PROFESSIONAL LTD
Houndmills, Basingstoke, Hampshire RG21 2XS
and London
Companies and representatives
throughout the world

Edited and typeset by Povey/Edmondson
Okehampton and Rochdale, England

Printed in Hong Kong

British Library Cataloguing in Publication Data
The problem of youth: the regulation of youth employment
and training in advanced economies.
1. Developed countries. Young persons. Employment
I. Ryan, Paul II. Garonna, Paolo III. Edwards, Richard C.
1944–
331.34091722
ISBN 0–333–49380–X

Contents

v

Preface

We dedicate this volume to the memory of Ezio Tarantelli, whose untimely death overshadowed the period during which this research project was conceived.

The project has brought together people engaged in research on youth employment and training in different advanced economies. Our goal was to produce from a process of collaborative research and collective discussion new insights into the ways in which youth economic activity is structured in advanced economies, as well as the desirability of its varying results. The research group decided to avoid the conventional collection of single country case studies, preferring where possible to use national comparisons, principally on a two-country basis.

The chapters in this volume have developed from papers previously presented and discussed at conferences in Trento, in 1986, and Palermo, in 1988. The editors thank the participants both for their own contributions and for their interest in those of their colleagues.

The project is indebted to the Agenzia del Lavoro of the Provincia Autonoma di Trento and the Social Science Research Council of New York for the financial assistance which made the two conferences possible. We also thank the Faculties of Economics at both the University of Trento and the University of Palermo for their generous assistance with facilities and their remarkable hospitality to participants.

Finally, we thank our editors at Macmillan for their patience and assistance in publishing the results of the research; Dr M. Franchi, Professor E. Fazio, Dr A. Imperato and colleagues for their hospitality during our visits to Trento and Palermo; and Gale, Daniela and Carolyn for support during our editorial labours.

PAUL RYAN
PAOLO GARONNA
RICHARD C. EDWARDS

Notes on the Contributors

Tinie Akkermans is Lecturer in the Department of Administrative and Policy Sciences of the Catholic University of Nijmegen. He directs the William Reynaerts Foundation, which is concerned with the dissemination of expertise in industrial relations in social market economies to the former Eastern Bloc countries.

Richard C. Edwards is chair of the Economics Department of the University of Massachusetts, Amherst.

Albert J. A. Felling is Professor of Methodology in the Social Sciences Faculty of the Catholic University of Nijmegen.

Paolo Garonna is Deputy Director of Manpower, Social Affairs and Education at the OECD in Paris. Since 1987 he has held the chair of Applied Economics at the University of Padua. Between 1983 and 1989 he was economic adviser to the Italian government.

Jean-François Germe is Director of ADEP (Agence pour le Développement de la Formation Professionnelle) in Paris. He was previously deputy director of CEREQ (Centre d'Etudes et de Recherches sur les Qualifications) and a staff member of CNRS (Centre National de la Recherche Scientifique).

David Marsden is Senior Lecturer in Industrial Relations at the London School of Economics. He has been a Visiting Professor at the University of Aix–Marseille and Visiting Research Director at LEST (Laboratoire d'Economie et de Sociologie du Travail), Aix-en-Provence.

Jan Peters is Senior Lecturer in the sub-Faculty of Cultural Sociology and Sociology of Religion of the Catholic University of Nijmegen.

Paul Ryan is Lecturer in the Faculty of Economics and Politics and Fellow of King's College at the University of Cambridge.

Karen Schober-Brinkmann is Research Officer at the Institut für Arbeitsmarkt und Berufsforschung of the Bundesanstalt für Arbeit, (Federal Employment Institute), Nürnberg.

Eskil Wadensjö is director of the Swedish Institute for Social Research, University of Stockholm.

1 The Problems Facing Youth

Paolo Garonna and Paul Ryan

1.1 INTRODUCTION

Youth issues range wide in modern society. They include the extent and quality of education; the age at which personal independence, responsibility and citizenship are attained; the control of social deviance; and sexuality and health. A further category, youth employment and training, provides the 'problem of youth' upon which this book concentrates.

The problem of youth has two dimensions: the problems facing young people themselves and the problems which youth poses to the wider economy. Taking the former first, the problem for youth during the last two decades has been to find employment and to acquire skills. Public policy in advanced economies has reacted strongly but unevenly to this set of problems.

A range of factors is responsible. The first group is well recognised: economic, social and technical change. Economic stagnation and recovery have pushed youth employment and training in varied and often adverse directions. New technology, international competition and industrial restructuring have come to be seen as dependent upon high and malleable skills in much of the workforce and, thus, upon the vocational preparation of young people. Demographic swings have caused major fluctuations in the size of the youth labour force.

A second set of factors pushing youth issues to the fore involves the demands of youth itself. Rising levels of income and education have fostered more independent attitudes amongst young people and encouraged reductions in the legal age of majority. To some extent youth inclinations towards earlier independence have come into conflict with fiscal restraint, particularly when governments have cut back youth eligibility for income support; to some extent they have proven complementary, as when government has promoted training rather than income maintenance for the unemployed young.

A third group of influences provides the distinctive area of interest for this book: the interdependence between issues of youth employ-

1

ment and training, on the one hand, and broader socioeconomic institutions, on the other. These linkages tend to be neglected, particularly by economists who study the youth labour market as a self-contained institution. They have become increasingly important in the contemporary period, as issues of job quality and life-cycle decision-making have come to the fore. To study questions of youth jobs and skills in isolation from their institutional context, as is commonplace in the economics literature, has become increasingly invalid. This analysis emphasises the institutional – in particular the industrial relations – context in which youth employment and training are determined.

Such considerations point towards the second aspect of the problem of youth – the problems *posed by* youth to the rest of the economy. It is difficult to devise institutions to introduce young workers to skills, jobs and careers in ways which suit the interests of all parties – employers, trade unions, the state and young people themselves – and which are simultaneously stable and capable of adaptation to economic change. These issues provide the focus of chapter 2 and arise thereafter throughout the book.

We begin this chapter by considering the nature of youth as a socioeconomic category (section 1.2). The two principal aspects of the economic problems facing youth in advanced economies during the last 20 years are then discussed: access to employment (section 1.3) and skills and careers (section 1.4). In each case we consider both the extent of the problem and its importance for public policy. Section 1.5 concludes and introduces the succeeding chapters.

1.2   YOUTH AS A CATEGORY: STOCK AND FLOW ATTRIBUTES

The existence and definition of youth as a category is often taken for granted. Yet some deny the distinctiveness of youth as a social or economic category, while those who accept it vary widely in the age range which they take to constitute 'youth.'

The Distinctiveness of Youth?

Scepticism concerning the viability of youth as a socioeconomic category is fostered by its attributes as both flow and stock. The fluidity of youth reflects its transitional status. Everyone is young at one stage; no one is young for long, particularly if the youth age range is defined narrowly (e.g. 16–21 years). The age frontier between youths and adults is ill-defined and flows across any particular boundary are large. Moreover, even when a youth category is defined, its attributes as a stock both overlap with those of adults and show internal heterogeneity, creating further doubt on the score of distinctiveness.[1]

Detailed consideration suggests, however, that the attributes of youth as a stock are moderately distinct from those of adults, while the high fluidity of youth as a group must be counted as its most distinctive, albeit ambivalent, trait.

The economic characteristics of youth as a stock are particularly marked in terms of labour supply. Youth stands out for its willingness to work for low pay; its low experience in and information about the labour market; the high level and the up-to-date content of its schooling; its high interest in obtaining vocational training; and its low and variable rate of labour force participation (Banks and Ullah, 1987; Ryan, 1987; section 1.3, below). Of course, these traits do not characterise all young workers and some, such as a low supply price, are shared with other groups of secondary workers, such as females and immigrants.

The separateness of youth is less clear on the demand side, where a variety of inferences concerning the substitutability or otherwise of youth and adult labour can be seen in the literature and the balance of evidence suggests that technical substitutability is significant.[2] The final economic aspect, the determination of the price of youth labour, is however distinctive for its variability by time and place and constitutes a central issue in this book.[3]

The distinctiveness of youth as a flow reflects two features. The first is a process of transition, involving rapid personal change as individuals move from childhood to adulthood. An important implication is an ambivalent and changing individual identity, along with an important role for plans, aspirations and dreams. A further implication is internal heterogeneity within the youth group along a spectrum of maturity from child to adult (Murphy, 1990).

The second feature of youth from the flow side is the high turnover of its membership, reflecting the narrowness of its age range (in most definitions) by contrast to those of other groups, whether classified by age (e.g. adults, prime-age workers) or other criteria (females, immigrants). A key implication of high turnover is an ambiguous and erratic group identity – an important source of difficulty in forming and maintaining youth organisations in trade unions, for example.

The importance of the process aspect of youth requires emphasis. Even were the stock characteristics of youths and adults indistinguishable, for example, in terms of labour market status and behaviour, the fact that young people share with each other but not with adults a key transitional status would make youth a distinct category. Conversely, even were the stock characteristics of youth clearly different from those of adults, the coherence and identity of youth as a group would still remain precarious in the face of rapid rates of outward mobility, as its members turn into adults.

At the same time, the continuous renewal of its membership maintains youth as a potential source of pressure for social and economic change, however uneven and episodic it may prove. The passage of successive generations through the labour market involves complex and delicate processes of adaptation, in which youth is simultaneously subject and object. Youth is the object in that it has to learn how to respond to its institutional context; but it is also the subject, in that it can trigger institutional change. The task facing institutions is simultaneously to channel youth and to preserve and utilise its vitality and capacity for change.

These developmental attributes of youth may, however, be becoming less distinctive in advanced economies, to the extent that retraining, lifetime learning, career development, etc. affect an increasing segment of the population.

Youth is thus simultaneously a stock with a distinct combination of socioeconomic attributes and a process of transition with strong development traits and an uncertain ability to express its own identity and interests. To capture the essence of youth, both attributes must be kept in view.

The Definition of Youth

The operational definition of 'youth' varies across countries. The lower bound of youth is generally taken to be the legal minimum school-leaving age, which varies between 14 and 16 years of age in advanced economies. Child labour, or paid employment at lower ages, is far from uncommon, particularly in small industry in Italy and in agriculture in the US, and its problems overlap those of youth labour (Fyfe, 1989). However, as the numerical importance of child labour is otherwise small in advanced economies, the custom of taking the minimum school-leaving age as the lower bound of the youth category is well justified.

The upper bound is more variable by country, ranging from a tendency to concentrate upon teenagers in the UK to the inclusion of all persons aged less than 30 years in Italy. It makes sense to vary the definition of youth with the context; no uniform age range is adopted here. Where (as in Italy) a large proportion of first job seekers are found amongst the 20–24 and even the 25–29 age groups or where (as in Germany) effective youth training displaces unemployment onto young adults, it makes sense to include those age groups with teenagers in considerations of the youth question.[4] At the same time, as youth issues and problems are generally most marked amongst teenagers, and teenagers and young adults differ in many respects, including for example residence and marital status, any extended definition of the youth category must keep in mind the ensuing increased heterogeneity of circumstances and problems within the youth group itself.

1.3 THE QUANTITY PROBLEM: YOUTH UNEMPLOYMENT

The problems which face youth in terms of employment and training have during the last two decades caused extensive concern in advanced economies. We distinguish quantity and quality: the availability of employment and the quality of employment and training, respectively. This section deals with the former, the next section with the latter.

Extent of Problem

The fluctuating fortunes of youth have been charted by a series of comparative studies of unemployment (OECD, 1980a, 1984b, 1988b). Taking youth as ending at age 24 and relying upon official measures of unemployment,[5] youth unemployment rates rose more rapidly than those of adults in most advanced economies during the 1970s, the principal exceptions being Japan and the US. The rise in adult unemployment in the early 1980s generally reduced the ratio of youth to adult unemployment rates relative to those of the late 1970s. However, both the youth unemployment rate itself and the absolute difference between youth and adult rates continued to rise, peaking in most countries during the early and mid-1980s respectively (Table 1.1).[6]

The severity of youth unemployment generally declined during the second half of the 1980s in both absolute and relative terms. A variety of factors contributed. Firstly, special employment measures became

Table 1.1 Youth unemployment rates and ratios of youth to adult rates in selected advanced economies, males and females, selected years, 1972–88.

Country	Youth unemployment rate[a] (14/16–24 years)					Ratio of youth to all age unemployment rates					Difference[b] between youth and all age rates				
	72	76	80	84	88	72	76	80	84	88	72	76	80	84	88
France	4.2	10.1	15.0	24.4	21.7	1.8	2.3	2.5	2.6	2.1	1.8	5.7	9.0	15.0	11.6
FR Germany	0.7	4.8	3.9	9.9	7.0	1.0	1.4	1.3	1.3	1.1	0.0	1.4	0.9	2.1	−0.4
Italy	13.1	14.5	25.2	32.9	34.5	3.5	3.9	3.3	3.3	2.9	9.4	10.8	17.6	22.9	22.5
Japan	2.4	3.1	3.6	4.9	4.9	1.7	1.6	1.8	1.8	2.0	1.0	1.1	1.6	2.2	2.4
Netherlands	2.7	7.3	9.3	25.2	17.3	1.2	1.7	2.0	1.8	1.5	0.5	3.1	4.7	11.0	8.0
Sweden	5.7	3.7	5.0	6.0	3.3	2.1	2.3	2.5	1.9	2.0	3.0	2.1	3.0	2.9	1.7
UK	5.0	11.3	13.5	22.1	11.9	1.6	2.2	2.1	1.8	1.4	1.8	6.1	7.0	10.0	3.6
USA	11.3	14.0	13.3	13.3	10.6	2.1	1.9	1.9	1.8	2.0	5.8	6.5	6.3	5.9	5.2

Notes
[a] Percentages of labour force of that age.
[b] Percentage points.

Source: OECD (1989b), Part III

extensive in many countries during the early 1980s and were often –
notably in Italy, France and the UK (Table 1.2) – slanted towards
youth, thereby reducing the ratio of youth to adult rates of open
unemployment.

Secondly, the marked revival of economic activity in the US, the
Netherlands and the UK at varying stages during 1982–7 reduced
youth joblessness in those countries, aided by the concentration of new
jobs in youth-intensive sectors (Wells, 1989). Thirdly, growing participation in post-secondary education has shrunk the size of the youth
workforce in all countries, particularly in France (chapter 6, below).
Finally, the rapid shrinkage of youth cohorts in the population in
European economies during the early 1990s has converted public
perception of the problem of youth from one of excess supply to one
of scarcity, an issue dramatised in Britain under the rubric of the
'demographic timebomb' (GB NEDO, 1988; GB NEDO/TA, 1989).

Table 1.2 Public expenditure on youth special employment and training
measures as share of all manpower spending and of GDP in
selected advanced economies, 1987

| Country | *Spending on youth[a] measures as percentage of* | | |
| | *Spending on* | | |
	active measures[b]	*all measures[c]*	*GDP*
Belgium	0	0	0.00
France	32	8	0.24
FR Germany	6	3	0.06
Italy	80	29	0.37
Japan	0	0	0.00
Netherlands	6	2	0.06
Sweden	8	6	0.15
UK	30	11	0.27
USA	13	4	0.03

Notes
[a] Definition of youth category not standardised.
[b] Active measures include employment services, training, youth programmes,
job creation and employment subsidies and measures for the disabled.
[c] Including income maintenance programmes.
Source: OECD (1988a), Table 3.1.

Talk of shrinking youth cohorts and a scarcity of young workers might suggest that youth unemployment has become a thing of the past. In fact, the severity of youth unemployment has declined more strongly in public perception than in reality. Even where economic activity revived most strongly, as in the UK and the US, youth rates still exceeded 10 per cent towards the end of the 1980s (Table 1.1). Elsewhere, youth unemployment remained particularly high in Italy, France and the Netherlands, where one-sixth to one-third of the youth labour force was still unemployed in 1988. In the most extreme case, Italy, young workers accounted at that time for 54 per cent of the unemployment rolls (OECD 1989b, Table 1.11).[7] Prolonged depression of economic activity, as reflected in high adult unemployment, has contributed to elevated youth rates in those three EEC economies. However, youth-specific factors are clearly present as well: in all three countries the youth rate has remained significantly higher than the adult rate (Table 1.1).

Furthermore, the incidence of unemployment remains particularly high amongst particular groups of young people: teenagers in general in Japan and the US; female teenagers in France and Italy; and ethnic minorities in all economies (Table 1.3; Freeman and Holzer, 1986; DEG, 1988).

In sum, youth unemployment remained high in absolute terms at the end of the 1980s in all countries except Japan and Sweden, and in relative terms in all except Germany. Youth joblessness has proved particularly severe and persistent throughout the 1980s in Italy and France, notwithstanding significant policy spending on young employment and training. Getting a job and staying employed both remain problems for many young workers in many countries.

Actual Policy Priority

The importance given to youth unemployment by public policy in practice varies greatly by country. The comprehensive accounting framework required to gauge the orientation of employment policies towards youth is unfortunately not available at present. What is available is a comparison of expenditure on programmes earmarked for youth – as opposed to simply open to youth – with both overall expenditure and national income (Table 1.2, above).[8]

The importance of programmes targeted specifically upon young people varies widely, from 80 per cent of 'active' labour market

Table 1.3   Youth unemployment rates by sex and age, selected advanced
economies, 1988 (percentages)

| Country | Teenage[a] | | Youth[b] | All ages |
	Male	Female	(M + F)	(M + F)
France	17.7	30.9	21.7	10.1
FR Germany	4.5	6.1	7.0	7.4
Italy	35.2	50.1	34.5	12.0
Japan	8.0	6.3	4.9	2.5
Netherlands	17.0	17.5	17.3	11.3
Sweden	2.9	3.3	3.3	1.6
UK	11.5	8.9	11.9	8.3
USA	15.4	14.4	10.6	5.4

Notes
[a] 14/16–19 years old.
[b] 14/16–24 years old.
Source: As Table 1.1.

expenditures in Italy to practically nil in Belgium and Japan in 1987
(Table 1.2). Perhaps the highest degree of concentration upon youth
was reached in Britain in the early 1980s.[9]

Some of the variation in policy orientation towards youth in Table 1.2
can be associated with the severity of youth unemployment, as high
youth rates, both absolute and relative (Table 1.1), coincide with high
outlays on youth in Italy and France, in contrast to low values for each
in Japan, Sweden and Germany. The nature of youth unemployment
appears relevant too. Low spending rates in the US in the presence of
moderately high youth unemployment may reflect the short average
duration of unemployment spells amongst American youth (Freeman
and Wise, 1982).

However, policy priorities clearly vary as well. Levels of expenditure
on youth unemployment in Belgium and the Netherlands have
remained low, notwithstanding youth unemployment rates, absolute
and relative, second only to those of Italy and France.[10]

How Important is the Problem?

International differences in the policy importance of youth unemployment are promoted in turn by limited evidence and complex criteria in
assessing its importance, particularly in relation to adult unemploy-

ment. Youth joblessness may or may not constitute a major cause of policy concern. The adverse effects of long spells of youth unemployment have been documented (Ashton, 1986; McRae, 1987) and no one is likely to argue that high youth unemployment is desirable. At the same time, some consider youth unemployment a lesser evil than its adult equivalent and concentrate their attention upon either unemployment as a whole or unemployment amongst young members of ethnic minorities (Rees, 1986).

The less controversial issue is the latter: the desirability of a policy response to high unemployment, whatever the age of the unemployed. Agreement on the issue is widespread, reflecting both the economic waste involved in leaving human resources idle (Gordon, 1973) and the potential damage to the individual, in terms of living standards, self-respect, skills, motivation and health, associated with long-term unemployment. Agreement is less widespread about the feasibility of effective policy responses, let alone about the choice of instrument. However, the undesirability of unemployment beyond the low levels necessary for labour market adjustment, as well as persistently high unemployment in much of Western Europe in the 1980s, is now widely accepted.[11]

There is less agreement on the desirability of attaching special policy importance to unemployment when it affects young people rather than adults. Some view youth unemployment as more serious than its adult equivalent; others, as less serious. Factors which might induce differences in policy priorities between youth and adult unemployment include average spell durations, the effects of unemployment upon the individual, income in relation to needs and student status. We now consider these issues in turn.

Spell durations and state dependence
Young workers who enter unemployment spend on average considerably less time unemployed than do adult entrants. Amongst youth, high unemployment rates are generated by high inflows rather than by long durations, while the reverse applies to adult unemployment (except in periods of rapidly rising unemployment). The share of the unemployed who have become long-term is therefore lower amongst youth than amongst adults in all countries for which data are available.[12] Differences between countries are however striking, with the share of long-term unemployment low for young workers in Sweden, the US and Germany, but as high as one third to one half

in Belgium and the Netherlands (Table 1.4). A major contrast is apparent between the average duration of teenage spells of unemployment in the US and the UK: in the mid-1970s the US mean duration was only one third of that in the UK, notwithstanding a slightly higher teenage unemployment rate in the US (Johnson and Layard, 1986, Table 16.6).

To the extent that, for all workers, longer spells of unemployment mean greater individual hardship and the decay of skills, attitudes and health – technically, 'state dependence'[13] – the shorter average duration of youth than of adult spells implies less policy concern for youth, given similar unemployment rates. Indeed, given the contribution which job search and mobility by the short-term unemployed makes to the matching of workers and jobs in the labour market (Layard and Nickell, 1987), a moderate level of unemployment may even be welcome, particularly when it involves short spells for young workers whose career paths have yet to be determined. Finally, to the extent that rapid youth movement into and out of unemployment reflects the pursuit of leisure, policy concern in the face of youth unemployment is again limited.

Table 1.4   Share of long-term unemployment amongst the unemployed by age, selected countries, 1987 (percentages)

| Country | All | *Share of long spells[a]* in all spells of unemployment | |
		Male 15–24	*Female 15–24*
Belgium[b]	68.9	41.2	55.7
France	45.5	24.5	34.8
FR Germany[b]	32.0	11.2	14.4
Italy	n.a.	n.a.	n.a.
Japan	19.8	18.2	9.1
Netherlands	53.2	32.4	38.5
Sweden	8.1	2.0	2.2
UK	42.6	29.4	27.5
USA	8.1	4.4	2.6

Notes
[a] spell durations (current, incomplete) of at least twelve months.
[b] 1986 data.
Source: OECD (1988a), Table 2.10.

However, the lesser importance of long spells in youth than in adult unemployment does not necessarily imply lower rates of long-term unemployment amongst youth. The fact that overall youth unemployment rates usually exceed those of adults acts as a countervailing influence. An above average rate of long-term (as well as total) unemployment is unlikely for the very youngest age groups, dominated as they are by recent entrants to the labour market, but it is a distinct possibility for young adults. Thus in Britain in 1982, the rate of long-term unemployment was higher for 18–24-year-old males than for all adult age groups except that aged more than 60 (Figure 1.1).

It is also possible that state dependence differs according to age, in that unemployment spells of a given duration may affect young people more or less severely than adults. Popular perceptions commonly hold that unemployment has more effect upon young people, as a result of lower maturity, greater impressionability and a longer subsequent working life to be damaged. 'These young people are at a crucial stage in their personal development . . . the motivation and abilities of a substantial proportion of the working population may be prejudiced for years to come' (GB MSC, 1977, p. 7).[14] An allied fear is that political unrest and violence becomes particularly likely when it is

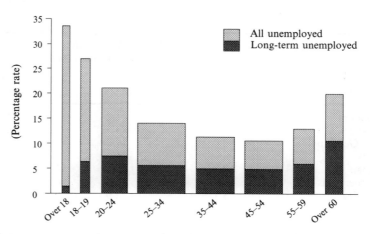

Note: The area of each bar is proportional to the total number unemployed in the age group.
Source: GB MSC (1982b), Diagram 1.

Figure 1.1   Unemployment rates by age group, males, Great Britain, July 1982

young people who bear the brunt of long-term unemployment, as in Italy (Statera, 1978).[15]

Economic theory and evidence also point to the importance of work experience for productivity and earnings growth, particularly at early ages (Ellwood, 1982). If these factors are strong, lower average spell durations amongst youth may be more than offset by greater damage per month, restoring the priority of youth in unemployment policy.

At the same time, youth shows certain advantages in responding to unemployment: resilience, low levels of responsibility for others, greater orientation towards peer-group support and time to recover from any damage induced. There can thus be no certainty that any given unemployment hits young people more severely than adults.

Moreover, much of the evidence of greater adverse effects from unemployment amongst youth is anecdotal and liable to evaporate when effective research techniques are employed – in particular when longitudinal data is used to compare the experiences over time of both the unemployed and a control group. Longitudinal evidence is based primarily upon the atypical US labour market and even then is less than conclusive, but it does cast doubt on the idea that scarring effects upon youth are absolutely large, let alone much greater than those for adults.[16] Controlling for personal characteristics amongst a sample of school-leavers in the US eliminates the association between a person's past unemployment history and present employment status (Heckman and Borjas, 1980). Amongst teenagers, unemployment spells do increase the probability of repeat spells in the near future and reduce earnings by way of forgone work experience, but the former effect is weak and the latter apparently 'one off' (Ellwood, 1982). Such evidence has led some, particularly in the US, to infer that youth unemployment constitutes a serious problem only amongst urban minorities (Feldstein and Ellwood, 1982; Rees, 1986).

However, any US-derived view that a given rate of youth unemployment is less serious than is a similar one for adults may not transfer to the higher levels and longer spell durations characterising youth unemployment in most of Europe in the 1980s. Longer periods of idleness, low income and loss of work experience may well mean blighted employment and earnings prospects amongst the youth generation of the 1980s in several European economies, over and above those involved for the adult unemployed.

The evidence is again limited and mixed. Recent longitudinal research on unemployed British youth finds state dependence in both a progressive decline of job search as spell durations lengthen and a 'one off' adverse effect upon mental health of entering unemployment. However, the negative effects of even long spells prove limited. Apart from a discouraged minority, young workers remain interested in work even after two years in unemployment and show no signs of any progressive decay in mental health. Although no comparable data were developed for adults, the research noted the resilience of most young people in the face of unemployment, a trait which was attributed to youthfulness and to the absence of dependents (Banks and Ullah, 1987).

The upshot concerning the effects of long-term unemployment upon young people is an intermediate position between extreme claims based either on sympathy combined with weak evidence, on the one hand or, on the other, complacency that the resilience of young people permits them to ride out adversity without long-term damage. Even were the latter true, the financial and social deprivation associated with being in long-term unemployment requires recognition; and there is some evidence that unemployment does affect young people's confidence and motivation adversely, though little on whether such effects are stronger than for adults.

Finally, it cannot simply be assumed that short spells of unemployment are of no concern. That may be true of spells spent in job search and leisure, but there is more than that to rapid youth turnover in the youth labour market. Young people may clock up considerable total time in unemployment through repeated spells. Much of that behaviour may be involuntary, resulting from the instability of the jobs open to them; or voluntary, but indicative either of the inaccessibility of well paid work or of an inability on their part to settle into steady work. On either score, a pathological element may be diagnosed which may be difficult to break out of in adult life, thereby slanting employment prospects towards low paid, secondary work (Doeringer and Piore, 1975; Osterman, 1980, 1982b).

Incomes and needs

A further attribute which distinguishes youth and adult unemployment is living standards. Differences between countries in this respect are marked and, as systematic information is hard to come by, this discussion refers primarily to Britain, which can hardly be taken as typical.

Unemployed young workers are disadvantaged in terms of eligibility for insurance benefits, and often in terms of lower benefit levels when eligible. The average replacement ratio (i.e. the ratio of net incomes out of work and in work) for British teenagers has been significantly less than that for the adult unemployed: in the mid-1980s, around 40 per cent for 16–19-year-old dependents as opposed to 60 per cent for all household heads (Bradshaw, Lawton and Cooke, 1987; Dilnot and Morris, 1984). However, as nine out of every ten teenage workers in Britain are unmarried and live with their parents (Bradshaw, Lawton and Cooke, 1987), their income needs are lower, and their access to family consumption higher, than those of adults, particularly household heads. Lower replacement ratios may therefore be associated with less, not more, financial hardship in teenage than in adult unemployment.

However, the 'turning of the screw' in terms of unemployment benefits in the 1980s (Atkinson and Micklewright, 1989) has been particularly severe for British youth (section 2.4, below). In particular, the denial of non-insurance benefit to 16–17-year-olds in 1988 has increased age-based disparities, creating widespread concern about hardship amongst the youngest unemployed, three-quarters of whom previously depended on non-insurance benefits (Cooke, 1985).

Problems may be more general in the next age group up the ladder, young adults (21–29 years), the income needs of whom are high in the face of family responsibilities and low assets. The tendency in many countries in the 1980s towards benefit restriction may not have been specific to this age group but it is likely to have borne particularly harshly on its members, given their rapidly rising and inflexible income needs.

Student status
The final consideration in a comparative assessment of youth and adult unemployment is the proportion of students amongst young workers, particularly teenagers. It is widely held that policy concern should be lower for student than for non-student unemployment, given that studying is an activity in itself, as well as one which leads normally to qualifications and lower future exposure to unemployment. Student status is also associated with a high incidence of short-term unemployment, reflecting high flows into and out of the labour force as students seek and relinquish part-time and vacation work (Feldstein and Ellwood, 1982).

In some countries, notably the US, but also the the Netherlands and the UK, significant proportions of both the youth labour force and the young unemployed are students (Table 1.5). To that extent, policy concern over unemployment is reduced in those countries for young workers, particularly teenagers, relative to that for adults. However, where studying and labour force participation are much more sharply distinguished, as in France, Italy and Belgium, student status has no significant bearing on the relative importance of youth unemployment.

Table 1.5   Participation rates, shares of labour force and unemployed currently in education, teenage labour force, selected countries, 1986 (percentages)

Country	Labour force participation rate[a]	Percentage of labour force in education[b]	Percentage of unemployed in education[b]
Belgium	11	5	7
France	24	3	4
FR Germany	42	8	19
Italy	26	4	6
Netherlands	22	36	41
UK	72	25	20
USA	59	56	51

Note: Teenage labour force defined as 16–19 years in UK and USA, 14–19 in Italy, 15–19 others; participation in education covers all who were following a course in a school or a university in the survey month.
[a] National definitions.
[b] Following a course in school or university in month of survey.
Source: OECD (1988a), Chart 2.1, Tables 2.1, 2.4.

Conclusion

It is not clear that youth unemployment should receive greater policy attention than its adult counterpart, particularly when the latter involves displaced persons facing long spells with heavy responsibilities and low prospects of finding work.

However, at a deeper level it matters little whether the youth unemployment rate receives greater or lesser weight in policy formulation than does the adult one. Youth unemployment would remain a serious policy issue even with a lower (but still significant) weight – as were its relative importance judged only in proportion to, say, numbers in long-term unemployment. High rates of youth unemployment bring with them, particularly in the EEC, prolonged spell durations and thus the possibility of long-lasting damage to the young people involved, in addition to the manifest immediate waste of resources and individual hardship.

Moreover, there is more to the youth unemployment issue than simply its importance relative to adults. Youth unemployment is from another perspective simply different from adult unemployment – and it is to that difference that public policy must respond.

Finally, although the young and the adult unemployed have often had to compete with each other for policy attention, youth unemployment has often catalysed action on unemployment more generally. The greater fund of social sympathy which is available for youth unemployment has allowed it to dramatise effectively the problem of unemployment as a whole, thereby bringing indirect policy benefits for adult unemployment. Thus, the extreme concentration of special employment measures upon youth in Britain in the early 1980s (note 9, above) had by the mid-1980s been greatly diluted by expansion of the Community Programme, aimed at adult long-term unemployment (Jackman, 1987): the relative neglect of the adult unemployed had become increasingly indefensible.

1.4 THE QUALITY PROBLEM: EDUCATION, TRAINING AND CAREERS

The second area of concern in youth activity involves the quality of youth activity: in particular, the degree to which young people learn skills and start a career. Low quality is typically reflected in a lack of vocational education, training or career prospects, and often also in low pay and insecure employment – the classic attributes of the 'secondary' labour market (Doeringer and Piore, 1971).

Extent of Problem

There are few internationally comparable data on the quality of youth activity. Two aspects are of particular interest: the extent of participation in education and the extent of education and training amongst those in employment.

The most accessible indicator is the rate of participation in education after the minimum school-leaving age. By 1986 more than one-half of all teenagers who had passed the minimum school-leaving age were following an educational course in all of seven advanced economies, Britain only excepted. More than three-quarters were thus engaged in the Netherlands, the US and (if apprentices are included) France and Germany (Table 1.6). The level is much lower for young adults, but in all countries a significant minority continues in education, with Belgium joining the same group of countries at the high end of the list. The quality of youth activity is therefore distinctly lower in this respect in Britain, reflecting high rates of labour force participation amongst British teenagers (Table 1.5, above).

Table 1.6   Shares of youth population in education, by age group, selected countries, 1986 (percentages)

Country	Teenagers[a] Definition of education[b]		Young Adults[a] Definition of education[b]	
	Normal	Broad	Normal	Broad
Belgium	57		22	
France	68	78	12	19
FR Germany	60	85	16	24
Italy	69		18	
Netherlands	85		27	
UK	43	48	8	14
USA	76		20	

Notes
[a] As in Table 1.5.
[b] Normal definition is as for Table 1.5; broad definition includes apprentices following educational courses and other vocational students, in countries for which data are available.
Source: OECD (1988a), Chart 2.1, Table A.1.

There are no comparable data on the proportion of young persons at work who receive job training, but limited evidence again suggests that Britain and Germany have again ranked at opposite ends of the scale. In 1979, 40 per cent of early school-leavers in Britain received no training at work, and 60 per cent less than eight weeks training (GB DE, 1981, p.6). Around the same time, only 6 per cent of West German 15–18-year-olds received no education or training and only 12 per cent of young people failed to obtain a vocational qualification (Schober, 1983; chapter 4, below; see also CEC, 1990, ch. 8).

Policy Activity

The wisdom of permitting large numbers of young people to miss out on qualification and to work without prospects of training or career development is a long established policy issue. Concern on that score goes back in Britain to controversies over child labour and 'blind alley' juvenile employment before the First World War.[17] The issue was raised also in the US in the 1960s by institutionalist analyses of poverty and manpower policy.[18] German social values have long emphasised the importance of the educational component in youth economic activity (*bildung*; Taylor, 1981).

During the last decade, however, the problem has been treated as one of increasing urgency. Countries which perceive themselves to be lagging behind in terms of youth vocational preparation have sought to catch up, even adopting the target of universal foundation training amongst young people which leading countries are taken to have achieved already (GB DE, 1981; d'Iribarne, 1982; OECD, 1988a; Keep, 1991). The expansion of youth qualification in France in the 1980s is set to intensify in the 1990s (chapter 6, below; White, 1989). Similar proposals for the revitalisation of education and training have emerged in the US, largely in response to deteriorating trade performance (US NCEE, 1983; Johnston and Packer, 1987; US DOL, 1988, 1989; Finegold, 1990; chapter 5, below).

The need for change has been perceived particularly keenly in Britain, which ended the 1970s with a majority of its young people leaving school at the earliest opportunity, of whom a further majority acquired little or no training, let alone qualifications (GB DE, 1981; GB NEDO/MSC, 1984; GB MSC/NEDO, 1985). The Youth Training Scheme (YTS), launched in 1982, set itself the goal of disseminating training throughout the teenage workforce, not just its immediate constituency amongst the 16–17-year-old unemployed (chapter 8, below). By the end of the decade, both the incidence of vocational education and training and the acquisition of qualifications amongst youth had risen significantly. Thus, nearly two-thirds (65 per cent) of British 16-year-olds had left full-time education in 1974; by 1988, the share had fallen almost to one-half (53 per cent; GB DE, 1987, p. 461; 1989, p. 263). The extent of youth training has also risen significantly in Britain in recent years. Between 1984 and 1989 the proportion of young employees reporting that they had received job-related training during the previous month rose from 20.2 to 23.0 per cent for 16–19-year-olds and from 13.5 to 19.4 per cent for 20–24-year-olds (GB DE, 1990).

The high policy profile of quality issues was affirmed when the British government responded, albeit only temporarily, to widespread pressure for the adoption of ambitious targets for youth qualification in the 1990s (CBI, 1989; Cassels, 1990).[19] However, rhetoric and action have not always coincided, nor have employers and young people proved highly amenable to government exhortations, particularly when demand picked up after 1985 and well paid jobs without training became easier to find (DEG, 1989). A significant minority of young Britons continues to acquire little or no training. As recently as 1986, around one-half of a sample of British teenage employees aged 17–19 reported that they had received no training in their current jobs (GB MSC 1987, Table D). Moreover, as the content of many of the 'qualifications' gained by young people continues to be trivial,[20] problems of low quality in youth employment remain far from solved in Britain.

Even Sweden and Germany, two countries where vocational education and training has become almost universal amongst youth, have taken steps to maintain their lead. Both the duration and content of vocational upper secondary education have been improved in Sweden. Although there has been little direct response to criticisms of the technical quality and occupational mismatch of much German apprenticeship, particularly in the artisan sector,[21] apprentice curricula have recently been overhauled in order to improve training content, linked to a smaller set of recognised occupations (Streeck et al., 1987). The small minority of early school-leavers who fail to get an apprenticeship place has been directed towards full-time training under either the Basic Vocational Year or work preparation courses (chapter 4, below).

How Important are Quality Problems?

Issues raised by low quality in youth activity fall into two categories: efficiency and equity (Marsden and Ryan, 1988a). In the earlier period, interest in the quality issue was stimulated primarily by concern for equity: the feeling that young workers relegated to casual, dead-end jobs were getting a raw deal. The recent upsurge of interest has been motivated more by efficiency, in particular by a perception that economic performance depends increasingly upon youth vocational preparation. In Europe a further boost has been provided by the impending completion of the single European market and the increasingly problematic status of other forms of public subsidy to international competitiveness (Marsden and Ryan, 1990a; Lindley, 1991).

Efficiency

The efficiency implications of low quality youth employment are nowadays discussed primarily in terms of economic change and adaptability. It is widely held that innovation in both products and processes has become more extensive and rapid; that productivity growth depends increasingly upon workforce skills; and that the skills of the whole workforce, not just of a skilled minority, must be upgraded, as unskilled work fades away. An allied perspective emphasises the importance for economic restructuring of a labour force sufficiently *polyvalent* to adapt smoothly and quickly to occupational change, including retraining and upgrade training – and asserts that this can be realised only if the quality of initial vocational preparation is universally high (GB MSC, 1982c; Eliasson, 1987; OECD, 1988d).

The evidence does indeed indicate a long-term upgrading of skill requirements in the workforce, albeit less extensive than that in educational attainments (Eckaus, 1964; Berg, 1970, Miller et al., 1980); an important role for workforce skills and qualifications in explaining differences in performance between otherwise comparable enterprises (Prais, 1981); and the importance of worker competence for the successful implementation of electronic technology (Fleck, 1983). Even when job requirements appear unremarkable, German and Swedish commentators justify the 'excessive' training of young people in terms of its contributions to subsequent career development and economic restructuring.

At the same time, the implications of economic change for youth training are more limited than is generally recognised. Job design and skill requirements depend upon managerial strategy as well as technology. Much of management remains wedded, not least in the UK and the US, to low skill requirements, whether or not efficiency suffers as a result (Campbell and Warner, 1991). Structural change slants new jobs towards the service sector, where a large segment of jobs continues to demand little skill.[22] More generally, inferior economic performance in Britain in particular results from a range of influences, including corporate and financial structures, industrial relations and management attitudes, and not just from initial vocational preparation – and changing the latter without changing the former is likely to produce disappointing results (Maurice, Sellier and Silvestre, 1986; Finegold and Soskice, 1988; Finegold, 1991).

The importance of quality in youth activity is thus easily oversold, not least in terms of what is implied for it by technical change and productivity growth. Training tends to become a panacea at times of high youth unemployment, distorting its true significance and producing an undesirable backlash when promises fail to materialise (chapter 5, below). At the same time, high quality youth vocational preparation is a necessary component in any broadly conceived package for a high productivity economy (Keep and Mayhew, 1988; Keep, 1991).

The efficiency implications of improving the working lives of young people depend also upon the alternative, which is usually unskilled and casual work, with skill learning being delayed until entry to internal labour markets as a young adult (Osterman, 1980; chapter 3, below). The drawback of such an alternative is partly that delaying training well beyond the start of the working life means shortening the subsequent period in which a return is earned on the investment (Ben-Porath, 1967). A more important factor, however, is the higher cost of trainee time, and, with it, training costs, when trainees are young adults rather than teenagers. Moreover, the quality of skill learning may not gain from the trainee's having spent his or her time in work with little learning content, particularly when training is conducted by an employer anxious to restrict the turnover of skilled workers.[23]

The efficiency case for training teenage rather than adult workers may however fail if the former are substantially less mature or slower to learn, as when prior work experience improves motivation and learning; when the cost of information about occupations makes it desirable for young workers to engage in job search and mobility before settling into skills training proper; or when young people themselves are intrinsically more interested in short-term rewards, including leisure (Osterman, 1982b). None of these conditions appears generally applicable, even in the US. Job search in secondary labour markets teaches little besides the value of stable, career employment; and the youthful instability and interest in leisure of which so much is made in North America is fostered by lack of access to skills and careers in the first place.

Equity
The second criterion of the importance of quality in youth activity involves social justice. Even when there is no case in efficiency terms for improving the quality of youth training and employment, a policy response may still be warranted, particularly on egalitarian grounds. A

widely held norm holds that it is unjust to leave any young people to idleness. Such values implicitly underlie the guarantee to all unemployed early school-leavers of a place on a public training scheme, as operated in Britain since 1980: efficiency arguments alone could hardly justify such expenditures on disadvantaged youths who face a future involving at best unemployment and unskilled employment (Lindley, 1983; Ryan, 1984b). A similar line of justification is required for similar measures targeted at unskilled unemployed youth in France (the *Travaux d'Utilité Collective* programme of 1984; Germe, 1986), as well as for non-employer training for the equivalent constituency in Germany (chapter 4, below).

However, egalitarian arguments for the improvement of the quality of youth activity are evidently limited, both practically and *a priori*. On the practical side, inequality remains marked in public subsidies to education and training within the youth cohort. In Britain in 1989 an average of £24,000 per capita was spent by the state on the first degrees of the 15 per cent of the age cohort who entered higher education, in contrast to a maximum of £5,200 for the 40 per cent who entered the Youth Training Scheme and nil for most of the 30 per cent who went directly to a job.[24] Fair treatment may have assisted the most disadvantaged young workers, but thus far it has done little more to level up public support for education and training amongst British 16–21-year-olds.[25]

Egalitarian concern for youth training is limited by two further considerations. The first is the transient status of youth, particularly relative to other secondary workers, notably non-whites and females, for whom secondary employment is more commonly a permanent feature and whose access to training is particularly low (Ryan, 1990). The reservation is underlined to the extent that the effects of temporary low quality employment prove non-durable (Brown, 1982; Metcalf and Richards, 1983). Secondly, quality itself may not matter much to young people themselves, particularly the disadvantaged young, to the extent that they aspire simply to getting a job, whatever its quality (Roberts et al., 1987, p.93).

However, these qualifications do not destroy the case for reducing social inequality both by improving the quality of youth activity for young workers as a whole and by reducing inequality within the youth cohort itself. Thus the approximation to the ideal of universal comprehensive education up to age 18 which has been achieved in Sweden (chapter 4, below) is attractive on egalitarian grounds, quite apart from its implications for economic performance.

1.5   CONCLUSION; CONTENTS OF VOLUME

An assessment of the priority which policy should attach to the problems facing young people, in terms of access to both jobs and skills, depends therefore on a wide range of issues and evidence, involving both economic efficiency and social justice. The balance is not easily drawn.

A simplifying factor is the fact that the issues of quantity and quality, hitherto discussed as if independent of each other, overlap considerably in practice – for both individuals and economies. At the individual level, they tend to be experienced in tandem. The young people most likely to end up in long-term unemployment are those who lack training and qualifications (White and McRae, 1989). Countries with inferior systems of vocational education and training are liable to have poor economic performance and, with it, high youth unemployment.

The relative importance of the two issues is also of interest. While no precise determination is possible, it can be argued that the increasing orientation of policy in recent years towards the quality issue, in the shape of initial education and training, and away from the quantity one, in the shape of youth unemployment, has proceeded further than is warranted by actuality. Youth unemployment remains high in many advanced economies. Universal youth training makes sense only in a wider context, particularly one in which problems of managerial quality and skill requirements are also addressed. Policy concern should move towards effective job creation for young people, with training as a desirable adjunct rather than an alternative.

In any event, the twin economic problems facing young people – finding and keeping a job, acquiring a skill and a career – must remain important sources of policy concern in most advanced economies in the 1990s. The employment problem remains most serious in Western Europe, the skill problem in the English-speaking countries, but no economy is immune from concern on either score.

Contents

The chapters which follow address various aspects of youth employment and training in advanced economies. The discussion falls into three sequential categories: multicountry studies, paired country comparisons and studies of youth and trade unionism in particular countries.

The present authors continue in chapter 2 to the less visible aspect of the 'problem of youth': the problems posed by youth in advanced economies to the organisation of work and production, along with the various regulatory structures through which those problems are addressed and the outcomes of such regulation for young people themselves. The goal is to develop a framework for the analysis of youth employment and training, one which contrasts, on the one hand, market and rule-based methods of regulating youth activity and, on the other, outcomes which include or exclude youth from particular workplaces. The content of the deregulatory initiatives of the 1980s, as they have affected youth, is analysed with a view to separating the desirable from the undesirable.

In chapter 3, David Marsden and Paul Ryan extend their previous research, which established a similar role for wage structures in patterning youth employment across six major EEC economies, to analyse differences across countries in pay structures themselves. The EEC economies fall broadly into two categories in terms of two key attributes of pay structures: the mean pay of young workers relative to that of adults and the dispersion of adult pay across sectors. These differences in 'pay regimes' are in turn interpreted in terms of labour market structure, the role of schools in youth training and the goals and strength of trade unions.

The paired country studies begin in chapter 4, where Karen Schober-Brinkmann and Eskil Wadensjö compare the experiences of youth in two economies marked both by success in terms of youth training and employment and by radically different routes to success: Germany and Sweden. The German system of early induction of most young people into workplace-based apprenticeship contrasts sharply with Sweden's preference for vocational preparation through extended secondary schooling. The two systems are shown to differ in their implications for status differentiation in the general education of children; in the occupational breadth of vocational preparation for teenagers themselves; and in the employment prospects of young adults, who have entered the mainstream labour market. The authors judge the Swedish system to have performed somewhat the better in terms of youth training and employment, while recognising that much of the difference results from the better macroeconomic performance of the Swedish economy in recent years.

The second paired national comparison, by Richard C. Edwards and Paolo Garonna (chapter 5), focusses upon training aspects of youth regulation in the US and Italy. In both economies, training, which had traditionally been largely left to employers to provide and finance, achieved in the 1980s the status of policy nostrum in response to problems of precarious international competitiveness and high youth unemployment. Emphasis on increased training as a response to the problems of both youth and the economy has dovetailed with politically popular flexibility strategies, emphasising private sector initiative and employer requirements. From a wider perspective, such training proposals are seen as part of the revision in both countries – more drastically in the US – of the wider postwar regulatory system or 'labour accord.' The longer-term prospects for this 'flexibility' model of training are seen as dubious, given its inegalitarian and anti-union attributes, but, beyond insisting that any reformulation of the role of training must conform to wider regulatory structures, the authors treat the future course of training in both countries as an open question.

In chapter 6, David Marsden and Jean-François Germe contrast patterns of entry to long-term and stable employment amongst young males in Britain and France. They find that a higher proportion of young workers function in jobs below the level for which they are qualified in France than is the case in Britain. This difference in the extent of 'occupational downgrading' amongst skilled young men is interpreted as a product of the greater importance of internal (i.e. employer-based) relative to occupational (external) structures in the French labour market, with its corollary of a lesser importance for industry and wage-for-age pay scales than has traditionally been the case in Britain. This feature of youth labour markets could be linked in both countries to the role of the special contracts (*formation-emploi* and *alternance* in France, YOP (Youth Opportunity Programme) and YTS in Britain) which have sought to facilitate the transition of young people into employment, including skilled work.

The final two chapters deal with different aspects of links between young workers and trade unions. In chapter 7, Tinie Akkermans, Bert Felling and Jan Peters analyse the sharp decline in union membership density amongst Dutch youth. Drawing upon a survey of youth attitudes, they find evidence amongst young people of a 'new worker', delineated by a set of attitudes marked by hedonism, individualism, the combination of an avowedly apolitical stance with an intrinsically conservative attitude, and an unfavourable view of the social and economic activities of trade unions. Such attitudes contrast to those of both the older generation and the dwindling proportion of union members within the younger generation. Interpreting the difference between generations as a cohort rather than an age effect, they infer a serious long-term threat to the viability of trade unionism in the Netherlands, as the ageing of the current younger generation diffuses attitudes less receptive to union membership and activism throughout the workforce.[26]

The direction of the analysis is reversed by Paul Ryan in chapter 8 to consider the reactions of trade unions to youth activity in public employment measures in Britain. The Youth Training Scheme (YTS) has reduced the pay and employment security of its participants relative to those enjoyed in regular youth employment and training. As YTS has depended primarily upon workplace activity for young participants, it has posed serious problems to trade unions. Although unionists have agreed on the importance of defending their regulatory role against the scheme's deregulatory intent, divisions over its content have run deep and wide. Unions have had to choose between boycotting YTS, implying the exclusion of young trainees from organised workplaces, or seeking to improve its content, implying the conditional acceptance of young trainees at the workplace. The arguments advanced in support of the two positions during public debates within the union movement are outlined and evaluated.

The contributors to this research effort have sought to ensure that the chapters in this volume constitute, if not an integrated analysis of the institutional aspects of youth training and employment, at least an interdependent and innovative sequence of analyses of such issues. If we have succeeded in that goal, the game will have been worth the candle.

Notes

1. Reubens (1983, pp. 10–13) denies the appropriateness of the concept of a 'youth labour market' to the US, pointing to extensive overlaps between youth and adult employment by occupation and the heterogeneity of the youth category. 'Differences among groups of young people emerge as a more significant feature of our analysis . . . than differences between youths and adults' (Hills and Reubens, 1983, p. 310). However, youth may constitute an important socioeconomic category without there being any separate youth market: distinctive youth characteristics within a common labour market suffice, given that the existence of a youth market is a matter of degree rather than kind. Thus Freeman and Medoff (1982) infer the existence of a 'reasonably distinct job market' for young people in the US from high and rising values of an index of structural differences in sectoral employment patterns.

2. For example, OECD (1980a), Grant and Hamermesh (1981), Freeman and Wise (1982), Lynch and Richardson (1982), Wells (1983, 1987),

Reubens (1983), Hamermesh (1985), Marsden and Ryan (1986, 1989a), Costrell, Duguay and Treyz (1986), Rice (1986), Junankar and Neale (1987), Hart (1988). While most of these studies assume or infer substitutability between youth and adult labour, they disagree on its importance and one study even suggests complementarity (Hutchinson, Barr and Drobny, 1984).

3. Merrilees and Wilson (1979), Wells (1983); chapters 3 and 8, below.

4. Prevailing concepts of youth have also altered during the postwar period, from an initial emphasis upon adolescence, particularly teenagers still in school, towards one upon students, mostly those of middle-class origin and aged 18–30 years, and subsequently again towards school dropouts and the young unemployed (Adamski and Grootings, 1989).

5. The standard index of the problems which young people face in obtaining employment – the youth unemployment rate – is in many ways a limited guide to the problem (OECD, 1988a, section 2.B). Many young people are students and, as such, may be more or less available for paid work and interested in finding it. Some fail to show sufficient evidence of availability for or interest in employment to be classed as unemployed on standard criteria, yet they may still be willing to accept a job if it became available. Others, notably amongst full-time students, are definitely outside the labour force, but that status results from the difficulty of finding a job – as evidenced by marked pro-cyclicality of rates of staying on in school at age 16 in Britain (Whitfield and Wilson, 1988). Further bias arises in countries, again with Britain to the fore, where unemployment is measured by registration for benefit rather than responses to surveys. An extreme instance of the distortions introduced by registration bias into official unemployment series involves the removal in 1988 from British 16–17-year-olds of eligibility for the main social security benefits (section 2.4, below). As the official British unemployment figures are based upon a count of benefit claimants, 16–17-year-olds cannot now be unemployed, even when sufficiently available for and interested in work on normal criteria. Their zero official unemployment rate clearly says more about measurement methods than about youth joblessness. Nevertheless, as alternative measures of youth joblessness – such as the non-student unemployment rate – show broadly similar patterns across all countries, except the US (OECD 1988a, Table 2.6), the youth unemployment rate provides a valuable general indicator of the problems which youth face in finding jobs.

6. The countries for which data are presented in this chapter are those represented in the remainder of the volume, plus (on account of its importance) Japan.

7. Although the youth unemployment rates in Table 1.1 are not strictly comparable across countries, international differences in them are too great for definitional factors to make more than a secondary contribution.

8. The data in Table 1.2 do not reveal the extent to which young people have access to other programmes not specifically targeted on young people, such as enterprise subsidies, income maintenance and job

creation. Thus the services, such as counselling, provided to young people by regional authorities in Italy are not reflected in Table 1.2; nor is the low access of young Italians to income maintenance programmes.

9.   The youth intensity of public intervention peaked in Britain during 1980–2, when nearly one in two jobless members of the labour force were covered in the age group 16–17, as opposed to only one in 100 in other age groups (Ryan, 1983).

10. Although no time series for Belgian youth unemployment is available for inclusion in Table 1.1 above, in 1986 the rate was 26.8 per cent for teenagers (15–19 years), 20.0 per cent for young adults (20–24 years) and 11.3 per cent for all ages (OECD, 1988a: Chart 2.1, Tables 1.7, 2.1, 2.4).

11. Only new classical macroeconomists, who interpret actual unemployment as an approximation to the equilibrium of a competitive labour market and as therefore essentially voluntary in nature, do not see high unemployment as a major policy priority, not least because they do not believe that goverment can act effectively against it (Lucas and Rapping, 1970). However, mainstream economics generally accepts the importance of demand deficiency in the persistence of high unemployment in Europe in the 1980s (Bean, Layard and Nickell, 1986; Blanchard and Summers, 1988).

12. A possible exception is Italy (for which comparable data are not available), where the large number of first-job seekers, accounting in 1987 for 48 per cent of the unemployed, contain many (older) young workers whose spell durations may be very long indeed (Ministero del Lavoro, 1988, Table 5.10).

13. The alternative to state dependence in the interpretation of statistical associations between the duration of unemployment spells and the characteristics of the unemployed (e.g. lower mental health on average amongst the long-term than amongst the short-term unemployed) is 'heterogeneity': the possibility that persons whose characteristics are intrinsically poorer are selected into long-term unemployment by their innately low access to employment. The relative importance of state dependence and heterogeneity in generating associations between unemployment and skills, attitudes, etc. remains unresolved. While popular perceptions and unsophisticated research undoubtedly overestimate the adverse effects of unemployment upon individuals relative to that indicated by longitudinal data (Stern, 1983), the adverse effects of long-term unemployment to which social psychology has long pointed (Jahoda, 1982) conform to indirect macroeconomic evidence of state dependence (Budd, Levine and Smith, 1988; Jackman and Layard, 1988). Moreover, the causal role of unemployment in the financial difficulties of the long-term unemployed is particularly clear (Dilnot and Morris, 1984). We assume here a significant degree of state dependence in long-term unemployment for both young and adult workers.

14. In Britain an allied argument held that cultural change had left young people generally more resistant to work discipline and reliability (GB MSC, 1977).

15. A strong link has been widely inferred in Britain between the urban riots of 1981 and intensified public intervention against youth unemployment

through the Youth Training Scheme (Moon and Richardson, 1985). Some connection is surely present, but those upheavals came too late to account for the most important extension of youth intervention: the guarantee of a place in a youth scheme to all unemployed early school-leavers in 1980.

16. A detailed review of the US evidence concludes that 'our knowledge about whether teenage unemployment has long-run scarring effects is still quite imprecise' (Ehrenberg and Smith, 1987, p.619).

17. Tawney (1909), Bray (1911), Keeling (1914), Dearle (1914). Only sporadic attention was paid to the issue thereafter (Gollan, 1937; GB DE, 1974) until it was restored to attention by studies of youth employment and training in the 1980s, including Ashton, Maguire and Garland (1982) Ashton and Maguire (1986), Roberts, Dench and Richardson (1987), Raffe (1987a, 1987b, 1988, 1990), Marsden and Ryan (1986, 1988a, 1989a, 1990b) and Lee, Marsden, Rickman and Duncombe (1990).

18. Doeringer and Piore (1971), Osterman (1980), (1982b), (1988), Wial (1988).

19. In 1989 the Department of Employment announced the objective of qualifying half of the employed workforce to NVQ Level III by the year 2000, implying a major increase in youth training levels. However, following a ministerial change, such plans were quietly discarded as excessively ambitious (*Financial Times*, 5 May 1990).

20. The value of the lower (Level I) qualifications promoted under the National Vocational Qualification system has been found wanting in international comparisons (Steedman and Wagner, 1989; Jarvis and Prais, 1989).

21. OECD (1980b), Taylor (1981), Casey (1986), Dougherty (1987), Raggatt (1988).

22. Skill requirements in services may also be depressed below efficient levels by defective managerial policy (Jarvis and Prais, 1989; Prais, Jarvis and Wagner, 1991).

23. The low opportunity cost of youth time reflects the same factors which generate willingness to work for low pay: low recent income levels, lack of labour market experience, dependency status within the family and low eligibility for social security (section 1.2, above).

24. The youth cohort shares of the various paths are approximations for the second half of the 1980s, derived from the Youth Cohort Study (GB TA, 1990, Table 2.2; GB DES, 1988, Chart 5). Costs per channel are estimated in 1989 prices as follows: higher education – recurrent costs per student year in universities and polytechnics in 1982 (GB DES, 1985, Tables 3,4) and average student maintenance grants in 1986 (GB DES, 1988, Annex B) adjusted for price inflation and average length of course; YTS – cost to the Treasury of £50 per trainee week in 1989–90, assuming completion of two year traineeship (*Employment Gazette*, May 1990, p. 282).

25. Adoption of the voucher system suggested by the national employer association for the encouragement of youth training would reduce inequality in public subsidy to post-16-year-old education and training

by ensuring a minimum to all, employed and unemployed alike (CBI, 1989).

26. Their conclusion contrasts interestingly to recent British studies of youth attitudes to unions, which agree about the long-term organisational threat but which relate it less to changes in social values than to economic restructuring and the decreasing availability of union representation in the workplaces where young workers are active (Spilsbury, Hoskins, Ashton and Maguire, 1987; Payne, 1989; Cregan and Johnston, 1990).

Part I
Youth Regulation: Methods, Outcomes and Sources

2 The Regulation and Deregulation of Youth Economic Activity[1]

Paolo Garonna and Paul Ryan

2.1 INTRODUCTION

In the previous chapter we distinguished two problems of youth: those which face young people themselves and those which youth poses to the wider economy. The latter set of problems, which has received much less attention than has the former, provides the subject of this chapter.

Youth itself poses problems for the organisation of work, production and industrial relations in advanced industrial societies. On the one hand, the reproduction of the labour force requires that young people be incorporated into employment and skills. On the other, those processes of youth incorporation can create threats to the interests of other parties, particularly adult workers and trade unions, deriving partly from widespread willingness among young people to work (or train) at well below established adult rates of pay. For example, the mean reservation wages of £43.60 reported in 1983 by unemployed 17–18-year-old British males amounted to only 35 per cent of the average weekly earnings of adult manual males (> 20 years). The equivalent figures for females were £39.60 and 37 per cent (Banks and Ullah, 1987, p. 13; GB DE, 1983, Part A, Table 1).[2]

The resulting threat from youth may imperil the stability of existing institutions, particularly in the area of industrial relations. The threat may result from the political or industrial activism of young people themselves but it emanates more generally from the use which employers and the state may seek to make of a passive, potentially low priced youth workforce.

This conjunction of factors is specific to youth. Other groups, notably married females and immigrants, share with youth the willingness to work for low pay which poses a threat to the earnings and job security of established employees. But their threat can be marginalised by *de facto* segregation and discrimination. The same is also possible for youth, but prejudice is an intrinsically weaker exclusionary force vis-à-vis youth,[3] and, as incumbent employees age, they must eventually be replaced by younger people, even if not necessarily by young workers themselves (Ryan, 1987a).

The difficulties associated with the industrial position of young people are resolved in different ways across time and place. In section 2.2 we propose a youth regulatory framework with two key dimensions: method and outcomes. In each dimension a dichotomy is proposed – in terms of methods, between market-based and rule-based procedures; in terms of outcomes, between the inclusion of young people at, and their exclusion from, the workplace. Our primary interest in that section is the nature of regulatory systems before the industrial turbulence of the 1970s.

Section 2.3 considers the influence upon youth regulatory systems of the goals and strategies of four key socioeconomic agents: employers, trade unions, the state and young people themselves. The objective is to understand the determination of the content of youth regulation in practice. The part played by one agent, the state, has come more clearly into focus during the 1980s. Proposals oriented towards deregulation, flexibility and market forces, discussed in section 2.4, have exerted increasing influence upon policy in most advanced economies. An important part of the deregulatory canon involves young workers. Their employment and training prospects are to be enhanced by some mixture of reductions in relative pay and employment security, on the one hand, and enhanced public support for vocational preparation, on the other. Such proposals have been taken up by many governments in the form of special employment and training measures.

These deregulatory initiatives have created tension with antecedent systems of regulating youth employment and training. The regulation of youth activity has thereby become more visible and more problematic. Although it has been forced to adapt to the problems of youth in new ways, it has often shown sufficient resilience to divert deregulatory initiatives towards unintended effects.

A widespread stalemate between deregulatory initiatives and established regulatory patterns leaves much of youth regulation at the start of the 1990s in an unresolved and unsatisfactory condition. Section 2.5 considers some implications of our analysis for public policy towards the regulation of youth economic activity. We urge the desirability of 'bargained flexibility': a policy stance which determines outcomes desirable for both youth and the wider economy, drawing upon the attractive elements of the deregulatory agenda, and, recognising the insufficiency of market forces as a vehicle for their realisation, pursues them within negotiated and prospectively stable frameworks – whether national, sectoral or occupational – for youth employment and training.

The analysis of deregulation requires a prior investigation of regulation, to which we now turn.

2.2 PROCESSES AND OUTCOMES IN YOUTH REGULATION

Our starting point is the set of institutions which govern the training, entry to employment and subsequent labour market experiences of young people, which is here denoted the youth regulatory system.

We adopt the term 'regulatory system' with some reluctance in view of the variety of meaning and nuance with which it is associated in the social sciences. It denotes here the wide range of social and economic institutions which structure the activity of young people in education, training and employment, including the labour market, the industrial relations system, the education system and the system of social reproduction (family structure and social security). As such our usage of 'regulation' is closer to that of the French *régulation* school than to its use in the US and UK economics literature as a 'shorthand for government intevention in private markets' (Piore and Sabel, 1984, p. 4). However, we do not pursue the issues of macro-systemic coherence emphasised by the *régulation* school (Boyer, 1988).[4]

Our analysis of youth regulation starts with a distinction between processes and outcomes. Regulatory processes are the structures which govern youth activity, particularly at the workplace but also in the wider educational, labour market and social security arenas. Regulatory outcomes are the resulting patterns of youth activity, notably access to jobs and training at the workplace.

A dichotomy may be made within each dimension. Regulatory process shows two main variants, that by rules and that by markets, here termed Institutional Regulation and Market Regulation respectively. The rules which pattern youth activity under Institutional Regulation include the formal provisions of collective agreements and the law, as well as the informal ones of custom and practice at the workplace and in society (Brown, 1972). Under Market Regulation, youth activity is structured instead by the price signals thrown up

directly by markets. In its competitive variant, excess demand
determines the price signals that induce young people, employers
and providers of training into courses of action which lead towards
market clearing.

Although for some purposes differences within Institutional Regulation are more important than those between it and Market Regulation,
the political importance of deregulation and flexibility in recent years
leads us to emphasise the latter distinction.[5]

In terms of regulatory outcomes, we distinguish situations according
to whether young people gain or do not gain access to jobs and/or
training at the workplace, termed respectively Inclusion and Exclusion.
Again, intra-category differences are of interest as well. The exclusion
of young people from particular workplaces may be desirable, as when
it is associated with high quality alternative activities, such as full-time
vocational education. Alternatively, youth exclusion may be undesirable, as when it is associated with inferior alternatives such as
unemployment or casual employment.

We dichotomise Institutional and Market regulation only for ease of
exposition. In practice, the two often function together, and it is their
relative importance which varies across time and place. Some
economies show a marked predominance of one form, such as
Institutional Inclusion in Germany. Others are more clearly mixed.
In the US, some sectors exhibit Market Inclusion, others Institutional
Exclusion. Britain shows an unusually varied combination, including
Regulated Inclusion (e.g. apprenticeship run under Training Board
auspices), Market Inclusion (e.g. low wage industries without statutory
wage protection) and Regulated Exclusion (e.g. statutory bars on
teenage employment in particular occupations).[6]

Market Regulation

The four possible permutations of regulatory process and outcome
begin with Market Inclusion, that is, youth inclusion at the workplace
as employees and trainees in the absence of legal or collective rules
(Table 2.1, Box 1).

Taking employment first, the contemporary US youth labour
market is often offered as an example, with prices driven by supply
and demand. Thus the fall in youth relative pay which accompanied
the 'baby boom' increase in youth labour supply in the 1970s has been
seen as the cause of a fall in the relative youth unemployment rate at a
time when supply factors alone would have increased it (Freeman,

1979; Welch, 1979). Low unionisation and low minimum wages certainly suggest unusual scope for competition to determine youth pay and employment in the US.

Table 2.1   Methods and outcomes in youth regulation: a taxonomy with examples

Method \ Outcome	Market	Institutional
Inclusion	1 Apprenticeship in British engineering before 1939 Secondary segment of contemporary US market Small employers (Italy, GB)	4 Statutory hiring rules (including quotas) Contemporary apprenticeship (Germany and GB) Employment under bargained wage for age rules (Neth, UK)
Exclusion	2 Internal labour markets in primary segment of labour market (large non-union US employers)	3 Statutory minimum school-leaving age Exclusionary and protective legislation (shiftwork; truckdriving) Compressed pay structures under law or bargaining (Sweden, Italy in 1980s)

Market Inclusion is exemplified also in the slanting of youth employment towards small plants and firms in most advanced economies. The weakness of external regulation of youth contracts in small firms by either collective agreement or law is most marked in Italy, where the proportion of young workers functioning in small firms is exceptionally high (Frey, 1988). The position of young workers in small firms in Italy is affected by both exemption from and evasion of public regulation.[7]

A historical approximation to Market Inclusion is provided by youth employment in British engineering before 1939. Although youth was paid according to set 'wage for age' scales, often laid out in apprenticeship agreements, those agreements had become increasingly informal. Wage scales were largely left to employer determination in the light of conditions in the labour market. The result was low rates of payment to young workers and large-scale access to employment, if not training (Ryan, 1986).

In these three instances, young workers and employers are under little or no external constraint in settling employment contracts beyond the standard requirements of employment law; youth pay proves low and responsive to the supply of youth labour; and young workers have little difficulty finding employment.

However, closer examination indicates that the inclusion of young workers under Market Regulation, like the working of competitive forces themselves, is at most partial and selective, and that Market Exclusion of young people (Box 2) is also important. Even when unconstrained by law or collective agreement, many employers, particularly those in high wage sectors, hire few young workers (chapter 3, below).

Such patterns are marked in the US, where Institutional Regulation is weaker than in any other advanced economy. The sectoral distribution of youth employment in the US involves the effective exclusion of teenagers, and even young adults, from 'primary segment' employment, in association internal labour markets and employer hiring policy.[8] In such cases, Market Regulation diverges from competitive expectation, fostering the 'selective exclusion' of young people from a range of desirable employment opportunities.

Market Exclusion applies also to youth training at the workplace, where it proves more extensive than for employment alone. Competitive theory predicts that, when employers and young workers settle employment contracts subject only to market constraints, young people will obtain from employers as much training for transferable skills as they are willing and able to finance themselves, in return for accepting low or zero pay (Becker, 1975). In practice, when young people do gain access to internal labour markets they find that job-based training is limited in breadth, depth and transferability, and that any willingness on their part to buy more skill by taking lower pay is of no assistance (Ryan, 1984a).

Market Exclusion thus prevails when employers develop internal labour markets without external constraint from unions or government. Young people may then fail to obtain jobs and thus miss out on the training which comes with jobs, or, if they do get into the workplace, receive less training than they wish or is economically desirable.

Institutional Regulation

Instances of youth exclusion from workplaces under Institutional Regulation (Table 2.1, Box 3) divide into two categories: formal (or direct) and informal (or indirect). The formal category refers to explicit rules which forbid youth activity at the workplace. The most important are statutory: for example, the minimum school-leaving age and the prohibition of child labour, which, when enforced, together debar persons below the specified age from most areas of employment (Fyfe, 1989). For young workers, 'protective legislation' widely vetoes employment below specified ages under particular conditions or in particular occupations or sectors. For example, the employment of persons aged less than 19 years on nightwork, piecework or repetitive assembly work is forbidden by law in Germany (Schober, 1983); persons aged less than 21 years cannot legally drive heavy goods vehicles in Britain, etc.

The informal variant of Institutional Exclusion involves the indirect consequences of rules concerned – at least ostensibly – with other matters. The leading example involves wage structures set by collective agreement, statute or employer personnel policy. If payment systems do not permit substantially lower rates for young workers, and if young workers are sufficiently less productive than adults, then pay rules indirectly foster the exclusion of youth from employment and training. Examples include the near-absence of youth and learner rates in collective agreements in US industry (Osterman, 1980; Ryan, 1984a) and the Italian legal requirement that apprentices be paid at 95 per cent of the qualified worker rate (Mariani, 1986).

Youth exclusion has also been fostered indirectly in postwar Italy by public regulation of hiring practices. Employers hiring workers through public employment services have been required to do so in strict order from the top of skill-based lists compiled in order of seniority. However, to the extent that it was widely evaded in practice, the lists system proved only a limited force for youth exclusion (Napoli, 1984; Garonna, 1986).

Finally, examples of the Institutional Inclusion of young people (Table 2.1, Box 4)[9] may be generated either by wage structures which provide employers with incentives to hire or train young people or by antidiscriminatory rules, such as hiring quotas, which require employers to do so if they are to avoid specified sanctions.

Legal compulsion of employers to hire young workers has been considered, and once even formally adopted as policy, by the British trade union movement.[10] However, hiring quotas are rare outside the US, even for non-white and female employment, and are practically unknown for young workers. The special lists for unemployed young workers set up in Italy in 1977, from which young people were to be hired in numerical order, also fail to qualify here as nothing required employers to hire from the youth list in the first place and the incentives to do so were weak (Garonna, 1986).

The more potent vehicle for Institutional Inclusion is pay structure. Pay rates stipulated by collective agreement or law sometimes permit young or trainee workers to be employed at lower rates than adult or experienced workers in the same job category. Leading examples include 'wage for age' schedules in the Netherlands at present; their pre-1939 equivalents in Britain; and apprentice allowances in the German-speaking countries. In all of these cases, trainees or particular young workers can be paid at less than half the corresponding adult rate (chapter 3, below; Jones, 1985; Ryan, 1986). Employers will then wish to hire young people unless their anticipated productivity is even less than their pay, relative in each case to that of adults. Moreover, if fixed-duration contracts are more readily adopted for young workers, the incentives to employers faced by uncertainty to hire young workers become greater still.

Institutional Regulation may also affect youth training. The outstanding example is contemporary German apprenticeship. German law stipulates that employers may normally take on persons aged less than 18 years of age only on contracts of apprenticeship, subject to a panoply of external regulations concerning training methods and outcomes. A weaker variant is found in British apprenticeship, as regulated by Industrial Training Boards after 1964, where collective funding was tied to the attainment of stipulated quality standards. Those young people fortunate to get a place secured a training of much greater quality than had their more numerous counterparts in previous generations (Marsden and Ryan, 1991).

Youth inclusion may also be affected by wider institutions. An education system which provides school-leavers with skills and qualifications of value to employers, as has increasingly been the case in Sweden and France, encourages their inclusion into employment and on-the-job training, unlike one in which many young people leave school early without qualifications, as in Britain. Similarly, an organisation of work which throws up an abundance of low skilled, repetitive job tasks will mean potentially greater interest in hiring young workers than one in which skill requirements are high.[11]

The preceding discussion of youth regulation has provided a descriptive taxonomy. It becomes analytically useful when linked to an account of the forces which select between the four boxes of Table 2.1 and the desirability of particular outcomes.

2.3 DETERMINANTS OF YOUTH REGULATION

Evidence on the determinants of youth regulatory systems can be found firstly in marked variability across time and place in the institutions which govern the training and employment of young people; and secondly in the interests and strategies of the socioeconomic agents involved.

An Initial Interpretation

A start may be made by focussing on employers and unions. Some employers find the employment of youth labour a valuable contribution to their objectives of profit and control, to the extent that they can take advantage of its lower price and greater pliability than those of adult labour. Unions, concerned primarily with the earnings and job security of their adult membership, are then threatened by the substitution of youth labour for that of their adult members.

In this scenario, employers favour Market Regulation, in which unions have no role, while unions favour some variant of Institutional Regulation, in which their interests are protected by collective negotiation or public authority. Unions, acting as representatives of the economic self-interest of their adult majority, do not favour youth inclusion. Only when employers are strong enough to prevail will youth inclusion characterise both forms of regulation.

This simple interpretation is consistent with the relative unimportance of Market Regulation during the period of high trade union influence under the postwar 'labour accord' in almost all advanced economies; and with its greater importance during the preceding (pre-1939) and subsequent (post-1974) phases of higher unemployment and greater employer power. It is also consistent with widespread union concern to defuse the threat of cheap youth labour, often by promoting youth exclusion from the workplace.

The interpretation is however only preliminary. It cannot explain the inclusionary tendencies of highly unionised economies such as the German and the Dutch; nor does it explain widespread youth exclusion in non-union workplaces in the US. The motives and methods of both employers and unions are more varied than it allows; the influence of the state and young workers themselves must also be considered. A fuller account of youth regulatory systems requires detailed consideration of the goals and strategies of four types of socioeconomic agent: employers, unions, the state and young workers themselves.

Employers

Employer goals and strategies show considerable variety in the youth context. While it is common to assume that private sector employers are interested primarily in high profitability, that says nothing about public employment; nor does it indicate for private employers the nature of profit-seeking strategy and its implications for youth activity.

We distinguish initially two broad variants of employer goals and strategy, one associated more with large firms and primary employment conditions, the other more with smaller firms and secondary employment.

Employer size

Large employers operating in concentrated product markets and offering 'primary' terms and conditions of employment tend to assess profitability over the long term and, in so doing, attach importance to both the ordered procedures of their internal labour markets and, increasingly, to high skill content within their workforces (Brown, 1989; Walsh and Brown, 1990).[12] Such employers show no interest in taking advantage of low youth supply prices in order to reduce production costs or undermine trade unionism. Indeed, many acquiesce in the hiring and training of young people only under government prompting, on grounds of public relations and social responsibility.

However, employers who operate in more competitive product markets and in the secondary segment of the labour market show more interest in using youth labour to cut production costs and to weaken trade unions. The smallest employers are well placed to evade (when not totally exempt from) union or public regulation of youth activity at the workplace. For some low wage firms, youth labour is all that is left once high wage firms have taken their pick. The result is a marked orientation of both youth employment and youth activity under special employment measures towards such employers (chapters 3, 8, below; Lee, Marsden, Rickman and Duncombe, 1990).

This distinction by employer size is subject to important exceptions. The social and economic status of the *Meister* in Germany is frequently associated with owning and running a small firm and favouring skill development amongst young people (Russell and Parkes, 1984; Rose, 1991). Small firms in the industrial districts of North Italy, relying on advanced production technology and high quality products, set great store by the skills of their employees and often train young workers.[13] Some large firms, particularly in the UK and the US, favour deskilling applications of new technology which favour youth employment (OECD, 1988d, chapter 3).

Peripheralisation?
The distinction between the two types of employer may also be changing. In some accounts, the large modern corporation, faced by heightened uncertainty in its operating environment, seeks increased flexibility by developing a core/periphery dichotomy within its workforce. A *core* of multiskilled, secure employees works in an occupationally fluid manner, while a *periphery* of partly trained employees, lacking job security, comes and goes according to short-term requirements.

Firms pursuing such strategies may find young workers, along with females and part-timers, useful sources of low wage, insecure labour for their peripheral workforces. Young workers' employment prospects then improve while their earnings and job security decline.

Such employer strategies, longstanding in Japanese manufacturing, have been adopted in the US and the UK in sectors as diverse as shipbuilding, retailing and automobile assembly (GB NEDO, 1986; Atkinson, 1987). However, their quantitative importance remains limited. In the UK at least, only a small minority of firms have adopted such a strategy (Hakim, 1990) and the growth of insecure employment has been largely compositional, arising from structural change (Rubery, 1989). Others treat peripheralisation as an open issue for employer choice, noting that most large employers seem reluctant to embark on it in view of the low levels of skill and commitment which it promises (Osterman, 1988, chapter 4).

A further distinction amongst employers is necessary in Britain: that between the public and private sectors. While the public sector has traditionally seen the employment and training of youth as a public service, the reversal of government attitudes towards public activities since 1976 has moved public personnel practices rapidly from the primary towards the secondary segment of the labour market. Pay restraint combined with the rapid extension of temporary contracts has made youth labour (as opposed to training) a matter of increasing interest to hard-pressed public sector management (chapter 8, below).

Control
Another factor is the high priority that employers generally place upon the control of skills and training at the workplace. What they seek to do with that control varies, reflecting the tension between the Taylorist inclination to reduce skill requirements in order to enhance control over worker activities and the 'human resource development' interest in capturing the technical and motivational benefits of high employee competence.

Employer resistance to external regulation of workplace training has been particularly intense in Britain, where employers have fought a prolonged campaign against regulatory initiatives from unions, government and even their own associations. Although German employers have acquiesced in a regulatory role for government, unions and employer organisations which their British counterparts would bitterly resist, they too have striven to maintain control at the margin over issues such as public training funds, apprentice intakes and the extent of training outside the workplace (Schober-Brinkmann, 1986). Although French and Italian employers have traditionally supported public vocational education and training, they too have insisted upon control over the workplace component of the *alternance* training to which they and government have turned in recent years (Sellin, 1983).

Such efforts to retain control of training are however qualified by the gap between ideology and practicality in employer preferences. The employer world view is, in the UK and the US at least, slanted heavily towards 'unitarism' and its corollary, Market Regulation, under which employers are entitled, as those who know best about the organisation of production, to take decisions unhampered by external constraint by unions or government (Fox, 1974). The unitarist view is clearly visible in employer attitudes towards initial training in the US and the UK. At the same time, the actions taken by many employers are implicitly pluralist, in the sense of acquiescing in some form of consultation with unions, employees and government over sensitive operational decisions and, to that extent, opening the door to Institutional Regulation.

Finally there is the role of employer organisation. The scope for particular employers to increase short-term profitability by intensive use of youth labour may be curbed by the employer collectivity, recognising the destabilising effects upon shared employer interests of either cuts in training quality or competition on pay. Employer support for joint regulation of youth employment and training in Germany can be understood partly in such terms, pointing to the scope and strength of employer associations as an influence upon the response of particular employers to youth labour (Streeck, 1989).

Employer goals and strategies, as they affect youth employment and training, are thus complex and varied. Employers have not generally sought in recent decades to use youth labour to undermine Institutional Regulation, even if a minority, which may have grown somewhat, has shown such inclinations. The problem for social policy has been rather to interest employers in shifting Institutional Regulation towards youth inclusion at the workplace.

Trade Unions

The goals and strategies of unions are more varied still than are those of employers. Problems of interpretation are also considerable, given that announced and actual objectives often diverge; that objectives are often multiple and ill-reconciled; and that objectives and methods can shift, often in conjuction with internal political conflict.

Adult interests
A central issue is the importance of youth interests to trade unions. Factors pointing towards low importance include the small membership shares of young people, the widespread absence of internal, recognised youth organisations and the low and erratic level of youth involvement in union affairs.[14] Thus the low and declining membership share of youth has been a cause as well as an effect of the low willingness and ability of Dutch unions to maintain the relative pay of young workers (chapters 3, 7, below).

If adult interests consequently dominate union goals, the implications for young people depend upon the nature of those interests. If adult interests are limited to their own pay and job security, young workers are likely to find themselves restricted at best to insecure marginal employment, if not excluded altogether. Such a scenario appears relevant to industrial unions in the US, where the gap between the interests of secure senior members and insecure junior ones is most striking and where responses to crisis commonly involve the buying out of employment rights by management (Griffin, 1984).

However, when adult interests include the reproduction of the community of adult workers, unions will seek ways of regulating youth entry to promote that objective without threatening the position of current adult members. Such issues are prominent amongst unions with a strong occupational or community identity, such as printers and miners in Britain. Craft unions often seek to include youth in training and employment under apprenticeship, while avoiding overinclusion through numerical quotas such as apprentice–journeyman ratios (Webb and Webb, 1920; Rottenberg, 1961).

The industrial unions of modern Germany, lacking any attachment to particular occupations, show no such interest in imposing quotas on apprenticeship. Yet in other respects they show similar concern for the reproduction of the adult workforce and the regulation of youth activity at the workplace to that end (Taylor, 1981; Schober, 1983). Swedish unions, by contrast, have preferred to pursue their interest in youth training and employment through public education rather than through early insertion of youth into the workplace (chapter 4, below).

Youth interests

Unions are not however simply vehicles for the pursuit of adult interests. Under some conditions, young people exert a marked influence upon union objectives. Young workers have featured prominently in waves of militancy and subsequently in union structures. In Italy, the incorporation of the young activists of the 1960s into union bodies in the 1970s contributed directly to the formation of the *egualitarismo* wage strategy and the associated increase in the relative pay of young workers and apprentices (Garonna, 1986). The youth-led upsurge of May 1968 in France led to increases in minimum wages.

The interests of youth will also count, as prominent marginal members, when leaders are concerned to increase membership and, with it, the union's strength and their own standing (Pemberton, 1988). Such tendencies are particularly marked under multiunionism, with inter-union competition for new members, as in much of British employment.

However, interpretation of youth influence within unions faces the problems of determining the actual content of youth interests and selecting appropriate means of promoting them. Is youth better served by minimal regulation of its conditions of employment and training, which encourages employers to engage young people in large numbers but on poor terms and conditions, or by insisting on similar levels of pay and protection as for adults, in which case terms and conditions are more attractive to young people but fewer are engaged? The strategy of Dutch unions in agreeing to a further steepening of wage-for-age scales in the 1980s may be interpreted either as favouring youth, in terms of its interests in greater employment, or as disfavouring youth, in terms of its interest in higher pay. The contrasting insistence by Swedish and Italian unions on similar or identical pay rates for young and adult workers raises similar problems of interpretation (chapters 3, 4, 5 below).

Other interpretations

Still other interpretations of these contrasting union policies are possible. The first reasserts the primacy of adult over youth interests; the second involves the indirect consequences for youth of union interest in other objectives.

An interpretation in terms of adult interests returns to the threat posed to adult union members by cheap youth labour. When employers pursue their interest in substituting youth for adult labour, threatening the position of adult employees, unions who are not strong enough to regulate it directly by restrictions on hiring may do so indirectly, by bargaining up the wage at which young workers may be employed. Such responses are visible in Britain in the 1980s (chapter 8, below), Italy in the 1970s (Garonna, 1986) and the US in the 1930s.[15]

Similarly, union policies which seek to apply protective legislation to youth as well as to adult employment, as in Sweden (Wadensjö, 1987b) and to raise the school-leaving age (Osterman, 1980) probably reflect in part the interests of their adult members. However, such efforts also reflect to some extent pro-youth concern on the part of adult unionists and the balance of motives is not readily discernible. An exception is provided by the efforts of British unions to raise the publicly-funded trainee allowance on the Youth Training Scheme. As such an increase has no effect on the employer's payroll costs, it does nothing to reduce any threat to adults from job substitution, but it does increase youth incomes directly – indicating a clear orientation towards youth interests in this union policy.

The balance between youth and adult interests within union goals is ultimately a political issue. Unions (and their federations) can become battlegrounds for multi-layered conflicts between the interests of young and adult workers and between rival interpretations of the interests of each group. Such strife became extensive in British unions during the 1980s as they sought a response to public employment measures. Argument raged over the importance of substitution-induced damage to existing members relative to increased opportunities for young people; and over whether access to low paid work experience was or was not in the interests of young people themselves. Policy varied from union to union, culminating in a public and damaging split in the union movement as a whole (chapter 8, below).

Union policies
Union strategies towards the regulation of youth activity at the workplace also vary across countries. Unions have generally opposed special youth or trainee rates in the US, Sweden, France and Italy. However, in Germany, Britain and the Netherlands such rates are widely accepted by unions (chapter 3, below).

Although traditional union attitudes towards youth pay have recently come under pressure, they have thus far given little ground. Conflict over the introduction of a youth subminimum wage in the US sheds light on union priorities. A 1989 compromise introduced for the first time a teenage minimum wage, set at 85 per cent of the adult rate, applicable to the first three months of a job (six months if the young person were shown to be in training). Unions had for some years preferred to block the introduction of a special youth rate than to concede it and gain an increase in the general minimum wage, which had remained constant in nominal terms since 1981. The AFL-CIO president, Lane Kirkland, argued that the 1989 compromise, in limiting the size and duration of the lower youth rate and linking its duration to certified training, provided 'adequate safeguards so youth are not exploited and older workers not displaced'. The centrality of union concerns in this protracted tussle is affirmed by the complaint of an employer representative that 'we were just cut out of the debate' (*New York Times*, 1 November 1989; Starobin, 1989).

Similarly, Swedish unions have in the 1980s strongly opposed government proposals to introduce youth or trainee pay rates below established adult rates in public job creation (Wadensjö, 1987b). In Italy and France (until 1983), publicly sponsored youth inclusion at workplaces under special training contracts has proceeded at normal rates of pay, with employers encouraged to participate by relief on social security contributions and grants toward training costs respectively. In the UK, by contrast, youths active at workplaces on public schemes have been paid at specially low rates, with partial union acquiescence (Garonna, 1986; Germe, 1986; Ryan, 1989). Recent union policies towards youth pay under public sponsorship have thus generally followed traditional patterns.

Little research has been done on these differences in union goals and achievements across countries. One influence is the extent of assurances against the 'exploitation of youth' which is provided to unions by the regulatory content of occupational markets and apprenticeship, on the one hand, and internal markets and informal training, on the other (chapter 3, below). A normative factor is also apparent, with unions taking different views of the importance of high youth pay and low differentials, on one side, relative to youth employment and training, on the other. Finally, given their objectives, unions vary in their power to achieve them. Ironically, the apparently weak US union movement has had more success in its policies of restricting youth and trainee differentials in statutory regulation than has the apparently stronger Dutch one (chapter 3, below).

In sum, trade unions constitute a leading force for Institutional rather than Market Regulation. Under Institutional Regulation unions get a say. Youth activity at the workplace can be directed towards union interests by some mix of direct and indirect methods. However, what unions say they want is variable and a pressing subject for further research. When unions are unable to regulate youth inclusion on acceptable terms, they tend to favour exclusion, whether through direct regulation or as the indirect consequence of wage policy.

The State

The interests and methods of government, and the state more generally, are directly relevant to youth economic activity. Variety of objectives is accompanied by plurarity of agents, reflecting the heterogeneity of the state apparatus.

One quasi-universal attribute of state activity stands out. As the agent primarily responsible for social control and stability, the state has reacted strongly to high youth unemployment and inadequate youth training. Its actions have been motivated in part by the threat to the incorporation of the rising generation into social roles in work and leisure. At its most acute this appears as the fear of youth revolt but, whether acute or not, such concerns help explain the concentration of public intervention towards the youth end of the age spectrum of unemployment in Italy, France and Britain in particular (chapter 1, above).

Three broad tendencies may be distinguished in the nature of state action in advanced economies. The first emphasises legal and administrative intervention in economic matters and is exemplified by the public traditions of France and Italy. In the second, the state acts as the corporatist reconciler of conflict between the major social groups, seeking progress through negotiated compromise, as instanced in particular by the Swedish, German and Dutch states. The third is the contractual state, erecting the rules governing economic activity and leaving it to a mixture of markets and decentralised negotiation to determine actual outcomes. The traditions of Britain and the US fit best into this mould.

The link to systems of youth regulation is direct. Institutional Regulation is a natural corollary of the first and second categories of public action, emphasising statutory regulation and tripartite negotiation respectively. Market Regulation is the logic of the contractual state, leaving actual outcomes to decentralised determination. Thus a major contribution to the divergent fates of apprenticeship in Sweden, Germany and Britain in the postwar period has been the willingness of the Swedish state to absorb vocational training into the secondary school system; the willingness of the German state, even under conservative governments, to push employers towards the tripartite regulation of workplace training; and the enduring reluctance of the British state, even under Labour governments, to do either (chapters 4,8, below).

However, adminstrative intervention has generally been associated with Institutional Exclusion rather than Inclusion. In France, Italy and Belgium young workers are underrepresented in or missing from large segments of industry and much initial training is conducted in public schools and financed by public funds (chapters 3,5,6 below). What distinguishes the administrative state in this respect is more the potential for vigorous pro-youth initiatives if political priorities shift towards youth interests (section 2.4, below).

The ideological content of national politics, which correlates only loosely with the various types of state, also influences youth regulation. An enduring commitment to active demand management in Sweden has contributed to the lower level of unemployment than in Germany, thereby limiting the effects of exclusionary tendencies. The dominance of social democratic politics in Sweden is also associated with the preference for preserving prior regulatory structures largely intact and injecting into them subsidies to youth recruitment and training, carefully designed to avoid major offence to union interests. Such a strategy is clearly visible in the decision to offer unemployed young workers part-time work at established hourly pay rates, instead of the initial proposal for full-time work at reduced rates of pay, while participating in Youth Teams (chapter 4, below; Wadensjö, 1987b). Elsewhere policy has been influenced to varying degrees by pro-market ideologies. Swedish measures contrast with the low wage, fixed-term contracts adopted under the flexibility banner in countries as diverse as Italy and Britain (section 2.4, below).

Heterogeneity within the state apparatus is also important for youth outcomes. Governments facing electoral constraints have been particularly active against high youth unemployment. In the 1980s the electoral popularity of deregulatory politics and fiscal retrenchment, notably in the US and Britain, has encouraged moves towards Market Regulation, in terms both of encouraging wage flexibility and of avoiding large-scale public expenditures on school-based youth activity.

At the same time, intervention to promote youth inclusion requires use of public bureaucracy, with its vested interest in Institutional Regulation, which requires more of its services and accords more with its procedural inclinations. The paradoxical position of the tripartite Manpower Services Commission in Britain in the 1980s – a public sector purveyor of large-scale training and employment interventions to a deregulatory Conservative government – is particularly striking here.

Similarly, educational interests have sought to mould public intervention towards educational objectives, delivered through secondary schools and colleges – which also favours Institutional Regulation. The conflict between these divergent interests within the state has been intense and prolonged in Britain, resulting in a mixed, uneven and unstable pattern of youth regulation.

The judiciary may also exert an influence, particularly under the administrative state. The tendency in Italy towards the elimination of youth differentials in pay was intensified in the 1970s by judicial interpretation – notably that of article 37 of the national constitution, stipulating equal pay for equal work – which struck down pay distinctions according to age (Mariani, 1986). In the US, the split between the executive and the legislative powers led during the 1980s to both the blocking by Congress of the Executive's proposals for a youth subminimum wage and the Executive's refusal of an increase in the general minimum wage without provision for a youth rate.

A final aspect of heterogeneity in the public sector is the territorial. In countries which provide a significant role for regional, state or local government, notably Germany, Italy and the US, regulatory interventions aimed at youth have on occasion emerged at such levels even when blocked at the centre. Italy saw in the 1980s an impressive proliferation of pro-youth local initiatives, suppported by local government and agencies and involving job creation, orientation and training. National politicians have at times wished to devolve responsibility for manpower policies to regional and local bodies, as in Italy and the US during the 1970s (chapter 5, below). Local government has also been able on occasion to adapt central initiatives to its own purposes. In Britain, local authorities controlled by non-government parties – notably town councils in London and Sheffield – have often altered the regulatory content of national youth initiatives, primarily by giving trainees standard, negotiated terms and conditions of employment instead of the low allowances and short-term contracts favoured by central goverment (Ryan, 1989).

In sum, the state is a central influence upon the structure of youth regulation. National political traditions slant regulation towards very different mixtures of Institutional and Market Regulation and, within the former, towards legal/administrative rather than tripartite/negotiated approaches. At the same time, as most governments have been influenced to some extent during the last decade by deregulatory ideas, an increasing inclination towards Market Regulation might be inferred. These issues are taken up in section 2.4.

Young People

The final socioeconomic agent is youth itself. Two roles may be distinguished for youth: a passive and an active one. A passive role for youth lies at the heart of the problem of youth regulation. Young workers need access to employment and training, depend heavily in most economies on the decisions of others to provide them and are available for employment at pay rates below those in most adult work. These attributes of youth make their inclusion problematic in the first place.

Passivity is also common amongst youth in terms of identity and concerted action in pursuit of its own interests. Youth status is ephemeral and transitional (section 1.2, above). Both the formation of a distinct youth identity and the operational continuity of youth organisations are correspondingly fragile. Moreover, to the extent that youth identity and organisation emerge, their colouring by the standard attributes of adolescent culture – introspection, orientation towards peers, concern for the underdog, hostility to authority and interest in change (Coleman, 1961) – promotes the marginalisation of youth within wider organisations such as unions and political parties. Stereotyping may contribute further to such outcomes.

A further restrictive force is active discouragement of the formation of separate youth identity and organisation. In Britain, most unions have been reluctant to follow the lead given by the Amalgamated Engineering Union when it set up in the 1940s a youth section and an annual youth conference (Wray, 1959). The leadership of the Trades Union Congress has since 1977 fended off three separate moves to give its own youth conference more autonomy, defending its position in terms of the lack of youth representation within most unions themselves and the corollary that any national youth body would be unrepresentative. But the TUC has done little to encourage unions to develop internal youth representation, fearing the promotion of left-wing activism.[16] Paternalist values, which expect youth to be easily led astray, thus discourage the articulation and organisation of youth identity.

However, a distinct youth identity does at times emerge and organise, with important implications for youth regulation itself. Britain, France and Italy all show important examples. The British evolution away from Market towards Institutional Regulation in the immediate postwar decades was heavily influenced by youth activism. The militancy of engineering (metalworking) apprentices, expressed in recurrent strikes in pursuit of union representation, higher pay and better training, was directly associated with the episodic increases in wage-for-age schedules between 1937 and 1964. As the attitude of union officials to such activity was occasionally supportive, generally ambivalent and sometimes distinctly hostile, the role of youth activism in altering pay structure appears to have been considerable (Croucher, 1982; Ryan, 1987a).

An important role for youth unrest is also apparent in Italy and France. Italian youth unrest was concentrated in the 1960s and early 1970s in factories; in 1977, in schools and universities. Both waves were directed against established authority – including employers, the state and trade unions. Such protests were influential in the formation of the unions' *egualitarismo* wage strategy in the early 1970s and subsequently in the erosion of the 'historic compromise', two developments which altered the course of Institutional Regulation in Italy, with the former a clear indirect source of intensified youth exclusion (chapters 3, 5, below).

In France, the youth-led upsurge of 1968 led directly during 1968–71 to the *Constat de Grenelle* and various sectoral agreements, the net effect of which was to raise substantially the proportion of adult pay rates payable under wage-for-age scales to workers aged less than 19 (Marsden, 1985). As in Italy, such changes benefited young workers who found jobs but simultaneously made it harder for youth to do so.

Differences in the goals of youth must also be recognised. Post-war apprentice activists in Britain put pay increases ahead of training improvements in their list of demands, whereas the reverse ordering characterised their West German counterparts' corresponding period of militancy after 1965. This difference in the expressed goals of the two groups is directly associated with the tendency of Institutional Regulation towards youth exclusion in Britain, where apprentice numbers shrank as training costs to employers rose, but towards youth inclusion in Germany, where stable wage costs favoured high quality and quantity in apprentice training (Marsden and Ryan, 1991).

Elsewhere, youth activism is rarely visible. Unrest amongst young Dutch workers in the early 1970s was readily contained and led to little alteration in the distinctive attributes of youth regulation (Akkermanns and Grootings, 1978). Young people have for the most part responded passively and individually rather than collectively and politically to high youth unemployment in the 1980s (Jackson and Hanby, 1982). Some infer a secular tendency away from youth collective identity and activism (chapter 7, below). The focus of youth activism has tended to shift, particularly in the US, from manual to more highly educated workers and from industrial to non-work issues, including defence (Vietnam and disarmament), housing (squatter movements) and the environment. Amongst an important minority of European youth more generally, youth activity may also have shifted towards intolerance, as articulated around such sources of identity as race and sport.

A final influence for youth activism is the indirect one operating through political reaction to it. Two strands appear relevant: first, the political violence practised in the 1970s and early 1980s, particularly in Italy and Germany, by groups composed mostly of educated young people; secondly, the role of minority youth in race riots in Britain in the early 1980s. Such pressures contributed to the policy priority in many countries of the unemployment problems of youths (section 1.3, above) – not least in Italy, the country which has suffered most from political violence.

Overview

The goals and strategies of the four categories of agent interact and adapt in determining youth regulatory systems. A more complex account of youth regulation is clearly required than the simple one with which this section opened. Large employers have not generally sought to abrogate established wage and employment structures in order to exploit the short-term advantages associated with excess supplies of low priced youth labour. Unions respond to varying degrees to youth interests and cannot be seen simply as instruments of the interests of the adult majority in the membership. The interests of the state and young workers themselves are also important, particularly for the content of Institutional Regulation.

A further issue involves the conditions under which Institutional Regulation tends towards youth inclusion or exclusion. In most of German industry, inclusion is the norm; in much of Italian and US industry, exclusion. Although a detailed discussion of the issue is not possible here, amongst the wide range of factors conducive to one outcome or the other trust appears central. Youth inclusion is most likely when the major agents trust each other not to abuse the position of young people at the workplace to their own advantage. Trust can be developed under either Market or Institutional Regulation but it is a precarious asset (Gambetta, 1988). In the youth context, adult workers and trade unions require reassurance that the activity of young people at the workplace will provide youth with access to jobs and skills without adversely affecting adult interests. The most successful route to widespread youth inclusion generates high levels of trust through the joint administration of apprenticeship training.[17]

2.4   DEREGULATION AND FLEXIBILITY IN THE YOUTH CONTEXT

A marked tension has emerged since 1970 in advanced economies between Market and Institutional approaches to the regulation of labour, including youth employment and training. Persistently high unemployment and mounting international competition have called into question the desirability of regulatory systems developed during the postwar boom. Institutional Regulation has come under widespread pressure, particularly where it is seen to promote youth exclusion from the workplace. Proposals to strengthen market forces in order to improve youth activity have abounded under the twin banners of deregulation and flexibility, advocating moves from Institutional Exclusion (Table 2.1, Box 3) to Market Inclusion (Box 1).

A notable example involves compressed pay differentials, both between young and adult workers and between trainee and qualified workers. Low differentials, widely favoured by employer personnel policy, collective bargaining and national incomes policy, have undoubtedly contributed to the exclusion of youth in many sectors in Italy, France and Britain, *inter alia*. They have become increasingly vulnerable to the charge of pricing young people out of jobs and training. At the same time, high unemployment and a changed political climate have weakened the power of unions to defend their interests under Institutional Regulation.

More generally, the tensions facing national industrial relations systems have proved interrelated with the difficulties facing youth labour, over issues such as flexibility in employment levels and pay; employment protection, particularly in small firms and service work; technological change, functional flexibility and initial training; union representativeness and legitimacy; and the decentralisation and curtailment of bargaining itself.

The importance of youth within this wider set of issues is particularly marked in Britain and Italy, where the centrality of youth issues in the attempted recasting of economic regulation has remained largely unrecognised in the literature.[18]

Categories of Flexibility

Analyses of flexibility distinguish three main dimensions: wage, numerical and functional.[19] *Wage flexibility* refers to a high responsiveness of pay levels and pay structures to economic forces, including the state of labour markets and product markets. *Numerical flexibility* denotes high response of employment to sales and output, through easy layoffs, one route to which involves low employment security. *Functional flexibility* refers to ease of reallocation of workers across jobs and occupations, primarily within the enterprise. Deregulatory politics tend to bracket wage and numerical flexibility together and to neglect functional flexibility. However, all three aspects have direct implications for youth employment and training.

Wage and numerical flexibility
Proposals for increased flexibility have in the youth context focussed in most countries on its wage and numerical dimensions. Economists have urged the importance of reducing youth relative pay and, to a lesser extent, job security in order to increase employer willingness to hire and train young people (OECD, 1984b, 1986b; Siebert, 1985; Jones, 1985; Marsden and Ryan, 1989b, 1990b). In countries as varied as Italy, Britain, France, Sweden and the Netherlands, governments have pursued such policies, sponsoring special employment and training interventions which have reduced the cost of youth labour and involved fixed-term contracts, principally for unemployed youth.[20]

Britain. The most striking instance of wage and numerical deregulation as applied to youth is provided by Britain since 1976. The British government has adopted a range of measures to reduce the pay and employment security of young workers. The most important measure is the Youth Training Scheme, which in the late 1980s involved two year contracts of training and work experience at low allowances.[21] A related initiative, the Young (New) Workers Scheme has – quite exceptionally – tied employment subsidies for teenagers to the payment of low wages (Bushell, 1986; Rajan, 1987). Until recently these flexibility-oriented youth policies had no adult counterpart.[22]

Further youth-oriented initiatives include the removal in 1986 of an estimated one-half million workers aged less than 21 from statutory wage protection by Wages Councils. The primary aim of the 1986 Wages Act was stated by the government to be to 'encourage the creation of new jobs, particularly by removing young people under 21 from the scope of the Wages Council system . . . this means that an employer is not prevented from employing young people at wages they are prepared to accept because the rates are below those set by Wages Councils' (DEG, 1986, p. 369).[23]

In the same vein, the government proposed in 1988 to eliminate protective legislation which has long prohibited 16- and 17-year-olds from dangerous work and unsocial hours. Faced with widespread opposition, it opted instead for reductions in the coverage of protective laws, less extensive for youth than that for females, and greater willingness to grant employers exemption from health and safety restrictions for the employment of 16 and 17-year-olds.[24]

The British government has also sought to reduce wage expectations by cutting access to social welfare. Again, the policy has been pursued more intensively for youth than for adults. A 1985 regulation required claimants aged less than 25 (only) to move to another district within between two and eight weeks (depending on age) in order to maintain eligibility for benefit (TUC, 1985, p. 114). The 1988 social security reforms introduced a reduced benefit rate for single people aged less than 25 which had by 1990 reduced the real incomes of 18–24-year-old single householders by 27 per cent (Oppenheim, 1990). The same changes removed from 16–17-year-olds any entitlement in their own right to Income Support (the principal non-insurance benefit) on the grounds that they enjoyed the guarantee of a place on the Youth Training Scheme (TUC, 1988, p.84).[25]

Finally, young workers have been affected more seriously than most adults by deregulatory policies not explicitly targeted on youth. The extension in the early 1980s of the qualifying length of service under employment protection law from six months to two years affects teenage workers more severely than others, given that, as recent entrants to the labour market who are frequently confined to unstable employment, they are least likely to have accumulated two years' seniority.

These varied policies are expected to lead under competitive conditions to lower pay and labour costs for young workers relative to adults. Similar, if weaker, results may be anticipated under collective bargaining as well.[26]

Taken together, these reductions in youth rights and incomes amount to a major qualification to Rubery's (1989) observation that flexibility policy has in Britain sought to weaken the rights of all workers rather than to reduce the rights of particular groups. Youth has in fact been singled out for special treatment.

Other countries. Neither the variety of youth policies in Britain nor the priority given to wage flexibility finds any close approximation elsewhere. Governments in other countries have also encouraged numerical flexibility through special fixed term contracts targeted on youth. The *contrats d'emploi-formation* (CEF) in France, the *contratti di formazione e lavoro* (CFL) in Italy and the Youth Teams in Sweden also involve fixed-term contracts of up to two years' duration geared largely or wholly to young workers. Such programmes have however sought to increase flexibility in youth labour costs through public subsidy to sponsoring employers rather than through lower youth pay: participating employers are required to pay young workers at established rates in order to receive public payroll subsidies (Germe, 1986; Garonna, 1986; Frey, 1988; chapters 4,5 below).[27]

However, neither wage nor functional flexibility has featured in the response of German government to youth problems, which has involved instead both the expansion of apprenticeship places and remedial provision for the disadvantaged (chapter 4, below). Continuing reliance on existing regulatory forms in Germany may well reflect the established characteristics of apprentice contracts, with their low trainee allowances and fixed contract durations. But the absence of policies to reduce the pay and job security of 18–24-year-olds is striking, particularly in view of their high unemployment rates and the federal government's increasing interest in numerical flexibility in the 1980s (Buttler, 1987).

Functional flexibility
A further item on the flexibility agenda has been functional flexibility, or the ease with which workers can change jobs and expand their skills, primarily within the enterprise but also within the wider labour market. Youth training is directly relevant, in that high quality initial vocational preparation may increase functional flexibility during an individual's subsequent working life, while an enterprise whose workers have been so prepared may expect greater success in dealing with technical change. The presumed benefits of universal youth training, polyvalence, etc. have been widely accepted in policy discussion (section 1.4, above).

Increased functional flexibility has featured in various policy initiatives towards young people. There is firstly the insertion or upgrading of training content in the special employment measures developed for unemployed young people in Italy, Britain and France. In Britain the transition in 1982 from the Youth Opportunities Programme to the Youth Training Scheme was announced as a major step towards universal youth training (GB MSC, 1982c; Keep, 1986).

A second aspect is the upgrading of the technical and vocational content of general secondary education, particulary in Britain and France (Senker, 1986; d'Iribarne, 1982). Thirdly, *alternance* training for young people has been promoted, both by injecting work experience into secondary education, as notably in Sweden, France and Britain (Watts, Jamieson and Miller, 1989), and by increasing the classroom content of workplace-based training, as in Germany, leading to some convergence in methods of youth preparation under Regulated Exclusion and Inclusion (Sellin, 1983).

The simple nexus between increased flexibility and deregulation breaks down when the discussion moves from wage and numerical flexibility to functional flexibility. Only the most enthusiastic advocates of market forces deny the importance of market failure and the need for public intervention to improve initial training (Matthews, 1989). Government rhetoric in Britain follows this line in insisting that lower youth pay will increase youth access to training as well as to jobs, as well as in relying on an 'employer led' training system (GB DE, 1988). However, government practice suggests otherwise, in intervening widely and spending heavily to revamp initial training. Indeed training has constituted in the 1980s one of the few policy areas in which the government has found it expedient to retain a classic tripartite instrument, the Manpower Services Commission (chapter 8, below). Although the government's deregulatory instincts have indeed shaped its training policy, the absence of any simple link between youth training and regulatory mode remains clear even in Britain (Ryan, 1991b; Marsden and Ryan, 1991).

Similarly, although the German federal government has since the mid-1980s encouraged increased numerical flexibility (Buttler, 1987; Brunhes, 1989), its actions in the context of youth training have remained marginal, seeking primarily to adapt apprenticeship to technical change, notably by the reform of occupational categories and training programmes (Streeck et al., 1987).

The ambiguous relationship between functional flexibility and youth regulation means that deregulatory policies aimed at youth have concentrated upon the numerical and wage (more generally, labour cost) aspects of flexibility and remained largely silent on functional flexibility, where Institutional Regulation in one form or another has retained widespread legitimacy.

A further deregulatory current is the tendency for pro-youth public interventions to focus upon employers, particularly profit-making firms rather than educational and charitable institutions, as delivery vehicles for youth employment and training under publicly subsidised contracts. Only in the relatively stable regulatory systems of Sweden and Germany has this development remained marginal or absent. Indeed, the Swedish public school system has been given enhanced responsibilities for the young unemployed, a development unthinkable in 1980s Britain (chapter 4, below).

Outcomes of Deregulation

Although the effects of deregulatory policies towards youth have yet to be studied in detail, a partial assessment can be attempted here.

International differences

The volume and status of youth activity under deregulatory initiatives in France, Britain and Italy suggest some success, particularly by contrast to the limited effects of policies seeking to increase aggregate wage flexibility. In Britain, more than one-half of all 16-year-old workers, and one-third of 17-year-olds, was active on YTS at any one time during 1987 (GB TA, 1990, Table 2.1). The extent of youth activity under the Italian CFL trainee contracts has remained smaller, but rapid growth after 1984 took it to 10.3 per cent of all placements by the public employment service in 1987 (Frey, 1988). The least extensive of the three is France, where the 84,000 young people active under CEF in 1984 amounted to less than 8 per cent of unemployment in the age group 16–25 years (Germe, 1986).

The extent of youth activity under special contracts appears related across countries to the scale of labour cost rather than numerical flexibility. Differences in the latter respect have been small: the British, French and Italian programmes of the late 1980s all stipulated fixed-term contracts of up to two years' duration. Differences in labour cost flexibility have however been marked. In Britain, the publicly financed trainee allowance, which has amounted to less than one-half of normal youth pay, covers the entire payroll cost of trainees under YTS for employers who do not concede higher allowances. Public support under the CFL in Italy has been limited to employer exemption from social security contributions, equivalent to a 30 per cent subsidy to payroll costs for Northern employers but only 6 per cent for those in the South, who already received similar relief. In France, the state's contribution has been lower still, being limited to a grant to cover training costs, with employers paying the recognised rate for the job –

until the introduction of youth payment at less than the minimum wage in 1984 (Ryan, 1989; Frey, 1988; Germe, 1986).

At the same time, youth programmes in Britain, Italy and France have not been able to bridge the gap between youth unemployment in those countries and in Sweden, Germany and Japan. The difference between youth and adult unemployment rates remains much greater in the former than in the latter group (Table 1.1, above). Patterns of youth activity under such programmes are biased towards segments in which youth employment is already most marked, especially towards small plants, non-union employers and the service sector (Ryan, 1989; Marsden and Ryan, 1988b; Frey, 1988).

Outcomes in Britain

The multidimensional deregulatory effort targeted upon youth in Britain has chalked up some achievements. The most important has been the replacement for early school-leavers of much ordinary employment and most apprenticeship by government-financed trainee-ships – quite apart from the effect on youth unemployment. At the end of 1988, an estimated 300,000 trainees on the Youth Training Scheme, mostly 16–17-year-olds receiving low allowances on fixed duration contracts, would have been in regular employment or apprenticeship in the absence of the scheme.[28]

The attributes of mainstream youth employment have been altered as well. Youth pay fell relative to that of adults during the 1980s. For 18–20-year-old females the decline was broadly continuous after 1979, amounting to 12 per cent by 1989. The decline was more moderate, at around 9 per cent, for the other categories (manual males, 16–17 and 18–20, females 16–17) and in all three cases relative pay had stabilised by around the middle of the decade (Table 2.2, columns 1–4).[29] To the extent that the demand for youth labour is price-sensitive, deregulation has increased youth employment through reductions in its price.[30]

However, deregulation cannot take sole responsibility for falling youth pay. The political triumph of deregulation in 1979 came after the start of the decline in youth pay around 1975–7, aided by the collapse of the Social Contract incomes policy and the growth of youth unemployment. Fluctuations in unemployment, government interven-tions and economic restructuring have clouded the picture further in the 1980s by inducing complex compositional changes in time series of youth earnings. However, the decline in youth relative pay in the 1980s has been too great to be attributable simply to compositional factors,

Table 2.2 Average relative pay of young workers and dispersion of pay within age groups, full-time employees, Britain, April 1974–89

	(1)	(2)	(3)	(4)	(5)	(6)	(7)	(8)	(9)	(10)
	Mean youth relative pay (percentage of adult pay)				Pay of lowest decile as percentage of pay of median[a]					
	< 18		18–20		< 18		18–20		21 +	
Year	MM	F	MM	F	MM	F	MM	F	MM	F
1974	46.3	55.7	73.9	73.7	67	71	70	72	73	69
1975	48.9	57.3	75.4	73.8	71	75	68	72	73	68
1976	47.9	53.6	73.5	72.0	71	71	69	69	74	67
1977	49.3	54.6	73.8	73.7	71	71	70	72	75	70
1978	48.8	54.0	74.9	73.0	73	72	70	73	74	71
1979	48.5	55.5	74.6	73.7	72	74	70	76	73	71
1980	47.7	54.6	74.6	73.0	71	71	71	74	72	69
1981	48.7	53.0	72.8	71.0	69	67	69	73	73	68
1982	49.2	51.9	71.6	70.1	68	68	70	73	72	69
1983	46.4	48.9	71.7	68.9	69	68	65	72	71	67
1984	43.7	48.1	70.5	67.8	65	65	67	74	71	66
1985	45.2	49.0	69.4	66.1	67	67	65	73	70	67
1986	43.4	50.6	68.7	65.6	67	69	67	72	70	66
1987	44.9	51.4	67.3	66.0	66	68	67	73	69	65
1988	45.8	51.7	68.0	65.0	66	70	69	73	69	64
1989	45.0	50.8	68.6	64.9	71	68	67	72	68	63

Notes: Pay variable is gross hourly earnings of full-time employees whose pay was unaffected by absence; MM denotes manual males; F, all females.
[a] Within age-sex category.

Source: GB Department of Employment, *New Earnings Survey*, Part E, Tables 125, 126.

particularly for 18–20-year-olds.[31] Moreover, whether or not it was caused by deregulation, falling youth pay has certainly been the outcome sought by deregulatory policy.

In any event, youth deregulation has in other respects been less successful at meeting its own goals – in terms of both its immediate objectives and the restructuring of youth regulation more generally.

Taking immediate goals first, YTS traineeships have been offered predominantly in occupations with low skill requirements, particularly in the service sector, and the quality of much YTS training has remained low. YTS has therefore made only a limited contribution both to scarce training for costly transferable skills and to functional flexibility more generally (Ryan, 1989; Begg et al., 1990; Lee et al., 1990).

Similarly, cuts in youth pay have not been uniform or extensive enough to match deregulatory requirements. In particular, the removal of young workers from coverage by minimum wages in 1986 appears to have had little effect, anecdotal evidence of cuts in youth compensation notwithstanding (*Youth and Policy*, 1990). The pay of young workers appears not to have declined systematically relative to that of adults in the two occupational categories where coverage of young people by wage minima had been greatest (Table 2.3, columns 1–5). Only a limited period has elapsed since 1986 and sampling error in the data is substantial, but there is no evidence here of any deregulatory effect upon youth pay.[32]

One widely noted attribute of deregulation does not however show up more generally in the youth context: a tendency towards increasing segmentation in the labour market (Rosenberg, 1989a). The orientation of deregulation towards youth in Britain might be expected to result not only in lower relative pay for the representative young worker but also in a more rapid growth in inequality amongst young people than amongst adults, particularly in the lower tail of the earnings distributions. Labour market inequalities have certainly grown strongly in the 1980s, as evidenced here in the decline in earnings at the lowest decile relative to those at the median for young and adult workers alike (Table 2.2, columns 5–10). However, the increase in inequality was if anything greater and longer-lived amongst adult than amongst young workers, for whom some recovery in the position of the lowest paid appears to have occurred since 1985.

The conclusion is unreliable for 16–17-year-olds, as the inclusion of YTS trainees would undoubtedly result in a particularly rapid growth of intra-group inequality in the 1980s. But it is more robust for 18–20-year-olds, few of whom participate in YTS and who have since 1987 been the target of subsidies to low wage employment under the New Workers Scheme.[33]

The effects of a decade of deregulation upon the wider regulation of youth activity have been less impressive still, not least in terms of activity at the workplace, upon which this discussion concentrates. Although the Youth Training Scheme developed during the 1980s into the main channel of labour market entry for 16–17-year-olds, it has not produced a basic transformation of youth regulation, even for early school-leavers. Its occupational coverage and legitimacy have both remained deficient (Marsden and Ryan, 1991). By 1990 it had

Table 2.3 Youth relative pay and inequality in pay by age group in two low-paid occupational categories, full-time employees, Britain, April 1985–9.

	(1)	(2)	(3)	(4)	(5)	(6)	(7)	(8)	(9)	(10)
						Pay of lowest decile as percentage of pay of median				
	Mean youth relative pay (percentage of adult pay)									
	Selling			Catering etc		Selling			Catering	
Year	M2	F1	F2	M2	F2	M2	F1	F2	M2	F2
1985	51.1	56.5	76.6	72.4	79.2	77	78	78	67	65
1986	52.9	60.3	80.1	73.5	80.0	75	80	77	70	66
1987	52.5	57.1	78.5	68.6	80.6	75	83	78	66	62
1988	55.6	55.8	75.1	71.5	78.6	72	76	78	71	69
1989	51.2	59.6	78.0	74.3	79.8	71	78	76	65	68

Notes: As Table 2.2 except: sex/age categories are male (M) and female (F), 16–17-year-olds (1) and 18–20-year-olds (2); occupational categories are VIII (Selling) and X (Catering, cleaning, hairdressing and other personal services).

Source: As Table 2.2 (Tables 128, 129).

begun to shrink in both scale of operation and *per capita* public funding, reflecting both increased youth employment and government desire to transfer training costs to employers. Its revamping in 1990 as '(New) Youth Training' further bolsters a prediction that it will be classed in retrospect in the legion of *ad hoc*, ephemeral public interventions.

Nor have changes in youth relative pay meant substantial change in this aspect of youth regulation. The recovery of 1987–9 has stalled, if not reversed, the decline in youth pay, even though youth unemployment remains high and initial training inadequate.[34] The similarities between youth pay and employment in Britain at the start and at the end of the 1980s are more striking than the differences, particularly compared to other countries. Britain occupies nowadays an intermediate position amongst major EEC economies, below France and Italy and above West Germany and the Netherlands, similar to where it stood in the late 1970s (chapter 3, below).[35]

Outcomes: overview
Outcomes disappointing from the standpoint of deregulatory aspirations reflect the tendency of deregulatory policies to misunderstand the

regulatory systems which they seek to replace. There are two aspects to this failing. The first is the widespread assumption that Market Regulation will automatically produce the outcomes associated with the textbook model of the 'perfectly' competitive market, including youth inclusion in particular. In practice, the prevalence of internal markets involves substantial barriers to youth incorporation even in the absence of union or public regulation.

The second misconception involves the realisability of Market Regulation itself, given the resilience of union power. Increased wage and numerical flexibility for young people resurrects the threat posed by cheap and insecure youth labour to trade union interests. Union reaction has been divided, given the political embarrassment of being seen to oppose pro-youth measures and the widespread impulse within unions to help young people. However, in Britain at least, the quest for increased flexibility in youth activity would arguably have been more effective had it been tied less closely to deregulation and pro-market ideology, and more willing to consider union interests, not least by a greater involvement of unions in its determination.

Thus a strikingly high level of union involvement in the formulation and administration of the Youth Training Scheme – *de facto*, not *de jure* – was probably essential to what limited success the programme achieved in industry. Only the government's recognition of that fact can account for its willingness to deal with unions on the issue, however informally (chapter 8, below).

Similarly, the fact that compressed wage differentials might be valued for reasons other than their implications for youth activity – such as egalitarian wage policy or increased worker willingness to change jobs – also dooms deregulatory calls for increased wage flexibility to failure unless unions can be convinced, as they have been in the Netherlands.

International comparisons of youth unemployment and training at the end of the 1980s suggest therefore that the secret of success lies more in the development of a suitable and stable form of Institutional Regulation than in indiscriminate attempts to move from Institutional towards Market Regulation.[36]

Flexibility: Positive and Negative

Deregulatory policies are often criticised from the left for being undesirable, quite apart from whether they are effective or not. Two negative attributes of flexibility have been widely recognised. The first involves efficiency: increased wage and numerical flexibility are criticised as myopic, 'defensive' responses to structural problems, in contrast to the farsighted, 'offensive' potential of functional flexibility (Boyer, 1988; Rubery, Tarling and Wilkinson, 1987; Brunhes, 1989). The second concerns equity: the tendency for increased wage and numerical flexibility to work only selectively and then largely upon groups whose pay and job security are already weak, thereby increasing 'the freedom of action of the more powerful social partners' (Meulders and Wilkin, 1987).

Such defects are clearly visible in the youth context, again particularly in Britain. The contribution of labour cost flexibility to firms' performance overall is particularly small when it concerns youth only, given the small share of employment accounted for by youth in most organisations. Market forces offer an at most limited contribution to the elusive goal of improved youth training. The scope of British deregulatory cuts in youth welfare benefits and pay aspirations lacks justification in terms of employment and training, given that youth supply prices have long fallen short of negotiated youth pay rates. The cuts represent instead a dismal example of the placing 'of the burden of . . . the necessary adjustments on the shoulders of the weakest' (Meulders and Wilkin, 1987).

However, the manifest defects of the flexibility agenda can easily blind criticism to the important issues which it points up for youth regulation – issues which involve not so much short-term adaptability in the face of unemployment, on which most of the controversy has concentrated, as longer-term structural defects. Increased wage and numerical flexibility are relevant not just to the short-term, defensive, pro-market attributes with which they are normally associated; they can also contribute to reform within Institutional Regulation.

Thus lower relative pay and fixed-term contracts for young trainees can contribute more powerfully to youth inclusion when they are embedded in a legitimate and stable system of youth incorporation, rather than in ephemeral special employment programmes. German apprenticeship has shown a highly desirable form of flexibility in its stability and resilience in the face of the upheavals of the last two decades. The task to which the flexibility agenda points countries such as the UK and Italy is therefore to develop effective and durable institutions of youth regulation in cases where they do not exist at present, without expecting that market forces can contribute much on their own.[37]

2.5   POLICY DIRECTIONS

Although the variability of youth regulation across advanced economies rules out generally applicable policy suggestions, some broad
statements follow from the discussion in the previous section.

General Issues

Firstly, there is widespread scope for improving upon the regulatory
status quo, particularly where youth exclusion prevails. The inclusion
of young people at workplaces under suitably regulated conditions can
avoid the unsatisfactory compromises of earlier regulatory systems
and, by improving youth development while protecting adult interests,
provide gains for all parties.

Secondly, for such policies to succeed, they must harmonise with the
wider regulatory framework, particularly its industrial relations
component. In particular, any policy which promotes youth inclusion
in unionised sectors must deal explicitly with trade union concerns, as
by effective regulation of the quality of training (as approximated in
Germany) and by recognising established rates of pay (as for 18–19-
year-old participants in Youth Teams in Sweden).

Finally, all countries face common issues in deciding the respective
merits of youth inclusion at or exclusion from the workplace and,
whichever outcome is desired, of Market and Institutional methods of
pursuing it.

Regulatory outcomes
Few will argue in favour of the desirability of youth exclusion from the
workplace taken by itself (chapter 1, above). To that extent, youth
inclusion may appear a universal *desideratum*. However, on closer
inspection, the issue is less clear cut, particularly for youth training, as
exclusion may be positive or negative in intention and effect.

If youth exclusion involves access to public vocational education,
while youth inclusion means casual, unskilled employment or low
quality training, exclusion appears preferable. Such considerations led
Swedish policy to favour secondary education over apprenticeship in
its reappraisal of training policy in the 1950s. However, the quality of
full-time vocational schooling itself may be poor, particularly in
Britain and the US, where it is often underresourced, technically
stagnant and held back by low attainments in early schooling. To
some extent full-time schooling also suffers from simply delaying the

problem of youth inclusion from 15 to 18 years of age. The qualified 18-year-old is indeed better placed to compete for employment with adult workers than is his or her unqualified counterpart, but the experiences of youth unemployment in France and Sweden (chapters 4,6, below) indicate the difficulties that even qualified young workers may face in finding suitable employment.

The appealing policy alternatives for teenagers thus involve either early youth inclusion, through apprenticeship-type arrangements, which entails problems of training quality control at the workplace, or full-time vocational education, which is more costly and which involves subsequent problems of youth inclusion. The former outcome appears superior in terms of the quantity, the latter in terms of the quality, of youth employment and training. However, both are superior to any concentration of youth activity in secondary employment, without significant training content or career prospects. Whatever about its quantity, the quality of youth activity is then unacceptably low.

Regulatory methods

The advantages of Market and Institutional Regulation were discussed in the previous section, in the context of deregulatory policies favouring the former. Taking a broader view, it is clear that the two approaches offer contrasting advantages. Market forces offer the prospect of increased allocative efficiency by moving prices towards market-clearing values. The pervasive and powerful effects of price incentives are commonly contrasted with the uneven and weak ones achieved by an administrative system based upon rules, inspection and enforcement (Siebert, 1989).

Such arguments presume that deregulation can approximate the competitive ideal, even though Market Regulation rarely does so in labour markets.[38] Even in the absence of union and government intervention, large firms and internal labour markets remain a pervasive fact of life, restricting the applicability of competitive models to small firms – where their applicability cannot be taken for granted either (Kaufman, 1984). Indeed, labour markets usually prove *more* segmented, unequal and inefficient under Market than under Institutional Regulation.[39] Youth activity at the workplace under Market Regulation consequently lacks both breadth and quality.

Institutional Regulation, by contrast, can deliver high quality youth vocational preparation combined with low youth unemployment and a moderately even spread of youth employment across sectors. Such outcomes are most evident in Sweden and West Germany, countries where Institutional Regulation tends towards the exclusion and inclusion of teenagers respectively. Sweden scores the more highly in terms of vocational training quality, Germany in terms of relative youth employment. What they share is the importance of Institutional Regulation, in which the interests of government, trade unions and young people themselves are explicitly recognised and influential (chapter 4, below).

Institutional Regulation may also promote undesirable outcomes. Compressed age differentials in pay tend to exclude young people from jobs unless accompanied by high aggregate demand – an outcome particularly evident for females in France and Italy (Table 1.3, above). Youth exclusion can be even more intense under Institutional than under Market Regulation.

We conclude that both the most and the least attractive outcomes for youth have been achieved under Institutional Regulation; and that the most attractive possibilities – inclusion under a regulated apprenticeship system or exclusion into vocational education – offer contrasting advantages, each of which is preferable to either exclusion into unemployment or inclusion in low quality employment.

Institutional Inclusion: Bargained Flexibility

The preceding considerations suggest that the inclusion of young people in employment and training at a wide range of workplaces is an attractive policy objective in a wide range of circumstances; and that the joint administration which characterises much of Institutional Regulation offers a more effective vehicle to realise youth inclusion than does the uneven operation of market forces under Market Regulation.

A policy which seeks to implement Institutional Inclusion for young people (Table 2.1, Box 4) seeks a durable basis for youth employment and training at the workplace and looks to negotiation and bargaining to achieve it. In an earlier discussion we termed such a policy one of 'bargained flexibility' (Garonna and Ryan, 1986).

The superiority of a policy of negotiating increased flexibility in youth activity to simple deregulation has already been discussed. It is also preferable to a third alternative: taking existing regulation as given and simply providing public subsidies to youth employment and training within it, as in Britain in the 1970s and in Sweden and Italy in the 1980s. The high fiscal cost of such a policy (outside conditions of low unemployment) makes it problematic in an era of downward pressure on public spending (OECD, 1985). Its effects are also limited: in both Sweden and Italy youth unemployment rates have remained considerably higher than adult ones (albeit at very different levels) and increases in overall unemployment still fall disproportionately upon youth (Table 1.1).

The negotiation of increased flexibility is familiar in terms of functional flexibility. In the UK it has been well established since the 1950s under the rubric of 'productivity bargaining' (Flanders, 1964). In the US it has grown rapidly since 1980 as part of 'concession' or 'giveback' bargaining (Strauss, 1984). In each instance, employers and unions bargain changes in rules which affect staffing levels, occupational demarcation, work assignment, job structures and technical change in return for improvements in pay, status and job security. The scope for such deals is promoted by their 'positive sum' attributes: the increased productivity of new procedures typically permits gains for all parties.[40]

Bargained flexibility may appear less familiar in the youth context, but it has long characterised German apprenticeship (Streeck et al., 1987). More recent manifestations include national collective agreements in the Netherlands in the 1980s, under which employers and unions agreed to encourage youth employment by induction contracts, the expansion of apprenticeship and worksharing (Van Rintel, 1986); the Youth Jobs and Youth Teams projects in Sweden, with their nationally negotiated mixture of wage and hours flexibility respectively (chapter 4, below); the insertion in 1983 of employer-level negotiability of the training content of the Italian CFL, previously set by government stipulation (Garonna, 1986); and the insertion in 1982 of similar provisions concerning trainee pay, contractual status and access to training, into the Youth Training Scheme in Britain as it superseded the non-negotiable Youth Opportunities Programme (chapter 8, below).

These varied instances of bargained flexibility for youth all promote the inclusion of young workers at a wide range of workplaces, whether at ages 15–17 for initial vocational training or, if that is conducted in schools, from around age 18 for regular employment.

The detailed direction which policies of bargained flexibility might pursue varies from country to country. Any attempt to provide such indications for a range of advanced economies lies outside our reach. We offer instead the implications of our discussion for the two countries which we know best: Britain and Italy.

Britain. Neither of the main policy stances towards youth regulation in Britain *circa* 1990 – simple deregulation and wholesale rejection of the flexibility agenda – finds favour in this discussion. The former is doomed to partial and unsatisfactory outcomes in the face of labour market realities; the latter condemns young people to a precarious and marginal existence, particularly while unemployment remains high.

A superior approach would encourage negotiation to extend the scope and quality of youth training, relying primarily upon the workplace. Lower pay and limited employment security for trainees should be envisaged in order to encourage employer participation in training. But it is also vital to provide for effective joint regulation of training quality in order to ensure that adequate skills are produced and to protect adult unionists and young people from the abuse of trainees at the workplace. The terms of such agreements should be negotiated by employers and unions in the first instance, but there is a clear role for youth representatives in their formulation and for the state in laying down broad guidelines before negotiation.

Such conditions have been approximated by apprenticeship, as regulated after 1964 by the Industrial Training Boards (Lindley, 1983) and, more recently, by parts of the Youth Training Scheme. However, the former suffered from limited coverage, employer hostility and the progressive withdrawal of government support; the latter, from inadequate quality control and low legitimacy in the eyes of trade unionists and young people (Marsden and Ryan, 1991).

An impressive example of bargained flexibility under YTS was provided by the 1983 national agreement between unions (EETPU) and employers (ECA) in electrical contracting for the reform of craft training. Significant alterations were made in all three dimensions of flexibility. Wage flexibility featured in the halving of the pay of first year trainees, aimed at cutting employers' training costs, and in union agreement to employers' use of YTS subsidies to cover almost all of first year trainee wages. Numerical flexibility was embodied in an employer guarantee of specified increases in trainee intakes and union acceptance that employers would not guarantee employment at the end of training. Functional flexibility was encouraged by the stipulation of a training programme with high quality objectives, along with procedures for their attainment (IDS, 1983). Such radical rebargaining of youth regulation remains exceptional in Britain.[41]

Italy. Bargained flexibility in the Italian context means primarily national politics and administrative regulation. The legislation of

1984–6 which gradually decontrolled hiring and firing reflected prior consultations with unions and employers. Youth training was an issue in central negotiations over incomes policy and annual wage rounds in the mid-1980s. The extension to smaller firms in 1990 of the coverage of worker protection and union rights under the Workers' Statute was partly the result of union pressure.

Institutional change is however required for bargained flexibility to contribute to the further improvement of the continuing difficulties of young people in the Italian labour market. A central issue in recent national discussions involves youth representation, particularly within trade unions but also in labour market regulation more generally. The issue is linked to interest in greater transparency and accessibility in worker representation. The late 1980s reform of the *Consiglio Nazionale dell'Economia e del Lavoro* represents a first step in that direction.

Limits to bargaining
Bargained flexibility clearly cannot offer a solution to the problem of youth in all contexts. The limits to the appeal of flexibility have already been considered, but bargaining is also a vehicle of limited capability.

Collective negotiations constitute an unlikely route for the unorganised sectors of all economies, notably in the services and in small firms. The difficulty is particularly marked in the US, where collective bargaining covers a small and declining share of employment. Institutional Regulation then requires the bargaining of rules in national politics and their judicial enforcement upon unorganised sectors, as over the youth subminimum wage in the US in 1989. Indirect methods may prove useful here, e.g. requiring firms to bargain in good faith and to appoint training representatives. Such rules can stipulate the terms and conditions of youth activity at the workplace, including the type and level of training to be provided. Mechanisms to enforce such rules have to be developed by the US government if it is to monitor the linkage of the youth subminimum wage to the provision of training at the workplace (section 2.3, above).

The fundamental difficulty in this respect is of course political. Employers prefer not to be obliged to bargain, not least over training, and in periods of union weakness there is little to force them to do so. At the same time, it is possible that, as the failings of simple deregulatory solutions become more clearly visible, many employers will come round to cooperation with nationally agreed and locally negotiated systems of youth employment and training which respect the interests of both young and adult workers.

Finally, there is the issue of youth representation in negotiations. Unions, employers and the state have all staked claims to represent the interest of youth, while youth itself, which might be expected to lay the strongest claim, often fails to do so and, when it does, usually meets with refusal. There is a strong case for public policy to promote youth representation within trade unions, at the workplace and on regulatory bodies in order to reduce the sway of paternalist values and to ensure a more effective representation of the interests of young people themselves.

2.6   CONCLUSIONS

The regulation of youth activity remains an unresolved issue in many advanced economies, most notably in Britain, France and Italy. Recent years have seen the articulation of widespread dissatisfaction with the regulatory systems developed during the postwar boom; the adoption to one degree or another of deregulatory policies aimed at greater flexibility in youth employment and training; and partial and unsatisfactory consequences for young people.

The debate remains stalled between positions entrenched for and against deregulation and flexibility. We urge the importance of breaking such stalemates, particularly by extending the quantity and quality of youth activity at the workplace; the futility of deregulation alone as means to that end; and the desirability of the long-term, structural potential of bargained flexibility, which seeks through negotiation to promote better outcomes for young workers.

Notes

1.   This paper revises and extends previous work (Garonna and Ryan, 1986, 1989). We thank David Marsden, Sergio Bruno, Sam Rosenberg and Vittorio Valli for comments.
2.   The adult pay figure for females covers all employees, not just manual ones. Further indirect evidence of low supply prices comes from the large numbers of young people who participated in non-compulsory public employment schemes such as the UK Youth Opportunities Programme, despite low payment, insecure employment and lack of

training (GB MSC, 1982a). However, low required earnings are not the same as low expected earnings, which can simultaneously be high amongst unemployed youth (Main, 1987).

3. Norms such as 'we were all young once' appear more influential than do the values which might favour the inclusion of female and immigrant workers ('we're all human beings', etc.).

4. We join the *régulation* school in its interest in the interdependence of socioeconomic institutions and macroeconomic performance, along with economic crisis and institutional renewal (Boyer, 1979, 1988; Marsden, 1986a, ch. 6). We share the interest of 'societal effect' analysis in the variability of regulatory institutions across countries, though we emphasise (i) differences within as well as between economies and (ii) industrial relations more than the organisation of work and education (Maurice, Sellier and Silvestre, 1984, 1986; Piore, 1987). Our primary interest lies in industrial relations systems and the forces which threw them into turmoil after 1974 (Edwards, Garonna and Todtling, 1986).

5. In adopting a dichotomy between Market and Institutional Regulation we do not deny the market's status as a regulatory institution (Marsden, 1986a, ch. 8) but simply adopt a terminology familiar in the literature (e.g. Piore 1987). The dichotomy corresponds to that made by Doeringer and Piore (1971) between the dominance of rules in internal labour markets and that of market forces in the external labour market. Our analysis extends however to the labour market as a whole, where rules may also predominate.

6. Raffe (1990) views British labour markets and training systems as a particularly mixed case by international standards. We avoid treating regulatory categories as historically sequential phases (e.g. Taylorism and Fordism) as opposed to concurrent structures. Although such periodisations can point up important changes in the relative importance of alternative modes of regulation, they also generate misunderstanding, as for example when the labour market segmentation which is increased by flexibility strategies is treated as a historical novelty (Boyer, 1988).

7. Worker protection under the Workers' Statute does not apply to small firms in Italy; nor, until 1990, did legal restrictions on unfair dismissal. Also, the evasion of social security contributions and social legislation and the wider black economy are well known to be widespread in the small firm sector.

8. Osterman (1980), Defreitas, Marsden and Ryan (1990).

9. The category 'regulated inclusion' in our earlier analysis (Garonna and Ryan, 1986) corresponds to Institutional Inclusion in this discussion.

10. A motion calling for 'legislation to compel employers to engage a proportion of their workforce in that [youth] age group in offices and factories in the same manner that they are now compelled under the Register of Disabled People' was passed at the 1978 conference of the Trades Union Congress. However, comments made on behalf of the General Council ('we have had problems with quota systems') implied that no vigorous pursuit of this objective was to be anticipated – and nothing more was heard of it (TUC, 1978, pp. 474–6).

11. The particularly strong attachment of British clothing employers to teenage female labour arises in part from their preference for highly sectionalised work and training (Steedman and Wagner, 1989).

12. The links between product market power, personnel policy and labour market outcomes are discussed by Krueger and Summmers (1987), McNabb and Ryan (1989) and Gross (1990).

13. Brusco and Sabel (1981), Piore and Sabel (1984), Brusco and Garonna (1984). However, the fall in labour turnover and the intensification of youth exclusion which characterised Italy in the 1970s was at least as intense amongst advanced small firms as amongst large businesses (Garonna, 1980b).

14. In modern economic theories of union objectives, which emphasise economic self-interest by individual members and preference aggregation by majority voting, the key factor is the smallness of youth numbers, which implies low influence, on the margin of union membership (Oswald, 1985; Carruth and Oswald, 1987).

15. US government proposals under the National Recovery Act in the 1930s for minimum apprentice or learner rates set at 80 per cent of the adult equivalent were opposed by trade unions on the grounds of potential substitution of youth for adults. Direct restriction was actually achieved by US unions: later NRA codes restricted payments to learners and apprentices to 5 per cent of payrolls (Osterman, 1980, pp. 69–74).

16. A motion to the 1978 TUC annual conference called for the annual TUC youth conference (a discussion body) to be allowed to determine its own agenda, to enjoy more time to discuss it and to be encouraged to draw up a Youth Charter for campaigning amongst youth. Similarly, a bakers union (BFAWU) motion in 1982 called for an independent TUC youth conference. Finally, a 1986 motion called for the same youth conference to be permitted to debate motions submitted by affiliated unions and to have its decisions considered by the General Council of the TUC. In the first two cases, the General Council declined to act until youth representation had become widespread within unions; it responded to the third by conceding a further conduit for youth issues – a Youth Forum, which was to meet thrice yearly – but insisted on keeping control of this new body by limiting its membership to union leaders themselves and those young people whom they selected from lists of union nominees (TUC, 1978, p. 489; 1979, p. 49; 1982, p. 624; 1986, p. 484; 1988, p. 449).

17. The conditions for Institutional Inclusion are discussed in chapter 3, below, and in Marsden and Ryan (1990b, 1991).

18. A verdict on Italy in the mid-1980s by one of the authors held that 'the question of youth unemployment is in fact at the centre of the industrial relations crisis and is therefore crucial to its resolution' (Garonna, 1986). Rubery's (1989) assessment of flexibility stands out for its appreciation of youth issues.

19. GB NEDO (1986), OECD (1986a, 1986b), Meulders and Wilkin (1987), Tarling (1987), Boyer (1988), Rosenberg (1989a, 1989b), Brunhes (1989), Rubery (1989). Secondary dimensions of flexibility are distinguished in

some analyses, including subcontracting (distancing) and working time, but none have direct implications for youth regulation.

20. Garonna (1986); Germe (1986); Ryan (1989); Crone (1986); chapter 5, below.

21. Although unions have since 1982 been free to bargain higher pay and contracts of indefinite duration (under employee status) for YTS trainees, only a minority has benefited from either (Ryan, 1989).

22. The New Job Training Scheme of 1987 extended wage flexibility to the adult unemployed under a 'benefits plus' formula, in contrast to the 'rate for the job' for which they had previously been eligible under the Community Programme (Carter, 1986; GB TC, 1988).

23. The estimate of one-half million was provided in an answer to a Parliamentary Question (*Employment Gazette*, November 1989, p. 573).

24. *Employment Gazette*, January 1988; February 1989, p. 107.

25. Welfare policy towards youth in Britain in the 1980s shows two contradictory impulses: cutting youth benefits and removing benefit differences between young householders and non-householders, which increases youth dependency on the parental household; and requiring young people to contribute more to the income of the parental household, by cutting adult housing benefit for non-dependant young members of the household, which increases parental dependence on children (Cusack and Roll, 1985; West, 1989).

26. For example, cuts in social security reduce wage settlements in bargaining models by lowering membership income levels in a dispute, thereby reducing union bargaining power (Binmore and Dasgupta, 1986). However, the pay effect of cuts in alternative incomes is weaker under bargaining than under competitive wage determination, where the whole youth supply curve moves down. Moreover, in models of unions as democratic organisations, reductions in the income of a minority group such as young workers *alone*, which do not affect the position of the median member, have little or no effect upon the desire or ability of unions to achieve their bargaining objectives, including youth relative pay.

27. Wage flexibility was however added in France in 1984, when the new youth contracts (*alternance*) for the first time permitted payment of young participants at less than established rates (Germe, 1986).

28. More than two-thirds (71 per cent) of YTS traineeships in a 1989 survey were estimated to have replaced regular jobs or apprenticeships for the same young workers ('deadweight') at a time when 420,000 young people were active on YTS (Begg, Blake, Deakin and Pratten, 1990, Tables, 2.1, 6.1).

29. Non-manuals are excluded from the male statistics in view of the greater occupational heterogeneity of that category and the distorting effects of rapid pay increases in the managerial occupations which contain almost no young workers. Sampling error makes year to year fluctuations unreliable, particularly for the small sample sizes underlying columns 5 to 8 in Table 2.2.

30. Chapter 1, note 2, above.

31. The greater abruptness of the fall in relative pay for 16–17 than for 18–20-year-olds, together with its timing in 1982–4, when the Youth Training Scheme was introduced, suggests that YTS may have had a substantial effect upon the composition of the employment and, thereby, the average pay of 16–17-year-olds. However, the nature of any YTS effect remains unclear, as the bias of traineeships towards low skill, low paid occupations creates an expectation that the introduction of YTS be associated with an *increase* in the average earnings of young employees.

32. The ineffectiveness of wage protection itself may contribute to the lack of a wage response to the 1986 reform (Pond, 1983; Brosnan and Wilkinson, 1988). The only evidence consistent with the expected effects of youth removal from wage protection is a fall in the pay of the lower decile (relative to that of the median) amongst 18–20-year-old males in sales occupations. However, as the opposite appears to have occurred for females in catering and cleaning, no general effects can be inferred (Table 2.3, columns 6, 10).

33. The low increase in wage inequality amongst 18–20-year-olds since 1982 contrasts with a considerable rise during 1974–82, when youth relative pay rose in sheltered and highly unionised sectors, where it was already high – and fell in the exposed and low unionised ones, where it was already low (Ryan, 1984c, Tables 6,7).

34. Tightening markets for youth labour have induced some major employers to increase youth pay rates substantially, particularly in retailing (e.g. 'Retail chains raise youth rates by 43 per cent', *Financial Times*, 18 June 1990).

35. We assume here no significant change in relative pay in other countries since the late 1970s.

36. A similar conclusion has been reached in the aggregate context by recent research on wage flexibility in relation to employment levels and quality. The highly regulated and 'rigid' Nordic variants of Institutional Regulation have outperformed the Market Regulation to which the US and Japan approximate (Rowthorn, 1989). The main difference between the two contexts is the superior position of Japan on youth than on aggregate criteria, where the quality of much employment growth is low.

37. The 'aim of flexibility is to maintain the stability of certain aspects of economic life' (Boyer, 1988, p. 227).

38. Deregulatory enthusiasts often fall into the error for which they attack critics of market forces. While the latter do indeed commonly bias the results by contrasting 'ideal' public intervention with 'real' markets, economic liberals often reverse the bias by comparing 'ideal' markets and 'real' intervention. A similar difficulty can be seen in the analysis of minimum wages (Ryan, 1990).

39. Rowthorn (1989); Ryan (1981). The non-competitive results of Market Regulation have gained recognition in modern theories of implicit contracts, staggered compensation, efficiency wages and insider–outsider phenomena (Azariadis, 1981; Lazear, 1981; Shapiro and Stiglitz, 1984; Lindbeck and Snower, 1988).

40. The potential losers (laid-off workers) are usually fully compensated by redundancy payments sufficiently large to induce voluntary departure.

41. An EETPU speaker to the 1987 annual conference of the Trades Union Congress, after contrasting a five-fold increase in apprentice activity in electrical contracting under the 1983 agreement with stagnation in other sectors, challenged trade unionists to take similar initiatives for the reform of training (TUC, 1987, p. 505).

3 The Structuring of Youth Pay and Employment in Six European Economies[1]

David Marsden and Paul Ryan

3.1 INTRODUCTION

The preceding chapter has argued that youth employment and training constitutes a sensitive issue within national systems of industrial relations. Countries differ greatly in the way in which such youth activities are structured. Young workers are employed in a much wider range of workplaces in the Netherlands, and trained in a much wider range in Germany, than is the case in Italy, for example.

This chapter analyses such differences in youth employment patterns primarily in terms of national pay structures, which are markedly less compressed in key respects in some countries – again, for example, in the Netherlands and Germany than in Italy. The determinants of national pay structures are therefore of particular interest. We relate them to underlying institutional attributes of education and training, industrial relations and labour market organisation.

Two aspects of the regulation of youth activity were distinguished in chapter 2: methods and outcomes. Taking outcomes first, differences in the extent of youth training and employment at the workplace in countries such as the Netherlands, Germany and Italy are interpreted here primarily in terms of the incentives which national training systems and pay structures provide to employers to hire and train young people.

In terms of regulatory method, the importance of market forces relative to administrative rules in determining pay structures varies greatly across time and place. Within the EEC, however, the leading differences are those within the latter category (Institutional Regulation). We argue that the two main determinants of youth employment patterns are (i) national institutions for vocational education and training and (ii) two attributes of pay structure, viz. youth relative pay and the dispersion of adult pay. These factors are in turn interpreted primarily in terms of the relative importance of occupational and internal labour markets. In particular, occupational markets are seen to foster the inclusion of young workers in a range of occupations and industries. Internal markets lack an institution akin to apprenticeship and, in the EEC as well as in the US, foster youth exclusion from the 'primary' segment of the labour market.

The analysis is based upon manual pay and employment in the six leading EEC economies in 1966, 1972 and 1978. As in studies of 'societal effects' (Maurice, Sellier and Silvestre, 1986), we analyse differences between countries for a given set of sectors rather than differences between sectors within countries. We find marked differences between two groups of countries: Belgium, France and Italy, on the one hand, and Germany, the Netherlands and the UK, on the other.

Section 3.2 describes sectoral patterns of youth employment and relates exclusionary patterns to employer hiring policy in a segmented labour market. Section 3.3 considers the implications of national 'pay regimes' for youth employment, focussing upon industry wage structure and 'wage for age' rules. The conclusions follow in section 3.4.

3.2 PATTERNS OF YOUTH EMPLOYMENT AND WAGE STRUCTURE

The Evidence

It is well known that youth employment is unevenly distributed across the economy. In the UK, few young people are found in manual work in heavy industry, while they account for substantial shares of the workforce in light industry, personal services and retail distribution (Reubens, 1983; Ashton, Maguire and Garland, 1982; Ashton and Maguire, 1986; Roberts, Dench and Richardson, 1987).

Patterns of youth employment may be compared across countries and time with the help of internationally comparable data on youth pay and employment, compiled for EEC countries in 1966, 1972 and 1978 (Eurostat, SEI).[2] Data for Great Britain have been compiled on a comparable sectoral basis (GB DE EMO, 1967, 1973), resulting in a dataset for six countries: Belgium, France, FR Germany, Italy, the Netherlands and the UK.

The SEI provides estimates of the employment and hourly earnings of adult and young (aged under 21) workers in establishments with

10 or more employees in industry (extraction, manufacturing and construction). We limit the analysis to manual workers in a 47-sector breakdown which excludes gas, electricity and water. Pay and employment are unavoidably missing for some sectors in all countries and years. The dataset excludes apprentices for all countries except Britain, consistent with their special contractual status in all countries except Britain.

Amongst males, the share of young workers in manual employment in industry was in all three years lower in FR Germany and Italy than in the other four countries, particularly the Netherlands (Table 3.1).

Table 3.1   Youth shares of manual employment by country and sex in six EEC economies in 1966, 1972, 1978 (percentages)

			Youth Employment Share[a]		
Sex	Country	Treatment of apprentices	1966	1972	1978
Male	Belgium	excl	11.9	11.8	9.1
	France	excl	12.5	10.8	7.1
	FR Germany	excl	6.9	5.6	4.8
	FR Germany	incl	n.a.	11.6	n.a.
	Italy	excl	5.8	5.3	4.8
	Netherlands	excl	13.8	10.4	11.4
	UK	incl	10.9	9.1	9.8
	All countries[b]		10.2	8.7	7.7
Female	Belgium	excl	31.6	30.2	19.3
	France	excl	34.3	23.5	15.5
	FR Germany	excl	16.6	14.1	14.4
	FR Germany	incl	n.a.	15.2	n.a.
	Italy	excl	21.8	20.4	11.9
	Netherlands	excl	53.3	37.2	27.1
	UK	incl	13.5	14.0	9.9
	All countries[b]	26.1	20.3	14.6	

Notes
[a] Employees aged less than 21 as a percentage of those aged 21 and over of the same sex in plants with 10 or more employees; part-time employees included.
[b] Weighted mean; apprentices included for GB only.

Sources: Eurostat, Survey of Earnings in Industry, various years; apprentice numbers for FR Germany from Wirtschaft und Statistik, November 1975, p. 771 (Produzierendes Gewerbe); GB DE EMO, 1967, 1973, 1979.

The difference is consistent with the importance of apprenticeship in industry in Germany and in artisanal workshops in Italy, as well as the persistence of high youth unemployment in Italy (Table 3.2; chapter 1, above).

Male youth shares declined throughout the period in the six countries taken as a whole, particularly between 1972 and 1978 in Belgium and France. The decline was not however universal, youth shares increasing in both the Netherlands and the UK between 1972 and 1978 (Table 3.1).

Female youth employment shares prove both higher and more variable across time and place. The difference between the sexes involves adults more than young people, given lower and more variable adult labour force participation amongst females (OECD, 1988a). The rapid growth of adult female participation is central to the decline in female youth shares, notably in the Netherlands; while high adult female participation in Britain contributes to a low female youth share.

Patterns of youth employment by industry show clear similarities in the six economies. The share of young workers in 1978 in branches of heavy industry such as oil refining and chemicals lay below the national average in all countries. Conversely, in light manufacturing (e.g. wood products and footwear), youth shares were generally well above average (Table 3.3). The similarity of youth employment

Table 3.2 Apprentice (and full-time trainee) numbers and employment shares, industry and construction, by country, 1978

Country	Numbers[a] (000s)		Employment shares (%)	
	Manual	All	Manual	All
Belgium	5.6	6.0	0.7	0.6
France	15.1	16.4	0.4	0.3
FR Germany	323.5	428.4	5.1	4.8
Italy	36.4	37.4	1.3	1.0
Netherlands	n.a.	9.8	n.a.	0.8
UK	251.5	297.1	4.2	3.7

Note
[a] Establishments with 10 or more employees; both sexes.

Source: Eurostat, Labour Cost Survey, 1978

patterns across place and their stability across time are both indicated by high correlations between sectoral youth shares across countries and years (Table 3.4).

At the same time, important differences do emerge between the youth employment patterns of the six countries, particularly in terms of the dispersion in youth shares and the degree to which young workers are employed in particular sectors. The Italian (for males) and the German (for females) economies show the most uneven spread of young workers across industry (Table 3.5), while the Dutch economy exhibits the least unevenness for both sexes.

We infer that the exclusion of young workers from employment is a matter of degree rather than kind, as young males at least are found in manual jobs in practically all sectors in all countries; that the exclusionary tendencies of particular sectors are highly similar across countries and years; but that the degree of youth exclusion from some sectors and crowding into others varies from severe (Italy) to moderate

Table 3.3   Youth shares of manual employment in selected industries by country, 1978

Sex	Sector	Belg	France	FRG	Italy	NL	UK
		\multicolumn{6}{c}{*Youth employment share[a] (%)*}					
Males	Oil refining	1.1	1.4	1.0	0.0	2.5	5.1
	Chemicals	3.1	3.7	3.0	1.0	3.8	5.8
	Foundries	6.1	4.9	3.5	2.6	8.7	10.2
	Mechanical eng.	6.9	6.3	4.1	4.8	8.5	10.4
	Wood prods, timber	14.6	12.1	7.7	6.6	13.0	15.3
	Footwear	12.7	10.3	13.7	13.0	7.5	17.5
	All industries	7.4	5.5	4.4	3.7	7.7	8.9
Females	Oil refining	0.0	0.0	0.0	0.0	19.6	2.1
	Chemicals	12.6	4.9	6.9	2.3	20.2	7.2
	Foundries	6.7	4.3	6.7	5.7	8.6	5.0
	Mechanical eng.	0.0	5.6	7.1	4.7	21.0	2.5
	Wood prods, timber	13.2	17.5	15.3	13.7	20.3	6.7
	Footwear	15.0	17.1	21.7	19.5	34.0	14.5
	All industries	14.5	10.0	12.2	8.6	20.9	5.4

Note
[a] Only the British figures include apprentices.
Source: As Table 3.1.

(the Netherlands). Full youth exclusion is most closely approximated in Italian industry, where young manual workers hardly appear at all on the payrolls of sectors such as oil refining, mining, cement and drink; while in the Netherlands, Britain and FR Germany, significant minorities of young males are found in manual work in all sectors – and young females in all sectors in which adult females are hired.

Table 3.4   Correlations between youth employment shares across paired country/year samples

		Average correlation[a]		Number of pairs
Dimension		Males	Females	
Across	1966	0.69	0.60	15
countries	1972	0.64	0.63	15
	1978	0.59	0.61	10
	All years	0.65	0.61	40
Across	Belgium	0.74	0.74	3
years	France	0.90	0.89	3
	FR Germany[b]	0.75	0.95	1
	Italy	0.77	0.81	3
	Netherlands	0.65	0.71	3
	UK	0.91	0.84	3
	All countries	0.79	0.81	16
Across both		0.69	0.67	56

Notes
[a] Pearson correlation (r).
[b] The 1978 West German classification was not comparable to those in other years and countries.
Sources: As Table 3.1.

Hiring policy in segmented labour markets
Such patterns of youth employment have been generally interpreted as simply facts of life rather than the outcome of economic behaviour, except insofar as technology is seen as making young people unsuited to heavy industry. Our interpretation analyses youth employment shares instead in terms of two attributes of national pay structures: the degree of labour market segmentation and the importance of 'wage for age' scales.

Table 3.5   Dispersion of youth employment shares by year, country and sex, manual employees

Sex	Country	1966	1972	1978	Average[b]
		\multicolumn{4}{c}{Coefficient of Variation[a] (%)}			
Males	Belgium	28.6	31.7	30.7	30.3
	France	33.7	26.3	29.7	29.9
	FR Germany	30.1	22.2	37.1	29.8
	Italy	38.0	42.5	54.8	45.1
	Netherlands	27.2	24.8	27.0	26.3
	UK	23.8	29.8	27.4	27.0
	Average[b]	30.2	29.5	34.5	
Females	Belgium	24.5	25.6	25.3	25.1
	France	29.3	26.3	35.1	30.2
	FR Germany	39.6	37.5	41.1	39.4
	Italy	27.9	36.5	38.0	34.1
	Netherlands	15.4	20.0	27.1	20.8
	UK	32.0	38.1	37.8	36.0
	Average[b]	28.1	30.7	34.1	

Notes
[a] Standard deviation divided by (weighted) mean ($\times$ 100 per cent); apprentices included for UK only.
[b] Unweighted average of country or year means.
Sources: As Table 3.1.

We assume that labour markets are segmented in all six economies, in the sense that there is considerable inequality in the job rewards (pay, fringe benefits, working conditions, etc.) offered by different firms and industries to comparable workers. In dualist terminology, there are good jobs and bad jobs; and the number of workers qualified for and willing to do the good jobs is greater than the supply of those jobs (McNabb and Ryan, 1989). However, rather than adopting a strictly dualist interpretation, we assume a continuous hierarchy of jobs, ranked in terms of rewards (amongst which pay predominates), with workers queuing for access to jobs in its higher reaches (Thurow, 1975). We also assume for each job category a well defined wage (i.e. a rate for the job) whose institutional basis in collective agreements, company wage structures, etc. renders it largely independent of the attributes or efforts of the incumbent employee.[3]

Employers are assumed to rank workers who apply for vacant jobs; and to be free to pick from the applicant queue so as to minimise unit labour costs. If a firm wishes to take on a young worker, it is free to do so; if it does not so wish, there is no statutory or contractual requirement to force it to.

A key constraint upon recruitment policy is however recognised: occupational segregation by sex. A wide range of evidence indicates that employers generally hire from one sex only for particular job categories, although they are free to pick young or adult applicants of the appropriate sex (OECD, 1988a, Note B; Rubery, 1988; Ashton and Maguire, 1986; Roberts, Dench and Richardson, 1987). Finally, we assume that young and adult workers are technically substitutable to some extent in all jobs, in the sense that a lower relative price for young workers is associated with increased employer willingness to hire a youth rather than an adult.[4]

In such a context, the attitude of employers towards young workers when hiring differs according to the firm's position in the industrial wage hierarchy. High wage firms can take their pick. They are not generally interested in young workers, given the lower experience, skill and job stability which characterise young people. Moreover, as such employers are assumed to pay a set rate for the job, the willingness of young workers to work for lower pay makes no difference. Such employers therefore prefer experienced adults, selecting only the minority of exceptional young workers.

The low wage firm enjoys less choice. Adult applicants are scarcer as a result of higher alternative incomes, including other jobs or social security (particularly amongst males with family dependants). Those adults who do apply to low wage firms tend to be disadvantaged in one way or another. Young workers are therefore better placed to compete for such jobs and secure a substantial share of recruitment.

An inverse relationship is therefore expected between the employer's pay level and the share of young workers in its workforce. 'The exclusion of young people from a large part of the general labour market' (Ashton and Maguire, 1986) may therefore be understood as the result of employer hiring policy in a segmented labour market.

Occupational and internal labour markets
Youth employment shares also depend on the relative strength of occupational and internal structures in the labour market. Internal labour markets consist of structured job groups based around particular workplaces or employers in which pay and labour alloca-

tion are governed by rules (rather than by the external labour market) and in which jobs above entry level tend to be filled by internal promotion rather than recruitment (Doeringer and Piore, 1971). Well known examples are found in public administration and the armed forces.

Occupational markets, by contrast, are bounded by the certified knowledge and skill possessed by individual workers and transferable across a range of employers. They tend to be organised either unilaterally by the worker collectivity or jointly with employers and/ or the state (Marsden, 1986a). Familiar examples include much manual work in construction and printing in the UK.[5]

Although labour markets often blend internal and occupational elements in practice, we analyse their implications for youth employment as if either one form or the other predominates.

Under internal labour markets, the analysis of youth employment shares can largely end with the preceding discussion of employer hiring policy in a segmented labour market. Young workers faced by rate for the job rules have typically to put on some years and gain some experience before being considered for entry jobs in internal labour markets associated with high wage employment (Osterman, 1980).

However, in occupational labour markets a further factor often intervenes: 'wage for age' schedules. Payment systems which exempt young workers from rate for the job rules and permit employers to hire them at lower rates of pay related to age (or trainee status) are common in occupational labour markets. Wage for age schedules characterise youth work under collective agreements or statutory minima in the Netherlands and Britain in particular. They may be associated with apprenticeship which, in FR Germany and Britain in particular, provides for young workers to be trained at rates of pay (or trainee allowances) well below that of qualified adults in the same occupation.

The exceptionalism of wage for age rules is not widely appreciated. They find a historical analogue in the lower women's rates which endured in British industry into the 1960s. However, now that it is illegal in advanced economies to offer women less than the established rate of pay for a given job – and indeed to do the same for immigrants, non-whites or other groups willing to work for less than the going rate – youth remains the principal category for which pay rates may legally be varied.

Although age–wage provisions are not totally absent in internal labour markets, they typically lack duration and depth as far as young workers are concerned. Internal markets are particularly extensive in France and Italy. In French collective agreements and minimum wages, the adult rate applies from 18 years of age, while Italian exceptions are limited to a 5 per cent discount for apprentices, who must be less than 21 years old (Marsden, 1985, 1987a; Garonna, 1986; Mariani, 1986).

This is not to urge that wages are unrelated to age under internal labour markets. Indeed, as internal markets commonly involve individually-related seniority pay and bonus pay and offer promotion prospects along job ladders to a greater extent than do occupational markets, wages tend to increase more strongly with age and length of service in internal than in occupational markets (Eyraud, Marsden and Silvestre, 1988; Marsden, 1990a). The absence of wage for age rules in internal markets might thus be seen as a matter more of form than of substance.

However, the greater overall progression of pay with age in internal than in occupational markets is relevant more to pay inequality amongst adult workers than to the access of young workers to employment. In particular, the general absence from entry jobs in internal markets of wage discounts conditional upon being, say 16 years old or a trainee, means that employers lack an incentive to hire young workers comparable to that provided by explicit wage for age schedules.[6]

Discounts in the price of young workers' services under wage for age schedules make young people more attractive recruits into training and employment than is the case under a simple rate for the job regime. The larger the discount, the greater the interest of employers. The price of youth labour relative to that of adults in the same firm is therefore a second prospective influence on youth employment shares.[7]

The Results[8]

In order to implement the preceding analysis, we measure the position of a sector in the industry wage hierarchy by the average gross hourly pay of adult workers (relative to the all-sector average for each country/year). The relative cost of youth labour is proxied by the relative pay of young workers (as a ratio of the pay of adults in the same sector). Youth employment shares are related by regression analysis to adult pay and youth relative pay, using the SEI dataset for each sex in six countries in three years.

The results of 12 separate regressions for each sex in the six countries, pooled in each case across all three years, are reported in Table 3.6. As all three variables are standardised by the relevant all-sector mean, the coefficients on the pay variables are elasticities (evaluated at the sample means). Thus the adult pay coefficient of −1.92 for Belgian males suggests that a rise of 10 per cent in adult male pay in a sector (relative to average pay in Belgium industry in that year) is associated with an approximately 19 per cent decrease in young males' employment share (again relative to the all-industry average in Belgium in that year).

A strong relationship emerges between youth employment shares and adult pay for both sexes in all countries. The elasticity of youth shares with respect to adult pay is significantly greater than unity in most cases, rising to particularly high levels in France and the Netherlands. It tends to be higher for males than for females and is typically stable over time. However, for both sexes in Italy and for males in FR Germany it increases strongly between 1966 and 1978, rising as high as six for males in Italy in 1978.[9]

The tendency for young workers to be excluded from high wage industries and crowded into low wage ones thus appears to be widespread and powerful. There are indeed striking and significant differences between adult pay elasticities. However, these differences contribute little to an understanding of inter-country differences in the degree of youth exclusion (Table 3.5). Thus, although Italy ranks high on each count for males, the Netherlands has the lowest dispersion of youth employment but a high adult pay effect. Similarly, the most unequal distribution of female youth employment is found in FR Germany, where the adult pay elasticity is amongst the smallest.[10]

Turning to youth relative pay, for males its association with youth employment shares proves no less strong than that for adult pay. Inter-country differences prove if anything smaller. For females the picture is more mixed. The relative pay effect is negative and significant in four cases, although the elasticities tend to be smaller than for males. However, in Italy and the UK the relative pay effect comes out positive, while the explanatory power of the analysis is weak in both West Germany and the UK.

The relative pay effect might be expected to operate differently in high wage from low wage sectors. For example, were jobs in high wage industries particularly demanding in terms of skill and responsibility, young workers might be considered particularly unsuitable and lower relative pay might do little or nothing to increase their access to jobs.

Table 3.6 Elasticities of youth employment intensity with respect to pay variables in regression analyses of national datasets pooled across three years, by sex and country

		Elasticity with respect to[a]			
Sex	Country	Adult pay	Youth relative pay	$\overline{R^2}$	n
Male	Belgium	−1.92[*]	−2.09[*]	0.50	113
	France	−3.44[*]	−3.19[*]	0.49	123
	FR Germany	−2.23[*b]	−2.66[*]	0.32	126
	Italy	−3.35[*b]	−2.92[*]	0.31	111
	Netherlands	−3.20[*]	−2.14[*]	0.52	104
	UK	−2.56[*]	−1.89[*]	0.52	107
Female	Belgium	−2.06[*]	−1.47[*]	0.30	81
	France	−3.67[*]	−1.25[*b]	0.59	100
	FR Germany	−1.71[*]	−1.82[*]	0.18	96
	Italy	−1.97[*b]	1.28[*]	0.75	86
	Netherlands	−2.11[*]	−1.17[*]	0.47	79
	UK	−1.05[*]	+0.97	0.18	71

Notes
[a] Full details are presented in Marsden and Ryan (1989a). Asterisks denote estimates significantly different from zero at five per cent level of significance. Apprentices included for UK only. Elasticities evaluated at the relevant sample mean.
[b] Average of three (significantly different) coefficients for each year.

Source: As Table 3.1.

The possibility is assessed by inserting into the regressions an interactive variable, the product of adult pay and youth relative pay, with the expectation of a positive sign. As the interactive variable proves insignificant in most cases, we conclude that lower youth pay is an effective force for higher youth employment in high wage as well as in low wage sectors.[11]

We conclude that the employment share of young manual workers is closely related to two aspects of labour market structure: the position of a sector in the manual earnings hierarchy and the extent to which payment systems permit young workers to be paid less than adults within a job category. Young workers tend in all countries to be excluded from the high wage segment. (The adult pay effect is interpreted in terms of involuntary youth behaviour, as young workers are unlikely to turn down highly paid jobs were they available, particularly as there is little or no link between low pay and skill acquisition; Marsden and Ryan, 1989a, Table 8). Furthermore, discounts on the price of youth labour increase youth employment in both high wage and low wage sectors, while at least some young people are employed in nearly all sectors.

Exclusionary tendencies are more intense for female than for male youth. Young females tend to be underrepresented in particular sectors in association not only with high pay for adult females but also with the exclusion of adult females as part of occupational segregation. Moreover, lower relative pay proves less effective at raising youth shares for females than for males.

For males at least, the stability of the relationship between youth employment and pay variables across the variety of institutional contexts in the six economies is striking. Both adult pay and youth relative pay have similar effects in FR Germany, on the one hand, where the great majority of young manual workers undertake an apprenticeship, and Belgium, France and Italy, where apprenticeship is unimportant in industry. Although price effects are not strictly uniform across countries, a high degree of similarity is visible. In terms of the structuring role played by the two pay variables, youth markets lie much closer to the pole of universality than to that of national specificity.

3.3 PAY REGIMES AND YOUTH EMPLOYMENT

Although the previous section found national differences to be at most secondary in the determination of youth employment patterns, they are important in setting the pay variables themselves. Differences in national 'pay regimes' are interpreted in this section in terms of labour market structures, youth training systems and pay bargaining arrangements.

A pay regime is taken to comprise the rules governing pay determination, as embodied in company pay scales, collective agreements and statutory minima. It is visible in both the content of those rules and the salient features of actual pay structures. The results of section 3.2 suggest that three aspects of pay regimes are potentially important for youth employment: the dispersion of adult pay, the overall level of youth relative pay and the correlation between youth relative pay and adult pay. National differences prove marked in each respect.

The Dispersion of Adult Pay

The size of the adult pay coefficients in Table 3.6 suggests that greater variability in adult pay across sectors is associated with greater inequality in youth employment shares. The dispersion of adult pay across sectors – a leading dimension of labour market segmentation – has generally been lower for manual males in FR Germany and the Netherlands than in France and Italy. It tended to fall between 1972 and 1978, most notably in Italy, but also in Belgium, France, and the UK. A similar pattern is discernible for females, but inter-country differences are smaller and the pattern of changes over time more disparate than for males (Table 3.7).

Institutional factors are potentially influential for adult pay dispersion. There is firstly the distinction between *occupational and internal labour markets*. Where occupational markets are highly developed, the boundaries imposed upon adult pay differentiation are likely to be narrower than under internal markets. Insofar as transferable skills result in higher intersectoral labour mobility, the reduction of labour supply to low wage firms associated with turnover is higher in occupational markets, which in turn limits their ability to pay less than firms in other sectors. Similarly, workers are better placed to compare earnings across sectors and to press for similar outcomes when qualifications are standardised across employers. If trade union structure follows that of worker qualification, as in some British sectors, the effect is likely to be still greater.

However, the difference in pay dispersion under the two types of labour market may be limited. Studies of occupational markets also find strong differentiation in pay between firms (Mackay et al., 1971). But pay differentiation is likely to be higher still when the more intense ties to employers under internal markets reduce workers' options for horizontal mobility and wage comparisons.

Our evidence is consistent with a mild effect for labour market structure on adult pay dispersion. The countries in which occupational markets are most pronounced (Marsden, 1990a), FR Germany and the UK, are amongst the three countries with the lowest levels of adult pay dispersion for males (Table 3.7). Conversely, France and Italy, which exhibit more extensive internal markets, show the highest levels of pay dispersion for both males and females. The differences are limited but consistent with our hypothesis.

A second institutional factor relevant to the size of industrial wage differentials is the degree of *centralisation in pay determination*. The familiar inverse association between centralisation of national bargaining and inter-industry pay dispersion (Freeman, 1988a; Rowthorn, 1989) appears also in our data. Adult pay dispersion is inversely associated with a standard index of bargaining decentralisation; Italy and the Netherlands occupy the opposite ends of each scale.[12]

Closer examination suggests that adult pay dispersion may be affected also, given national bargaining structure, by the degree to which trade unions pursue lower wage inequality, together with their ability to achieve such an objective. Changes over time are particularly relevant here. The marked declines in pay dispersion during the 1970s in Italy and Britain coincided with the announced egalitarian objectives of union bargaining and public incomes policies in the face of inflation (Garonna and Pisani, 1986; Coates, 1980).[13]

Table 3.7 Dispersion in adult pay, manual employees in industry, by sex, year and country

Sex	Country	Coefficient of Variation of Adult Pay[a] (%)			
		1966	1972	1978	Average[b]
Males	Belgium	8.9	11.1	7.6	9.2
	France	11.7	12.0	8.5	10.7
	FR Germany	6.0	6.0	6.0	6.0
	Italy	12.8	12.6	7.5	11.0
	Netherlands	8.5	6.3	8.0	7.5
	UK	9.5	10.4	7.4	9.1
	Average[b]	9.6	9.7	7.5	
Females	Belgium	6.4	9.2	10.2	8.6
	France	11.7	8.5	6.9	9.0
	FR Germany	6.0	6.9	9.4	7.4
	Italy	10.7	10.8	7.8	9.8
	Netherlands	8.5	7.8	3.9	6.7
	UK	5.9	9.9	11.0	8.9
	Average[b]	8.2	8.9	8.2	

Notes
[a] Based upon country–year means weighted by adult employment; apprentices included for UK only.
b. Unweighted
Sources: As Table 3.1.

Narrower inter-sectoral pay differentials are associated, according to the above regression results, with a lower dispersion of youth employment shares. It is not surprising therefore to find that the three countries with the lowest pay disperion for males, taking the three years as a whole, (viz. FR Germany, the Netherlands and the UK) are also the ones with the least uneven intersectoral distribution of young male employment. For females, the picture is less clear-cut but again the Netherlands shows low dispersion of both adult pay and youth shares, while Italy is marked by high dispersion for each indicator (Tables 3.5, 3.7).

The relationship between the dispersions of pay and employment shares is however less clear-cut over time than across countries. Although in France and the UK reductions in adult male pay dispersion between 1972 and 1978 were associated with the expected reduction in the dispersion of youth shares, the most substantial change in pay dispersion over time, the large reduction in adult pay dispersion in Italy after 1972, was accompanied by a substantial increase in the dispersion of youth shares for both sexes, the result being a marked increase in the adult pay coefficient (Table 3.6).[14]

The weakness of the link between adult pay dispersion and youth employment shares across time may result from adjustment lags, industry-specific fixed effects or changes in youth labour supply, none of which can be captured with these data (Marsden and Ryan, 1989a). In any event, links are visible between the relative importance of occupational and internal labour markets, the centralisation of national pay determination and the strength of egalitarian wage policies, on the one hand, and the degree to which young workers are crowded into a subset of low wage sectors, on the other, with the dispersion of adult pay as the key intermediary influence.

Youth Relative Pay: Evidence

Young manual workers work at lower wages (relative to adult workers in the same sector and skill level) in some economies than in others. The six EEC countries can be broadly dichotomised into 'high' and 'low' relative pay groups, although the classification varies somewhat by sex, age, and trainee status.

Amongst males, the treatment of apprentices affects the grouping of countries by youth relative pay. When apprentices are included for the two countries in which they are present in significant numbers (FR Germany and the UK; Table 3.2), the high relative pay group comprises Belgium, France and Italy; the low group, FR Germany, the Netherlands, and Britain. In 1972, the year for which the most comprehensive statistics are available, mean relative pay of young males was nearly half as high again in the former as in the latter group (unweighted averages of 75 and 51 per cent respectively; Table 3.8, cols 1, 2).[15]

However, given the compositional differences in youth employment associated with apprenticeship, such pay ratios may give a distorted picture of the underlying relative pay of comparable young workers. The importance of apprenticeship in both FR Germany and Britain and vocational schooling in both Belgium and France means that the average member of the youth labour force is both younger and less skilled in the former than in the latter economies. The low school

Table 3.8   Youth relative pay in industry by sex, manual employees, 1972 and 1978 (Mean hourly earnings as % of earnings of those aged 21 and over)

	(1)	*(2)*	*(3)*	*(4)*	*(5)*	*(6)*	*(7)*	*(8)*
	Males				*Females*			
	1972		*1978*		*1972*		*1978*	
	apps excl	*apps incl*	*apps excl*	*apps incl*	*apps excl*	*apps incl*	*apps excl*	*apps incl*
High group								
Belgium	70.6	n.a.	77.4	n.a.	79.2	n.a.	83.3	n.a.
France	77.7	n.a.	75.7	n.a.	86.4	n.a.	86.1	n.a.
Italy	77.9	n.a.	84.8	n.a.	84.3	n.a.	89.9	n.a.
FR Germany	78.2	47.2[a]	76.9	n.a.	83.9	79.1[a]	83.3	n.a.
Low group								
Netherlands	54.0	n.a.	59.7	59.1[b]	63.3	n.a.	66.8	67.6[b]
UK	58.6[c]	52.3	n.a.	61.6	n.a.	63.3	n.a.	65.8

Notes
[a] Assumes that all manual apprentices are aged less than 18 years.
[b] Full-time trainees of all ages included (Marsden 1987, Table 2.2).
[c] Assumes that one-third of male manual employees aged under 21 are apprentices (Marsden 1985, p.403) and that the 0.70 ratio between the hourly earnings of apprenticed and non-apprenticed manual males found for 1974 applied in 1972 as well (Jones, 1985, p.30).

Sources: As Table 3.1.

leaving age in Italy has a similar effect. The importance of the resulting compositional bias may be assessed both by the exclusion of apprentices and by further breakdowns by age within the youth category.

When apprentices are excluded, the low relative pay group comprises only the Netherlands and Britain, where youth pay ratios lay in 1972 in the range 50–60 per cent, as opposed to 70–80 per cent in the other four economies (Table 3.8, cols 1,2). The inclusion of apprentices makes little difference to youth relative pay in either the Netherlands or Britain, either because they are few in number, as in the

Table 3.9   Youth relative pay in industry by age group and country, manual males, 1972 and 1978 (Mean hourly earnings as % of earnings of those aged 21 and over)

| | | Age category | | | |
| | | < *18yrs* | | *18–20yrs* | |
Country	*Apprentice treatment*	*1972*	*1978*	*1972*	*1978*
High Group					
Belgium	excl	55.4	62.5	80.4	82.7
France	excl	66.1	65.3	80.3	77.5
Italy	excl	65.8	81.0	81.2	86.0
FR Germany	excl	57.8	n.a.	84.2	n.a.
	incl[a]	(26.1)	n.a.	(84.2)	n.a.
Low Group					
Netherlands	excl	39.0	44.2	60.7	64.4
UK	incl[b]	40.3	48.9	66.7	74.9
Group means[c]					
High Group[d]	excl	61.5	n.a.	82.3	n.a.
Low Group[e]	mixed	31.9	n.a.	65.5	n.a.

Notes
[a]   Assumes that all apprentices are aged less than 18 years.
[b]   Whole economy, 1974 and 1978.
[c]   Weighted by youth employment.
[d]   Comprises Belgium, France, Italy, FR Germany (apprentices excluded).
[e]   Comprises Germany and the UK (apprentices included in each) and the Netherlands

Sources: As Table 3.1, plus GB Dept of Employment, New Earnings Survey, 1974 and 1978, unpublished tabulations.

Netherlands, or because their pay is not much lower than that of other young workers, as in Britain (Jones, 1985).

When the youth category is subdivided into those aged less than 18 and those aged 18 to 20, the same dichotomy emerges. FR Germany remains in the high group except for the category 'under 18, apprentices included' (Table 3.9), consistent with the completion at that time of most German apprenticeships by 18 years of age.[16] Similarly, breakdowns by occupational category suggest that the classification of countries does not depend upon whether the work in question is skilled or not (Table 3.10).

Turning to females, relative pay is in all countries higher than for young males (relative to adults of the same sex). However, the same country grouping applies to the relative pay of young females as to non-apprenticed males, with FR Germany in the high group and Britain and the Netherlands constituting the low group (Table 3.8). In contrast to the situation for males, the number of female manual apprentices is too low for their inclusion to lead to the reclassification of Germany.

We conclude that the grouping of countries according to youth relative pay in Table 3.8 provides a broadly reliable guide to that

Table 3.10   Youth relative pay in industry by skill and age, manual males, excluding apprentices, 1972 (Mean hourly earnings as % of earnings of those aged 21 and over)

| | Age Group | | | |
| | Less than 18 years | | 18 to 20 years | |
Country	Less skilled[a]	skilled	Less skilled[a]	skilled
Belgium	57.3	60.8	82.9	81.0
France	70.1	70.1	87.8	79.9
Italy	69.7	66.6	86.2	76.5
FR Germany	60.8	70.4	86.9	83.1
Netherlands	40.9	37.7	63.0	59.6
UK	n.a.	n.a.	n.a.	n.a.

Notes
[a] 'Less skilled' comprises 'unskilled' and 'semi-skilled' occupational categories.
Sources: As Table 3.1.

aspect of national pay regimes and the cost of youth labour to employers. Although the categorisation of countries depends upon the treatment of male apprentices, in all cases Belgium, France and Italy are classed in the high relative pay group and the Netherlands and Britain in the low one. Germany joins the high pay group, except for the category 'males aged less than 18, including apprentices'.

Youth Relative Pay: Interpretation

We analyse national differences in the relative pay of young workers in terms of the same two factors as for adult pay dispersion: the relative importance of occupational and internal labour markets and the centralisation of pay determination.

Taking labour market structures first, we noted above that internal labour markets tend to permit little or no reduction for trainee or youth status, while occupational markets commonly permit pay reductions for trainees or young people under the rubric of apprenticeship. The greater importance of occupational markets in West Germany and Britain (than in Italy and France) thus corresponds to lower youth relative pay (when apprentices are included).

The reallocation of FR Germany from the low to the high category when apprentices are excluded suggests that the association of labour market structure with youth pay reflects methods of youth vocational education and training. Apprenticeship (or its equivalent) is central to initial training under occupational markets, for male manual occupations at least. Its role is at most marginal under internal markets, where employers tend to rely on a succession of limited doses of job-specific training linked to recruitment and internal mobility.[17]

The link between youth pay and apprenticeship is clearest is Germany, where apprenticeship and youth employment are clearly distinguished in both law and industrial practice; where large numbers of young people function as apprentices at low allowances; and where, for non- and ex-apprenticed youth, relative pay is amongst the highest of all countries. These features suggest a clear implementation of occupational principles for the relative pay of trainees, together with rate for the job payment for qualified young workers. In the Federal Republic youth pay is low primarily in conjunction with certified trainee status.[18]

While recent policy discussion in the UK has typically proceeded on the assumption of high youth relative pay (section 2.4, above), comparison to other EEC economies, as opposed to British history, indicates a low youth pay regime – even in 1978, when youth relative pay was close to its historical peak. At that time occupational markets and apprenticeship were still influential in British industry. At the other extreme, in Belgian, French and Italian industry, apprenticeship is relatively unimportant and youth pay relatively high (Tables 3.2, 3.8).

The association between labour market structure and youth relative pay can be given a technical or an institutional rationale (Marsden and Ryan, 1989b). From the technical standpoint, occupational markets tend to function with both a higher level of skill and less employer specificity of skill content than do internal markets, and to develop skills at the workplace rather than in public educational institutions. Lower trainee relative pay provides incentives to employers to provide apprenticeships when faced by occupational markets to which they may lose skilled labour. There may be no comparable requirement under internal markets, given the lower cost and greater specificity of employer training and the greater role of public vocational education (Marsden, 1987a).

However, training costs and skill transferability are often high under internal labour markets as well (Ryan, 1984a). The association of low youth pay with apprenticeship then reflects institutional rather than technical factors. The acceptability of low youth pay to trade unions is intrinsically precarious. It provides employers with an incentive to substitute youth for adult labour, to the detriment of the job security and bargaining power of adult workers (Ryan, 1987a; chapter 8, below). The key function of apprenticeship is then to provide, through external regulation of activities and outcomes, the safeguards against employer abuse of trainee labour for which it is difficult to develop any equivalent in internal labour markets. Low youth pay then achieves under well regulated occupational markets a legitimacy in the eyes of trade unions and employees for which there is no equivalent in internal markets.

On either interpretation, youth pay regimes are then understood in the first instance in terms of labour market structure in general and the organisation and location of vocational training in particular, be it apprenticeship (FRG and the UK) or a combination of public vocational education followed by job-specific training (Belgium, France and Italy; CEDEFOP, 1984).

The two non-German members of the low relative pay group in Table 3.8 suggest further influences. In both the UK and the Netherlands, the relative pay of *non*-apprenticed young employees, both male and female, is also low, lying in the 1970s roughly 20 percentage points below its counterpart in the other four countries.

Low youth pay for non-apprenticed youth reflects the importance of wage–age progression in ordinary youth employment, particularly in the Netherlands. Dutch collective agreements and minimum wages show marked wage progression over a substantial age range. The 1974 minimum wage for youth employment started at 40 per cent of the adult rate at age 15, moving in annual increments of 7.5 points to 100 per cent at age 23. In 1981 and 1983, two further cuts were implemented in the ratios of the minimum wage applicable to ages under 23 (Crone, 1986).

Similarly, British payment systems have long exhibited wage for age progression for mainstream youth employment, albeit to a lesser degree and over fewer years of age than for either British apprentices or young Dutch employees. Thus at present manual female employees in the UK typically attain adult rates only at 18 years of age; young males, at 19 or 20 (IDS, 1987). The upshot is that, in contrast to FR Germany, pay rates are differentiated more by age than by trainee status in the British and Dutch labour markets.

Low relative pay for non-apprenticed young workers may result from an extension of the methods and norms of apprenticeship and occupational markets to youth employment in general. Such an interpretation is plausible for the UK, where apprenticeship has historically been more widespread (for young males) than in the Netherlands and where trade unions, singly or in federation, have commonly bargained simultaneously for the pay of apprenticed and non-apprenticed young workers alike; and where employers have often treated the services of apprentices and other young workers as close substitutes (Ryan, 1986).

Historical developments must also be considered. The gap between the terms and conditions received by apprentices and young employees in Britain has narrowed during this century, reflecting (and in turn contributing to) the erosion of apprenticeship and occupational markets, in contrast to their consolidation in West Germany (Marsden and Ryan, 1991). An important facet of British development has been the erosion of the low youth pay regime for all young male workers. The relative pay of young manual males increased more rapidly between 1966 and 1978 in the UK (from 51 per cent to 62 per cent) than in any of the other five EEC countries. The increase appears to have applied at least as strongly to apprentices as to other young workers amongst males, although it was negligible for manual females (Marsden 1987a, Table 3.3).

The Dutch case is still more distinctive. Youth relative pay has remained the lowest amongst the six economies, at less than 60 per cent for males and 67 per cent for females in all three SEI surveys. The international distinctiveness of the Dutch youth pay regime has if anything increased over time. Although the relative pay of Dutch youth rose between 1966 and 1978, the rate of increase was the lowest of all six economies, with the possible exception of West Germany (Marsden, 1987a, Table 3.3).

The Netherlands also possesses an apprenticeship tradition, particularly in heavy industry and construction (Van Dijk, Akkermans and Hövels, 1988). However, to explain low youth pay in such terms is less plausible than in the British or German cases. Industrial training in the Netherlands relies more on vocational education after compulsory school than on workplace training (CEDEFOP, 1984; Van Dijk, Akkermans and Hövels, 1988). The Netherlands ranks with Belgium, France and Italy, rather than with West Germany and Britain, in terms of the numerical importance of apprenticeship (Table 3.2; OECD, 1979, Table 1).[19] Apprenticeship in the Netherlands has typically provided only a brief supplement to a spell in public vocational school (CEC, 1966), yet pay progression with age in youth employment can last up to eight years.

The Dutch case suggests again a role for wider institutions of wage determination, whose distinctive attributes in the Netherlands include neocorporatist centralisation of negotiations, strong government influence, well organised and active employer associations, weak and bureaucratised trade unions, strong obstacles to industrial action and a marked orientation of all three actors towards the 'national interest'.[20] None of the other six economies exhibits a comparable mix.

Such institutions may foster low youth pay by reducing the responsiveness of union wage bargainers to the immediate interests of a majority of the membership, adult as well as youth, in high youth relative pay. Young members themselves welcome higher incomes, as the increased probability of unemployment which accompanies higher pay may be of little consequence when the great majority of current members are employed and could expect to retain their jobs.

However, as young members are neither numerous nor influential within most trade unions, particularly in the Netherlands (chapter 7, below), the interests of adult members are potentially more relevant to union policy. Adults also tend to favour high youth pay, motivated both by the widespread union norm of a single rate for the job irrespective of who performs it and the need to protect employment opportunities and bargaining power from employer use of cheap youth labour. However, adult attitudes may be complicated by perceptions that higher pay for young workers means lower pay potential for themselves, and, to some extent, by an altruistic inclination to promote youth activity at times of high unemployment (Ryan, 1984a, 1987a).

In some industrial relations systems, such membership interests prove influential in directing union wage policy and setting wage structures. The erosion of the low relative pay regime in the UK during the postwar period was fostered by youth activism and broad union support under conditions of employer and government indifference. Youth activism in pursuit of higher relative pay also became prominent in the Netherlands, in the early 1970s, coinciding with a wider movement seeking, as in other EEC countries,[21] reductions in pay differentials. The demands of Dutch youth included coverage by minimum wages and an end to wage for age scales.

However, the outcome of youth activism fell short of youth demands to a much greater extent in the Netherlands than in the UK. National lobbying did indeed lead to the application of minimum wages from the age of 18 rather than 23, but that was as far as it went. Dutch wage for age scales not only survived the attacks of the 1970s but were subsequently extended during the 1980s in both depth and duration.

Although the attitude of Dutch adult union leaders and members to youth demands for higher relative pay remains obscure, it is clear that the wage gains made by youth proved limited in the face of an unresponsive union leadership,[22] of a determined stand by employer associations against egalitarian wage demands, and of an increasing government inclination in the 1980s to deepen age–wage schedules as a means of encouraging higher youth employment shares.

A weak trade union movement may not be in a position to act effectively on membership concerns. The leaders of a centralised movement locked into neocorporatist structures are likely to respond more to government interest in high youth employment than to the complaints of its membership, young or adult. The Dutch combination of union weakness with employer and government activism has provided an exceptional and enduring source of support for a strikingly low youth pay regime.

We therefore infer two institutional conditions which favour low youth relative pay: a predominance of occupational over internal labour market structures and the combination of centralised and weak trade unionism with neocorporatist industrial relations. The latter is less well established than the former, as it relies on one observation rather than upon six and as it is impossible with one observation to distinguish between national and universal determinants.

The strength of the link between youth pay and employment (Table 3.6) means then that youth pay regimes raise youth employment shares in the Netherlands, West Germany and the UK relative to those of Belgium, France and Italy. The role of relative pay is suggested most strongly by the extreme cases of Italy and the Netherlands, which come respectively top and bottom of a six country ranking of youth relative pay, but whose positions are reversed in the ranking of male youth employment shares (Tables 3.1, 3.8).

The difference between the twin extremes of Dutch and Italian youth employment shares is influenced by several factors beside relative pay: youth population shares, activity rates, shares of service employment and unemployment rates. However, only the differences between youth population shares and youth/adult unemployment ratios contribute in the required direction; and neither is sufficiently large – ratios of 11.0 versus 10.2 per cent and 3.60 versus 4.74 respectively in 1979 (Eurostat, 1981) – to account for much of the difference in youth employment shares between the two countries. The difference in youth pay regimes therefore contributes powerfully to the contrasting youth employment shares of the Dutch and Italian economies in particular.

Interaction of Youth Relative Pay and Adult Pay Dispersion

Youth employment patterns are also affected by the interaction between the two preceding features of pay regimes. If youth relative pay is particularly high in sectors which themselves stand high in the adult earnings hierarchy, then the exclusion of youth will prove even more intense than were youth relative pay and adult pay unrelated.

However, in no country does a significant positive relationship emerge (Table 3.11, cols 1,2). The relationship is typically negative; in France and Italy, strongly so. Consequently the tendency towards the exclusion of young workers from high wage sectors is softened in France and Italy from that implied by the adult pay effect alone, while in Belgium, West Germany and the Netherlands the two influences are largely independent of each other.

At the same time, the evidence does not support a view of France and Italy as possessing segregated youth markets with similar absolute levels of youth pay across sectors, as in the standard image of secondary employment. In all six countries, sectors which pay adults highly also tend to pay young people highly. The difference is that in France and Italy the relationship between youth and adult pay is less highly geared than in Belgium and West Germany, where it is effectively one-to-one (Table 3.11, cols 3,4).

Table 3.11 Relationships between adult pay and youth pay, by sex[a]

Country	Correlation between youth relative pay and adult pay		Slope coefficient[b] in regression of youth pay on adult pay	
	Males	Females	Males	Females
Belgium	0.22	0.14	0.89*	0.96*
France	−0.61*	−0.63*	0.48*	0.49*
FR Germany	0.12	0.36	0.87*	1.06*
Italy	−0.64*	−0.68*	0.47*	0.44*
Netherlands	0.03	−0.37	0.68*	0.39
UK	−0.41	−0.28	0.33*	0.50*

Notes
[a] Asterisks denote statistically significant difference from zero (p = 0.05); significance indicated is the least of the three results; all figures are average of estimates (Pearson correlation coefficients or regression slope coefficients) for each of three years.
[b] Youth and adult pay in units of national currency.
Source: As for Table 3.1.

These results might be generated by payment systems which embody similar wage–age discounts across sectors within both Belgium and West Germany but which involve larger wage–age discounts in the high wage sectors in France and Italy. However, as wage–age provisions are distinctly restricted in both France and Italy, it is more plausible to interpret the French and Italian results in terms of upgrading by seniority in enterprise internal markets. If job ladders and pay progression for adults are more extensive in high wage than in low wage sectors in both countries, then rate for the job payment systems are consistent with an inverse association between youth relative pay and adult pay. The average adult in high wage sectors stands further up a job ladder in relation to young entrants than does his or her counterpart in low wage sectors.[23]

3.4 CONCLUSIONS

This chapter has related patterns of youth employment in the industrial sectors of six European economies to institutions of vocational education and training, on the one hand, and to labour market structure and systems of pay determination, on the other.

The first finding is familiar: all countries show a tendency towards the exclusion of young workers from specific sectors, particularly heavy industry. At the same time, exclusionary tendencies are, firstly, less than absolute in all countries; secondly, more pronounced in some countries (notably Italy and France) than in others (notably the Netherlands); thirdly, where most pronounced, best interpreted as the outcome of cost-minimising employer hiring policy subject both to given sectoral pay levels (in segmented labour markets) and to pay rules which make no allowance for youth or trainee status (in internal labour markets).

The data suggest a dichotomous classification of the six economies in terms of two dimensions of national pay structures. Belgium, France and Italy exhibit high adult pay dispersion and high youth relative pay; Germany, the Netherlands and Britain, low adult pay dispersion and low youth relative pay. The classification is by no means unambiguous; it diverges from that implied by other criteria, notably educational objectives (Campinos-Dubernet and Grando, 1988); and its origins require further research. But the data permit little doubt about its importance.

Our analysis has focused mainly upon youth relative pay, which we interpret as determined by institutional rather than competitive forces. National differences in youth relative pay are marked. In the countries where relative pay is high (Belgium, France and Italy) the employment share of young workers is consequently low, relative to that in the countries with low youth pay (the Netherlands, the UK and, for apprentices, Germany).

Differences in national youth pay regimes are associated with two factors: firstly, the relative importance of occupational and internal labour market structures in general and apprenticeship in particular; secondly, the degree of centralisation of pay determination and the strength of trade unions. Occupational markets and apprenticeship promote, through lower youth pay, higher youth shares and, through lower adult wage dispersion, a more even sectoral spread for youth employment. Centralised institutions for national pay bargaining may foster similar outcomes. They favour lower adult wage dispersion if

trade unions seek it and are strong enough to achieve it, as in Italy
after 1974, as well as lower youth relative pay if government and
employers favour it but unions are either uninterested in opposing it or
too weak to prevent it, as in the Netherlands.
The links between institutions, pay regimes and youth employment
are however only partly explicable in terms of the above framework.
Actual outcomes depend upon the norms and strategies of employers,
unions, young workers and the state as well as upon the institutions
within which they interact. National differences are visible in these
respects amongst the three countries with low youth pay regimes – FR
Germany, the Netherlands and the UK. Historical processes are also
important, as in the cumulative divergence between British and
German labour market structures and the different outcomes achieved
by youth movements in Britain and the Netherlands.[24]
The results attained in this chapter are limited by the period and
countries to which our data refer: in terms of time, to the last phase of
the postwar boom and the early stage of adjustment to the first oil
price shock; in terms of country, to the highly structured labour
markets of European economies before the upsurge of deregulatory
policies in the 1980s. We cannot therefore assess the degree to which
the structure of youth markets has subsequently altered under the
impact of large-scale unemployment and deregulation. Other institutions capable of sustaining a low youth pay regime might be found in a
wider range of experiences, historical as well as national, even if the
deregulatory policies of the 1980s have had limited success in this
respect (Marsden and Ryan, 1990b; chapter 2, above).

Notes

1. We gratefully acknowledge financial assistance from the Joseph Rown-
    tree Memorial Trust and permission from the Department of Employ-
    ment to use unpublished results from the New Earnings Survey. We
    have also benefited at various stages in the research from comments and
    suggestions provided by Paolo Garonna, Tinie Akkermans, Bob
    Buchele, Richard C. Edwards, J-F. Germe, Rien Huiskamp, Robert
    M. Lindley, David Metcalf, Andrew Oswald, S. J. Prais, David Raffe,
    Ray Richardson, Jill Rubery, Karen Schober-Brinkmann, Eskil Wa-
    densjö and Keith Whitfield, none of whom can be held responsible for
    our responses. We are grateful above all to B. W. Kim for unstintingly
    helpful research assistance.
2. The SEI was not conducted in 1984, although a comparable national
    survey was undertaken in France in 1986.

3. By 'rate for the job' we mean not a standard rate which an occupationally based trade union seeks to impose upon all employers, as in British craft practice, but simply a well defined job structure together with a particular rate of pay attached to each job category irrespective of which worker fills it.

4. Although the assumptions appear extreme, they need not be precisely realised in order to be useful. Thus, although pay is frequently influenced by worker attributes and actions, through merit rates, output bonuses, etc., our analysis requires only that pay for a particular job depend more upon sectoral affiliation than upon individual characteristics: i.e., that its 'worker' component be small relative to its 'job' one. (The importance of sectoral effects in wage dispersion has received increasing recognition; Dickens and Katz, 1987; Krueger and Summers, 1987). Concerning hiring policy, the main qualifications to our assumptions involve legal exclusion of young workers from particular occupations (e.g. truck driver) and legal limitation of employer discretion in filling vacancies in Italy (Garonna, 1986). The relevance of the assumptions is discussed in more detail in Marsden and Ryan (1989a).

5. Occupational markets are commonly, but misleadingly, termed craft markets in the US literature (e.g. Osterman, 1982a), following Doeringer and Piore (1971). Descriptions of the internal market in the US also require modification when applied to the European context. In French enterprises, for example, pay structures are heavily influenced by national job classifications and associated pay scales.

6. The special (CEF and CFL) contracts under which many young workers have gained access to internal labour markets in France and Italy during the last 10 years involve the introduction of an age–wage dimension to the internal market (section 2.4, above; Brunetta and Dal Co, 1987, ch. 5). The permanence of the change is however an open question. These contracts reflect a political response to a crisis of youth unemployment which, as they have not been formally absorbed into the rules of internal markets, is best interpreted as a temporary and contingent revision of normal internal market procedures.

7. Youth shares might also be expected to vary positively with employer recruitment (because of high rates of labour market entry amongst youths and employer use of seniority in allocating layoffs) and inversely with size of firm (because young workers are overrepresented in small firms). We do not include these prospective influences in the empirical work because of lack of comparable data, but there is also reason to doubt their significance as independent determinants of youth shares (Marsden and Ryan, 1989a).

8. The results are presented here in summary fashion. Technical details are reported in Marsden and Ryan (1989a).

9. The major increase in the Italian adult pay effect between 1972 and 1978 coincides with the increasing public constraint upon employer discretion in the filling of vacancies, in the shape of mandated acceptance of applicants provided by rota from public lists of the unemployed. However, the expected and actual effects of this change diverge: the

adult pay coefficient should fall when employers enjoy less discretion in the hiring of young workers, whereas in fact it rises strongly (Table 3.6).

10. Simple correlations across countries between the dispersion (CV) of youth employment (Table 3.5) and adult pay coefficients (Table 3.6) are not statistically significant (0.31 for males and −0.34 for females).

11. Although we do not report the results in detail, it is worth noting that in two out of the twelve regressions (Dutch males and German females) a significant positive interaction coefficient does indeed emerge; however, in one case (Italian males) the estimate is significantly negative, while the other nine display a mix of signs, all insignificant.

12. When the Calmfors–Driffil (1988, Table 1) index of (de)centralisation in pay bargaining is ranked alongside our measure of adult pay dispersion for the six economies (Table 3.7), the only discrepancy between the two rankings involves the UK, which stands fifth on decentralisation but third on pay dispersion. FR Germany and the Netherlands occupy the bottom places, and Italy the top one, on both criteria.

13. The levelling of sectoral wage inequalities in Italy associated with egalitarian wage policies and flat-rate inflationary adjustments proved so powerful as to move Italy from the highest to the lowest level of sectoral wage dispersion amongst the four largest EEC economies between 1970 and 1983 (Marsden, 1988, Figure 1). Changes in statutory wage floors can also affect the dispersion of adult pay, depending upon the level at which they are set. The increase in the French minimum wage during 1968–70 may have contributed to the marked reduction of adult female pay dispersion between 1966 and 1972. The apparent absence of any effect for males is consistent with the low level to which the minimum wage had fallen by the late 1960s in relation to the male earnings distribution (Saunders and Marsden, 1981, pp. 52–3).

14. A poorly defined relationship over time between the dispersion of adult pay and that of youth shares is the principal reason for the lack of a significant relationship between the dispersions of adult pay and youth employment at the detailed country–year level. Simple correlations across the 18 observations in Tables 3.5 and 3.7 are insignificant (0.20 for males and 0.06 for females).

15. The distinction between apprentice allowances and youth wages in West Germany does not matter for this analysis.

16. Although roughly 85 per cent of minimum age school leavers enter apprenticeship in West Germany, the presence of significant numbers of apprentices aged 19–20 in the recent period (Table 4.4, below) reflects recent trends towards later entry to apprenticeship, primarily after completion of secondary education (Casey, 1986; chapter 3, below). Nevertheless, during the period 1966–78, entry to apprenticeship appears to have been overwhelmingly at ages 15–16 and few apprentices would then have been aged 18 or more.

17. Occupational markets need not depend upon apprenticeship, either formally or informally. Training arrangements for professional occupations (lawyers, accountants and physicians) do not formally involve apprenticeship, even though the mix of classwork and work experience has much in common with it. Training for many female-dominated

clerical occupational markets in large cities in the UK is devoid of apprenticeship in name or reality, relying instead upon pre-employment formal training courses. Similarly, initial training through vocational education (as in Sweden and France) could in principle support a system of occupational markets, even if in reality it tends to be limited to compensating for the deficiencies of employer provision under internal markets.

18. Age–wage schedules in fact apply in FR Germany to regular youth employment as well as apprenticeship. However, as in France, they apply mostly to workers aged less than 18 years (Table 3.10, above; chapter 6, below; Marsden, 1985) while persons aged under 18 cannot be employed (as opposed to apprenticed) in Germany without special dispensation (Schober, 1983).

19. The actual coverage of apprenticeship in the Netherlands is somewhat higher than suggested by Table 3.2, given its relatively short duration.

20. Chapter 7, below; Akkermans and Grootings (1978), Van Voorden (1984), Van Dijk, Akkermans and Hövels (1988).

21. Egalitarian wage policies adopted by trade unions contributed to the narrowing of youth–adult pay differentials in Italy during the 1970s (Garonna, 1986).

22. The response of union leaders appears to have been mixed. On the one hand, by the 1970s two out of the three leading union federations contained parallel youth organisations; on the other, the association of youth groups with unofficial local disputes 'led to some friction with the unions . . .' (Akkermans and Grootings, 1978, p. 180).

23. The interpretation is not readily assessed empirically, but it is weakened by the lack of a similar relationship in Belgium, whose pay regime in other respects resembles that of France and Italy; by its presence in the UK, which is otherwise quite different from France and Italy; and by the lack of marked differences between the sexes, given that women are less likely to gain access to job ladders than are men.

24. A fuller assessment of the influence of institutional factors on pay structures and youth employment shares would require the development of a range of empirical measures for a wider set of economies (Marsden, 1990a).

Part II
Paired Country Comparisons

4 Contrasting Forms of Youth Training and Employment in Sweden and FR Germany

Karen Schober-Brinkmann and Eskil Wadensjö

4.1 INTRODUCTION

In most Western countries the youth unemployment rate is high, much higher than the total unemployment rate. Germany and Sweden are two exceptions to the rule. In FR Germany, the youth rate is less than the overall unemployment rate. In Sweden the youth rate is higher than the total one, but both the youth and the overall rates are low by international standards and the difference between them is smaller than in most other countries (Table 1.1, above).

The fact that both countries have low youth unemployment rates is, however, not explained by any similarity in systems of youth introduction into the labour market. On the contrary, those systems differ considerably between the two countries. How effective are the respective systems at eliminating unemployment and increasing youth employment? Are young people included in the ordinary labour market or are they excluded from it and placed instead in special jobs, schools and training programmes?

In Germany youth activity after compulsory (intermediate) schooling divides into two parts, although this division has become less sharp in recent years, between those who continue with theoretical education and those who continue with vocational training. The majority of those who do not continue in school enter apprenticeship, the predominant means of vocational training and a form of Institutional Inclusion in the labour market (chapter 2, above). However, the apprenticeship system, reinforced by the occupational structuring of the German labour market, leads in practice to the exclusion of the youngest workers from the ordinary adult labour market.

In Sweden, by contrast, very few young people undertake an apprenticeship. After compulsory education (at age 16), the great majority continue on to upper secondary school, for theoretical or vocational studies. It is relatively easy to change from one form of education to the other; it is also possible to take one or more years off and return later. Most of those aged between 16 and 19 years who are not in school or working are placed in labour market programmes aimed at youth.

The great majority of those aged 16–19 years in Germany and Sweden are in school or apprenticeship. They are excluded, in practice, from the ordinary labour market, both the desirable and the less desirable jobs. On the other hand, these years give them skills and prepare them for subsequent entry to the labour market. In a way, the crucial test for educational and labour market policies for youth comes in both countries when young people leave their teens.

In both countries the main programmes for youths are targeted on those below the age of 20. Although efforts for those aged 20–24 have been extended, they do not benefit from the same safety net as do teenagers. What happens to youth when they leave their teens in Germany and Sweden? Do we get a wave of unemployment at the age of 20? Are some of them excluded from the ordinary labour market and confined to a secondary labour market?

Section 4.2 gives a short overview of divergent developments in the aggregate labour markets of the two countries. The central parts of the formal systems of youth integration into the labour market – education, vocational training and labour market programmes – are presented in sections 4.3 and 4.4, followed in section 4.5 by links between youth labour market development and industrial relations systems. Section 4.6 summarises the analysis. Links between youth employment and training and industrial relations are discussed in more detail elsewhere (Schober-Brinkmann, 1986; Wadensjö, 1987b).

4.2   OVERALL LABOUR MARKETS IN FR GERMANY AND SWEDEN IN THE 1970S AND 1980S[1]

The 1960s saw favourable economic development, in terms of high growth rates, low inflation and low unemployment, in both Germany and Sweden. In both countries workers were recruited from abroad. The 1970s and 1980s were, in comparison, years of severe economic difficulty. Growth rates slowed; inflation and unemployment initially increased; industry underwent major structural change; stagnation and stagflation were key words. Reactions to the crisis differed, however. In Sweden the highest priority was given to full employment, in Germany to low inflation.[2]

Germany, with a long tradition of social insurance but not of labour market policy, has leaned towards the cash principle in supporting the unemployed. Since 1969, moves towards an active labour market policy have been made, emphasising the training of both the unemployed and the employed. These programmes, however, have been neither extensive nor integrated with the social security system.

Sweden, on the other hand, has a long tradition of labour market policy and adherence to the work principle. This principle was already applicable to the support of the unemployed in the early 1920s. In the 1930s public relief work at normal wage rates was established as the main policy against cyclical unemployment. In the postwar period, the Rehn-Meidner model, a combined governmental and trade union policy, was accepted as the guide for employment policy. It consists of three parts: first, a restrained monetary and fiscal policy, to hinder inflation; secondly, a solidaristic wage policy, to further equality and foster structural change; and thirdly, an active labour market policy, to combat, with public relief works, labour market training and mobility allowances, the unemployment caused by its first and second components. Swedish response to the crisis of the 1970s and 1980s was therefore an expansion of existing labour market policy. In part it meant an expansion of existing programmes, in part new programmes and new job security legislation. Consequently unemployment was not allowed to increase to German levels.

In the global 1974 recession, the labour market situation in Germany deteriorated rapidly. Unemployment rose from 170,000 in 1970 to more than one million in 1975; employment dropped from a peak of 26.8 million in 1973 to 25.5 million in 1976. Despite a cyclical recovery in the late 1970s, unemployment persisted on a fairly high level and doubled again during the further recession of 1981–3 (Figure 4.1). The economic recovery which began in 1986 and which still continues failed until 1989 to reduce unemployment below two million despite the fact that almost 500,000 persons were active in labour market programmes (Autorengemeinschaft, 1987).

Difficulties in the German labour market were aggravated by an increase in labour supply. From 1977 young cohorts produced by the high birth rates of the 1960s entered the labour market at a time when the retiring age cohorts were small. Female labour force participation

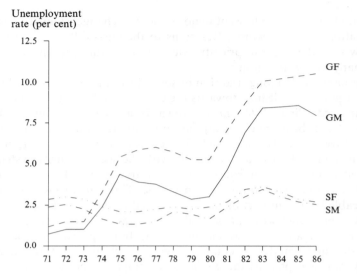

Legend: Germany (G) and Sweden (S), Females (F) and Males (M)
Source: Statistics Sweden, Labour Force Survey, various years.

Figure 4.1   Unemployment rates by sex, FR Germany and Sweden

continued to increase. The potential labour force rose by almost 2 million between 1975 and 1985, a period of stagnant employment. Women, unskilled workers, older persons and (until recently) young entrants were overrepresented among the unemployed.

Institutional arrangements in Germany during the 1960s and early 1970s became advantageous to those already employed. Co-determination for workers and unions was strengthened and job security extended to cover long-term employees, older workers, the disabled, young people in training and women on maternity leave. Unions successfully pursued egalitarian wage policy with respect to wage differentials between skilled and unskilled workers. Working hours were reduced to 40 hours a week and the retirement age was made more flexible.

In the 1980s labour market policy was redirected towards deregulation and flexibility. Thus the 1985 Employment Promotion Act permitted fixed-term contracts, while employers turned increasingly to subcontracting. Flexible working hours were pursued with the objective of detaching machine operating hours from working hours. The unions' fight for a further cut in working hours (to 35 a week) with full wage compensation, so far only partially successful, encouraged various flexible hours initiatives, including increases in part-time work, shift work, a four–day working week and irregular working hours.

In Sweden, both labour force participation and employment rose impressively, the former from 73 per cent of the 16–64-year-old population in 1970 to 84 per cent in 1988. Changes in the composition of the labour force were even more pronounced. Male participation did not increase but female participation increased from 59 to 82 per cent, attaining almost the same rate as for males. The span of the male working life has also fallen, as participation has decreased both among the young and the old.

Unemployment in Sweden gradually increased after the 1960s, becoming, with one exception, somewhat higher in every business cycle than in its predecessor (Figure 4.1). The (at least temporary) reversal of this tendency in 1987–9 has returned unemployment to very low levels, although, from an international perspective, unemployment has remained low throughout. The composition of unemployment developed parallel to that of the labour force. Unemployment rates are now practically the same for males and females, whereas previously the female rate was higher. The rates for youth and older workers both increased until the early 1980s, since when youth rates have fallen (section 4.5, below).

The Swedish labour market has also seen an important change in wage structure, with considerable compression of wage differentials, especially in the 1970s under the influence of the solidaristic wage policies adopted by trade unions. The most marked reductions in differentials occurred between males and females, as well as between adults and youths.

The 1970s and 1980s saw major institutional changes in the Swedish labour market. Labour legislation of the mid-1970s increased job security for those in employment by requiring the employer to give cause for layoffs and to implement them according to inverse seniority unless otherwise agreed with trade union. In a certain sense this law broke with the Swedish policy tradition of 'job security not in the firm but in the labour market'. The 1970s reorientation towards in-plant job security was promoted also through large-scale industrial subsidies, as well as such labour market programmes as inventory subsidies and in-plant training.

However, the 1980s have seen a revival of the traditional policy aimed at increased flexibility through the labour market. Industrial subsidies have almost disappeared. The two groups of labour market programmes to have expanded are those directed at the disabled and at youth. The latter provide part of the theme of this chapter.

4.3   TWO SYSTEMS OF YOUTH INTEGRATION: EDUCATION AND VOCATIONAL TRAINING

This section provides the outline of the systems of education and vocational training in the two countries which is required in order to understand the functioning of the youth labour market. The key differences are, firstly, the reliance upon full-time education in Sweden and the importance of apprenticeship, combining part-time education and workplace training, in Germany; and, secondly, the dominance of comprehensive schools throughout the entire age range in Sweden, in contrast to the three-part German school system, in which the crucial decision concerning educational and occupational careers is taken as early as age 10 or 11. In both respects Sweden has moved historically from a position much closer to that of Germany.

Germany

Despite many reforms, a three-part educational system has persisted since early in the century. Schooling is typically compulsory for nine years, ending at age 15. After four years in primary school, children are placed at age 10–11 in one of three types of school, with little possibility of subsequent change: the *Hauptschule*, or main upper primary school, leading to the basic school-leaving certificate at age 15 or 16; the *Realschule*, or intermediate school, leading usually to a certificate, acquired at age 16 or 17, which gains entrance to technical schools, as well as higher vocational education and apprenticeship training; and the *Gymnasium*, or upper secondary school, running through 13th grade, usually completed at age 19 or 20, and providing a certificate (*Abitur*) which permits university entrance. There are also a few comprehensive schools covering all lines of study. An increasing proportion attend the schools offering longer courses of study (Table 4.1).

Vocational education and training also consist of three systems, each roughly corresponding to one of the three parts of general education: firstly, apprenticeship (the 'dual system' of in-plant training and part-time schooling); secondly, full-time vocational and technical school; and, thirdly, university and technical college.

Table 4.1   Secondary school students in Germany by type of school, 1970–86
(per cent)

Type of school	1970	1975	1980	1982	1984	1986
Upper secondary (Gymnasium)	23.8	24.8	27.7	27.7	27.7	27.9
Intermediate (Realschule)	18.7	21.0	27.9	28.5	28.9	28.7
Upper primary (Hauptschule)	51.4	44.6	34.7	34.0	32.9	31.7
Comprehensive (Gesamtschule)	0	2.6	3.4	3.7	4.1	5.0
Special (Sonderschule)	5.8	7.2	6.3	6.1	6.3	6.6
Total (per cent)	100	100	100	100	100	100
(absolute 000s)	4 622	5 631	5 661	5 227	4 507	3 931

Source: BMBW (1987a), pp. 34–35, 52–53.

Apprenticeship is the most important type of vocational training. Around three-quarters of the young people who finish upper primary school and two-thirds of those with the intermediate school certificate take an apprenticeship. Recently apprenticeship has also attracted graduates of the Gymnasia: nowadays roughly one-third of those acquiring the Abitur (or equivalent) enter apprenticeship training.

Apprenticeship, regulated by the Vocational Training Act (1969), covers around 360 occupations spanning a wide variety of economic activities including agriculture and the public sector. Manufacturing and the artisan (handicraft) sectors are the main training areas (Table 4.2). For each occupation, a curriculum specifies the content, organisation and duration of training (2–3.5 years), related theoretical instruction in a part-time vocational school for up to two days a week, and the final qualifying examinations.[3] Instructors, who are required to have passed pedagogic examinations, are often senior craftsmen or owners of small firms.

Apprentices have the status of full-time employees, are covered by social insurance programmes and collective agreements and have special representatives on works councils. Their allowances, set by collective bargaining, vary between 20 and 50 per cent of the skilled rate for the occupation, depending on sector and training year. The Vocational Training Act provides for increased allowances in successive training years and stipulates that apprentices, after a three-month probationary period, may not be dismissed during the training period.

The main responsibility for apprenticeship training lies with employers and their associations. Employers decide individually on the number of training places offered and, thus, their regional and

Table 4.2   Apprentices by sector, FR Germany 1970–85 (thousands)

Sector	1970	1975	1980	1985
Manufacturing/commerce	725	634	787	875
Artisan/handicraft	420	505	702	688
Agriculture	38	33	47	53
Public sector	20	46	54	73
Professions/household, etc.	66	111	126	143
All sectors	1 269	1 329	1 716	1 831
As percentage of 16–19-year-old population	53.4	48.5	53.8	62.9

Source: BMBW (1987a), p. 96.

occupational distribution, as well as bearing most of the costs of training at the workplace. Young people are placed in apprenticeship either by direct agreement with the employer or, in 70 to 80 per cent of cases, by the local employment office.

Trade unions are by law integral to decisions concerning apprenticeship. In-plant training at the level of the firm is controlled by the works council and is influenced to some extent by collective agreements. Unions are also represented on the committees (local, regional and federal) responsible for examinations, operational control and the development of legislation, training fields and curricula.

In response to the uneven distribution of training and training costs among firms and sectors, unions have pressed, thus far with little success, for an independent financing system. An attempt to establish a national apprenticeship fund through a training levy failed in 1980 in the face of employer resistance.

Much apprenticeship is provided by small firms, where it is less expensive and often directed to less skilled occupations. In contrast, training in large industrial firms and some service occupations involves highly skilled work. These differences in the quality of training correspond partly to those in entrants' qualifications. Those who possess the *Abitur* tend towards the more skilled training places whereas those with only compulsory education usually apply for the less skilled ones.

Despite these differences, minimum training standards prevail even in the less skilled and less attractive fields. Curricula and examinations are identical for all apprentices in an occupational field and the qualification obtained allows the young person some flexibility on the labour market.

Both employers and trade unions support the apprenticeship system. The rights enjoyed by, and the participation of, trade unions contribute strongly to its stability and flexibility (Streeck et al., 1987) along with the strong support for it shown by youths and parents.

In addition to apprenticeship, a variety of full-time vocational schools, ranging from low-level work preparatory courses to multi-year, full-time technical schools, offer recognised vocational credentials. In 1986 more than 750,000 teenagers were enrolled in full-time vocational schools below university and technical college level (BMBW, 1987a). The majority of them studied in occupational fields or levels where apprenticeship is absent or scarce, including health, kindergarten teaching, business administration and clerical occupations. Vocational schools are also important in the preparation of girls for predominantly female occupations.

Enrolments in vocational schools expanded during the youth labour market crisis of the late 1970s and early 1980s, when the demand for apprenticeship places exceeded the supply. After finishing their courses, many young people entered an apprenticeship in order to improve their labour market prospects. At the same time, those who complete apprenticeship may subsequently proceed to higher education.[4]

About 12 per cent of an age cohort enter the youth labour market without a recognised vocational training or higher education certificate (Stegmann and Kraft, 1987; BLK, 1987). This group includes dropouts from school or the vocational training system, and those who never started any kind of training or further education after compulsory schooling. Their labour market chances have deteriorated because even for 'bad jobs' employers prefer young people with apprenticeship qualifications, regardless of occupational field.

Sweden

In 1962 Sweden adopted a common comprehensive school system (*Grundskola*) for ages seven to sixteen; the system was fully established by 1970. Almost all pupils in the *Grundskola* follow the same course. Those aged less than 16 who work do so mainly during vacations, weekends or evenings, in addition to schoolwork. Most students continue after *Grundskola* to upper secondary school (*Gymnasieskola*). A 1968 parliamentary decision led to the reorganisation of upper secondary schooling, with the *Gymnasieskola* replacing three antecedent categories of school: the *Gymnasium*, offering theoretical lines of study in preparation for university; the *Fackskola*, with its two year theoretical curricula; and the *Yrkesskola*, concentrating on vocational courses.[5]

The greatest change concerned vocational education, which was greatly reorganised, expanded, lengthened and standardised. Thus the last step was taken from the old apprenticeship system to school-based vocational education, following earlier changes in the same direction in the 1910s, 1930s and 1950s (Marklund, 1982). Although radical, the change was little discussed: political parties, unions and employer organisations all favoured it.

The 27 lines of study available in upper secondary school vary between two and four years in length and are intended mainly for those finishing compulsory school.[6] Vocational courses involve unpaid external work experience, varying between five and 25 per cent of study time according to subject. The *Gymnasieskola* has developed towards longer (three- and four-year) lines of study, both theoretical and vocational (Table 4.3). In addition, upper secondary schools offer 550 special courses, varying in length between eight weeks and three years. In autumn 1986, 100,000 were enrolled in a line of study and 27,000 in a special course.

The great majority of young people leaving compulsory education proceed nowadays to upper secondary education: in recent years 86 per cent of *Grundskola* leavers continued directly to a 'study line' (*Utbildningslinjer*: programme of study) in the *Gymnasieskola* and a further 3 per cent went to similar but less formal special courses. The rate of transition might be expected to be even higher, given that vacancies at the *Gymnasieskola* exceed numbers leaving the *Grundskola*. However, the distribution of places by study line does not always accord with applicant preferences and some places go to others than those who have just left the *Grundskola*.

Since 1980 the school system has also had responsibility for non-students aged 16–17, as well as for organising special programmes for the unemployed (section 4.4, below). Although the *Grundskola* has changed little since 1971, a governmental committee proposed in 1986 that most vocational lines be lengthened to three years, with three days a week being spent at a workplace during the third year (SOU, 1986). The experimental adoption of this scheme in some study lines led to conflict between employers and unions, who were initially unwilling to accept that trainee work should be unpaid.

Table 4.3   Admissions to upper secondary school in Sweden by line of study, 1978–86 (percentages)

Line of study	1978	1980	1982	1984	1986
3–4 year theoretical	36.6	38.3	39.4	39.5	43.1
2–year theoretical	19.5	17.5	13.8	12.7	9.3
2–3 year vocational	43.9	44.2	46.8	47.7	47.5
Total	100	100	100	100	100

Source: Statistiska meddelanden U50 SM8701, Statistics Sweden.

Comparison

Until the early 1960s, the non-vocational components of the Swedish and German school systems were similar, not least because the Swedish system was in many respects modelled upon the German one. However, subsequent changes in the Swedish system, primarily towards the integration of theoretical education, vocational education and later occupational choice, have made the differences more striking than the similarities.

The Swedish educational system is much the more comprehensive of the two. Sweden has one school for all children up to 16 years of age, whereas in Germany a choice made after only four school years determines subsequent occupational opportunity. At upper secondary level, Sweden's single system comprises both theoretical and vocational education, while Germany differentiates institutionally between theoretical education and (mainly) apprenticeship-cum-vocational education. The difference is particularly marked for vocational education, reflecting the broadly continuous development since the 1910s from an apprenticeship-based to a school-based vocational educational system in Sweden.

Vocational curricula are directed in Sweden not towards specific occupations but towards broad occupational areas. In Germany the division between theoretical and vocational education is sharp. Vocational education occurs mainly as part of apprenticeship and is directed much more towards specific occupations than are vocational lines in the Swedish *Gymnasieskola*, reflecting the greater importance in the German labour market of occupational structures, including regulations concerning who is allowed to do particular work tasks.

In Germany a considerable expansion of theoretical education took place during 1960–80 with fewer young people starting apprenticeship and more going into higher education. However, the labour market crisis of the 1980s has seen a reversal towards apprenticeship, especially among those with the *Abitur* (Table 4.2, above).

Most people aged 16–17 are nowadays still in school in both countries (Table 4.4). The majority leave school at 18–19 years in Sweden, after finishing two year or three year courses, vocational or theoretical. In Germany, if apprenticeship is included in view of its part-time educational content, school-leaving extends over one more year (18–20), though from the age of 21 the percentage studying is similar in the two countries.[7]

Why has Swedish but not German vocational education developed from apprenticeship to schooling? We discuss here some of the many influences upon this divergent development. In the first place, the Social Democratic Party has been in power in Sweden since 1932, 1976–82 only excepted. Promotion of vocational schooling can be seen as a part of the party's integrative and egalitarian social policy. It minimises differences in the length of schooling and ensures that different social groups go through the same school. The policy has been supported by unions and, with minor exceptions, employer organisations.

Trade unions are also stronger in Sweden than in most other countries, including Germany. For many decades Swedish unions have been organised according to industry rather than occupation or

Table 4.4   School students and apprentices as a percentage of age cohort, Sweden and FR Germany, autumn 1984

Age	16	17	18	19	20	21	22	23	24	25
Sweden students[a]	92	85	52	27	21	23	23	23	21	18
Germany students[a]	74	49	35	24	18	17	18	17	16	14
apprentices	23	42	41	30	16	8	3	2	1	1
total	97	91	76	54	34	25	21	19	17	15

Note
[a] Full-time study only.

Sources: Yearbook of Educational Statistics 1986, Official Statistics of Sweden, Stockholm 1986; IAB, Educational Accounting System, Nurnberg March 1988 (unpublished).

craft, an attribute which helps explain their support for an educational orientation towards sector-wide rather than occupational criteria.

Moreover, the major Swedish employer organisations are dominated by big companies, which, prior to the change in national training policy, made less use of apprenticeship training than did small firms. Several had even set up their own internal vocational schools. The favourable attitude of employer organisations to expansion of public vocational schooling may reflect the cost saving involved for such firms.

In Germany, trade unions wish similarly to change the existing three-part school system, with its early determination of occupational chances. The Social Democratic government of the 1970s supported moves towards a comprehensive school system. Success was however meagre, reflecting the location of responsibility for the educational system at state (*Länder*) level, where most governments remained conservative and opposed comprehensive schooling.

Apprenticeship benefits from a long historical tradition in Germany and enjoys the strong support of employers, unions and the population in general. The unions obtain through it a degree of influence and control which they would never acquire under school-based vocational education (Streeck et al., 1987). They also value the early access which apprenticeship provides to the new generation of union members, particularly given that union membership is more widespread among skilled workers than among the unskilled or those with higher education.

For German employers, especially small firms, apprenticeship training is a source of cheap labour. Even large firms prefer to recruit ex-apprentices from the handicraft sector mainly because such youngsters already have work experience, irrespective of the occupation involved, and additional training costs are much less for young people with apprenticeship training than for those with theoretical education. Employers also have an important influence on the content and organisation of apprenticeship training, whereas they have no influence at all on school education.

4.4 TWO SYSTEMS OF YOUTH INTEGRATION: LABOUR MARKET PROGRAMMES

Educational and vocational training have been used as means of counteracting youth unemployment in most countries. Not only are young people who are active in school or in apprenticeship not unemployed, but also both institutions improve young people's preparation for the labour market. Special programmes for youth integration into the labour market have also been adopted in most countries, their content varying greatly according to institutional setting and industrial relations system. In Sweden proportionately more people participate in labour market programmes than in any other country, whereas in Germany such activity is close to the European average.

Youths in German Labour Market Programmes

Special youth programmes in Germany involve predominantly training and education, with emphasis on the apprenticeship system and on work preparation for school leavers. Special schemes to raise youth employment directly are of minor importance (Table 4.5). A variety of other schemes are open to both young people and adults (Strikker, 1987).

A special one-year, in-school, work-preparatory programme was established in the mid-1970s for underachieving school leavers who failed to obtain an apprenticeship place or a job. The additional year of full-time school was designed to improve the chances of getting a training place or a job, acting as a substitute for compulsory part-time vocational schooling until the age of 18, since employers very often refuse to hire people under 18 for regular jobs because they have to pay them for the one day per week spent in school (Stegmann and Kraft, 1988).

In 1987 the Bundesanstalt für Arbeit, the German central labour market authority, administered programmes for around 170,000 youths aged between 15 and 24. The most important programme is the one-year, out-of-school work-preparatory courses directed towards those finishing school who have failed to obtain an apprenticeship. This scheme, which antedates its in-school counterpart, is more attractive to young participants because it gives access to a means-tested training allowance. In most cases these courses also provide better training than do in-school ones because they are conducted in training centres and workshops similar to industrial or craft-training places. Both training and theoretical instruction are provided in courses conducted by a variety of bodies, including charitable organisations, churches, chambers of industry and commerce, craft-

Table 4.5 Number of workers aged 15–24 participating in labour market programmes in Germany, 1980–7 (thousands)

Programme	1980	1981	1982	1983	1984	1985	1986	1987
A Out-of-school work								
preparation courses	29.6	34.5	35.1	26.4	54.6	58.1	62.2	62.1
Further training	29.0	32.6	34.2	32.5	39.8	41.2	45.1	52.5
Retraining	10.1	13.1	13.8	12.3	13.7	13.6	16.2	17.4
OJT allowance[b]	3.9	1.8	1.0	1.9	2.0	2.8	4.6	5.4
Settling-in allowance	n.a.	5.8	5.5	5.2	6.1	6.5	7.4	6.4
Public job creation[a]	10.6	10.2	8.0	15.4	24.8	30.0	26.7	26.5
B Programme for the								
disadvantaged	0	0.6	1.7	6.0	10.5	18.5	25.8	32.2
C In-school work								
preparation courses	50.5	46.8	45.4	46.1	47.2	41.7	36.8	n.a.
All	n.a.	144.9	144.7	145.8	198.7	212.4	224.8	n.a.

Notes: Programmes in block A are run by the Bundesanstalt für Arbeit (Federal Employment Institute); B by the Federal Government; C by regional (Länder) government.
[a] Includes the 'working and learning' scheme, involving part-time job creation and part-time training or education (1986–7 activity levels around 11 000).
[b] OJT: on the job training.

Sources: Bundesanstalt für Arbeit (various years); BMBW (1987), pp. 54–5; Schober (1988).

training centres and trade unions. As the majority of course participants seek apprenticeships after completion, the main effect is to postpone the demand for apprenticeship places by one year. The courses are often characterised as queues and criticised for not providing recognised skills or certificates (Schober, 1986b).

Several programmes administered by regional (*Länder*) governments subsidise private and public employers who provide additional apprenticeship places for target groups such as young women, children of migrant workers and disabled youth. The number of subsidised training places is not known but educated guesses put it at around 10 per cent of all apprenticeships in the country as a whole, i.e. roughly 180,000 places (Strikker, 1987).

During 1981–7 the Federal Government also administered an out-of-firm apprenticeship programme for disadvantaged youth. This programme is in all aspects (training contract, remuneration, curricula, examinations) equivalent to regular apprenticeship but it is run by non-profit organisations providing special pedagogic services. The programme, although quite successful, was opposed by employers, who feared the undermining of their sole responsibility for apprenticeship training.[8]

Youth activity in public job creation programmes also rose during the crisis, although such programmes are aimed mainly at the older and long-term unemployed. One particular youth programme combines part-time work in a public relief programme with a part-time training course. The regular remuneration of the part-time job is intended to encourage participation in training. Further training and retraining courses are open to all age groups but people under 25 are overrepresented (Schober, 1986a).

In total, more than 200,000 people aged 15–24 years participated annually in labour market and vocational training measures in the mid 1980s, corresponding to more than half the number unemployed in the age group. Thus the strengthening of the apprenticeship system and the withdrawal of young people from the labour market received much greater priority than direct employment creation. The strategy was supported by both employers and unions, although unions voted for additional employment programmes (Schober-Brinkmann, 1986).

Youths in Swedish Labour Market Programmes

Sweden has a long tradition of large-scale labour market programmes. In the 1930s, for example, public relief work with normal wages was introduced as a policy against cyclical unemployment. In the 1950s the government adopted union proposals in the shape of the Rehn-Meidner model, which involved an active manpower policy, a solidaristic wage policy and monetary–fiscal restraint. The policy has typically involved subsidies to training and labour mobility, added to the pre-existent public relief work. Since around 1960 labour market programmes have gradually expanded and various new programmes have been added.

The labour market programmes of the 1950s were predominantly targeted at prime-age, male, blue-collar workers who had been laid off or made redundant. Public relief usually involved physically demanding outdoor work, unsuitable for youth. In the 1960s it became evident, however, that other groups had greater problems than had adult men and programmes were gradually reoriented towards the needs of women, immigrants, the disabled and youth.

The initial policy strategy in regard to youth was to rearrange existing programmes. Training courses were introduced designated especially for labour market entrants. Public relief work, which had previously been dominated by 'investment jobs' (road construction, etc.), was also arranged in public services (health, nursing) until, within a few years, most places were in the latter sector. Some public relief jobs in the service sector are in practice part of a vocational training programme, given that public relief work is one way of getting the experience required for some special courses.

Variations in youth activity in labour market programmes are large (Table 4.6). Some fluctuation is explained by business cycles, some by changes in youth cohort size. But the most important factor is policy shifts. In the 1980s special programmes were introduced initially for 16–17-year-olds (Youth Jobs) and subsequently for 18–19-year-olds (Youth Teams), leading to the absence of persons aged under 20 from public relief work after 1984.

The shift in policy was a response to increases in youth unemployment rates and the associated intensity of public debate. Youth unemployment became an issue in the mid-1970s. The first policy reaction was in 1976, when parliament gave to employment offices and local school administration joint responsibility for youth for two years after the end of compulsory schooling (changed in 1979 to include all persons aged less than 18). When unemployment rates continued to increase, a new policy was adopted in 1980. Public relief jobs were abolished for the youngest age groups and education became the favoured policy. The number of places in the upper secondary schools increased and support to other forms of education was extended. However, the 16–17-year-old unemployment rate failed to fall and in 1982 Youth Jobs was established, following agreement between SAF (the main employer organisation) and the major trade unions in December 1981.

Since July 1982 sole responsibility for 16- and 17-year-olds has been allocated to the local community, which means in practice the school administration. Although employment offices are supposed to try to place youths in vacant jobs, in practice they do not do so. Young people are steered instead into the Youth Jobs programme, where pay is low and the employer is subsidised to the extent of all wage costs in the public sector and around one-half in the private sector. The period spent in a 'youth job' may not exceed six months. According to a 1983 survey, 25 per cent of participants get a permanent job in the same firm (SIFO, 1983).

Table 4.6   Youth participants by principal labour market programmes and age group, Sweden, 1977–87 (annual average in thousands)

Year	Labour market training 16–19	20–24	Public relief jobs 16–19	20–24	Youth jobs 16–17	Youth teams 18–19	Total Numbers 16–19	20–24	Total Population share (%) 16–19	20–24
1977	3.9	12.1	10.8	4.5			14.7	16.6	3.5	3.0
1978	5.4	13.5	19.5	9.1			24.9	22.6	5.9	4.0
1979	5.6	14.1	20.0	9.4			25.6	23.5	5.9	4.2
1980	3.7	11.6	8.2	4.4			11.9	16.0	2.7	2.9
1981	2.3	8.7	6.9	5.6			9.2	14.3	2.0	2.6
1982	2.7	9.6	16.7	13.2	4.3		23.7	22.8	4.9	4.2
1983	2.6	10.3	18.4	19.6	14.0		35.0	29.9	7.1	5.4
1984	2.2	10.9	4.7	14.6	14.4	30.5	51.8	25.5	10.6	4.6
1985	1.6	10.3	0	7.9	11.3	30.5	43.4	18.2	9.1	3.1
1986	1.6	10.4	0	6.4	9.9	23.7	35.2	16.8	7.6	2.8
1987	1.4	11.1	0	5.0	9.5	17.9	28.8	16.1	6.4	2.6

Note: Only the main programmes are reported. In 1985, for example, there were twenty different labour market and training programmes for youths (AMS, 1985), including Induction Opportunities (700 and 1800 participants in 1987 and 1988 respectively) which replaced Youth Teams as from July 1989.

Source: Labour Market Board; National Board of Education.

Since 1982 very few 16–17-year-olds have been unemployed. Most of those not in school have participated in Youth Jobs or follow-up programmes, also administered by the local school authority. National School Board statistics, available since 1983, show that the percentage in school has increased continuously (Table 4.7). Among the remainder, the share in Youth Jobs and follow-up programmes has fallen more rapidly than that in ordinary employment, consistent with favourable developments in the general labour market.

Unemployment amongst 18–19-year-olds continued to increase, however, reaching record levels in 1982 and 1983. A new programme for 18–19-year-olds (and up to age 25 for the mentally retarded), the Youth Teams, was accepted late in 1983 and introduced on a massive scale in January 1984. It means in practice jobs in the public sector, paying the hourly wage rate established in collective agreements but providing only half-time work.[9] Apart from budgetary considerations,

Karen Schober-Brinkmann and Eskil Wadensjö   1

Table 4.7   Activities of 16–17-year-olds, Sweden, September, 1983–
(percentages)

Year	Upper secondary school	Employment	Follow-up programme	Youth Jobs	Unemployed	Other
1983	85.6	3.0	2.4	6.2	1.7	1.7
1984	88.6	2.8	0.9	5.0	1.3	1.4
1985	90.4	2.1	0.7	4.5	0.9	1.4
1986	90.6	2.4	0.6	4.2	0.9	1.0
1987	91.2	2.5	0.5	3.8	0.7	1.3

Source: Skolöverstyrelsen, 'Kommunernas uppföljningsansvar 1987/88', Table 6.3.

the combination of full pay rates and part-time work under Youth Teams reflects two factors. Firstly, there is the desirability of providing youth with free time to look for jobs and incentives to do so. Secondly, trade unions successfully opposed a proposed format involving full-time jobs but lower wage rates. A lower wage rate for youth was seen as a threat to the solidaristic wage policy pursued by the unions.

Unemployment amongst 18–19-year-olds dropped dramatically as a result of Youth Teams. Participants in 1984 and 1985 stayed in the programme for an average of seven months (AMS, 1986a). Slightly more than one-half (53 per cent) ended their spell by getting a job. Of the remainder, as many as 19 per cent went into unemployment, while the others went on to other programmes, military service or school studies. The main criticism levelled against Youth Teams has been that it provides only part-time work and that the jobs are in the non-expanding public sector.

A further programme was introduced in 1987 in response to such criticism: Induction Opportunities, providing 18–19-year-olds with subsidised private sector employment for up to six months. One-half of wage costs are publicly subsidised, at wage rates laid down in collective agreements. Unemployed youth and Youth Team participants are eligible. In 1988, 1,800 on average took part. Proposals by the Labour Market Board that Induction Opportunities should completely replace Youth Teams and be extended to the public sector were accepted by government, to become effective from July 1989.

Although there are also some special programmes for young adults (ages 20–24), the main programmes for this age group are those open to adults in general: public relief work, training and mobility allowances. Young adults are markedly overrepresented in these programmes. Public relief work is highly counter-cyclical (Table 4.6) but training is more stable and mobility allowances are strongly pro-cyclical.

Thus public policy towards the youth labour market in Sweden strongly favours direct employment creation, with Youth Jobs, Youth Teams and public relief work as leading components.

Comparison

Although both Germany and, especially, Sweden have in the 1980s operated encompassing labour market programmes for young workers, important differences are present. In Germany training programmes dominate, in Sweden employment programmes. Youth programmes are in Sweden more concentrated on those with weak labour market prospects than is the case in Germany. One explanation for these differences is the much lower rate of unemployment in Sweden, which has meant fewer problems for non-disadvantaged youths than in Germany. Another explanation involves differences in the two countries' systems of youth introduction into the labour market. A third looks to the more integral status of labour market policy within general economic policy in Sweden.

Both countries responded to increased youth unemployment by strengthening their regular systems: Germany by intensifying apprenticeship, Sweden by expanding upper secondary schooling. Problems remained nevertheless, especially for the less able and the less motivated. For those groups again two different strategies have been used. German government tends to withdraw them from the labour market by providing a variety of full-time courses below apprenticeship level, whereas Swedish government subsidises their entry into the labour market through the Youth Jobs and Youth Teams programmes.

The Swedish strategy corresponds to a country where young people enter the labour market without work experience even when they have attained a high level of education. In Germany, where the apprenticeship system provides three years of work experience at a low wage rate, other subsidised, low-paid youth jobs seem out of place.

We argued in section 4.1 above that the acid test of the functioning of the youth labour market comes when young people have finished their period of initial education and training. Germany lacks a comprehensive employment programme for those who have finished apprenticeship. According to a broad consensus, public relief work and employment subsidies should be given only to the disadvantaged and the unemployed, and not made available for hiring well-trained young people. Trade unions fear in particular strong windfall profits, with employers acquiring subsidies for the employment of young people whom they would have hired anyway. Although Social Democrats and trade unions strongly favour public job creation, such programmes have not won wider acceptance either in the public or in the private sector. In Sweden, on the other hand, all political parties have for many decades accepted public jobs and subsidised private jobs as part of labour market policy.

4.5 DEVELOPMENT OF THE YOUTH LABOUR MARKET IN THE TWO COUNTRIES

We now compare developments in the youth labour markets of the two countries and relate them to systems of youth introduction to the labour market. The comparison is not without problems, particularly given the importance of differences in general employment situations.

The comparison is restricted to the age group 16–24 years, with a major division at age 20. In both countries special arrangements, including schools, apprenticeships and labour market programmes, apply mostly to 16–19-year-olds. Few teenagers are tested on the open market and, of those who are tested but do not get a job, most are placed in special programmes. Teenage unemployment rates are thus kept low.

Labour force participation, on the other hand, depends strongly upon whether those participating in special programmes are classified as in employment or outside the labour force. Thus the labour market situation of 16–19-year-olds as measured by unemployment and labour force participation, indicates both the aspirations of special programmes and the nature of classifications rather than outcomes in youth markets *per se*.

The situation of 20–24-year-olds, on the other hand, provides more of a test of the effects of youth-related institutions. Are youths in school, apprenticeships and labour market programmes sufficiently prepared while teenagers to establish themselves in the market in their early twenties? If they are employed, do they get good jobs or only unstable ones in a secondary labour market?

Youth Labour Force Participation

Patterns of youth participation in the two countries show similarities and differences. For 16–19-year-olds, the main characteristic in each country is the long run downward trend, particularly for 16–17-year-olds. School enrollment rates amongst 16–19-year-olds increased in Germany from 28 to 53 per cent between 1970 and 1985 (Tessaring, 1988) and Sweden showed a similar development. These changes reflect mainly the trend towards longer periods of general education, but increased unemployment also plays a part, as school attendance may be for some students a way of disguising unemployment.

Measured labour force participation rates are higher for male teenagers in Germany than in Sweden. Girls show a more mixed pattern: for 16–18-year-olds, participation rates are similar in the two countries but the rate for 19-year-olds is much higher in Sweden. The latter reflects mainly higher female participation in Sweden, but also the fact that the large numbers active in Youth Teams are officially classified as employees. Finally, differences in measured participation rates between German and Swedish teenagers have diminished over time.

For various reasons, official statistics are misleading guides to both levels of and trends in participation, interpreted as the occupation of an established position in the regular labour market. The major difficulty involves the classification of trainees. German apprentices, who attend school part-time, are counted as in the labour force, whereas, in both countries, those training full-time in school or attending school part-time and getting part-time training at a workplace are counted as out of the labour force, even though the combination of education and work can be similar across all categories. The latter categories dominate in Sweden (Table 4.4, above), apprentices in Germany. Were apprentices removed from the 'employee' category, the difference between teenage participation rates in the two countries would disappear.

Moreover, Sweden counts those active in the Youth Jobs and Youth Teams programmes as within the labour force, whereas those in labour market training programmes, relatively more common in Germany, are not so classified. Other difficulties arise in association with military service and the greater importance of part-time work amongst Swedish teenagers.[10]

Labour force statistics for 16–19-year-olds are thus more a measure of the high ambitions prevailing in each country than of the results of educational and employment policy. The situation of 20–24-year-olds gives a better measure of success. Their participation rates have been considerably higher in Sweden (Figure 4.2), particularly for women. If the employment rate is preferred to the participation rate, the Swedish advantage becomes even greater, reflecting higher unemployment in Germany, and its development over time much more favourable.

The difference in participation rates amongst young adults derives only to a minor extent from the higher rates of participation in labour market programmes (notably public relief work) in Sweden and in higher education in Germany (Table 4.4). We conclude that Swedish youth become well established in the ordinary, non–subsidised labour market by their early twenties but that the same is true only to a lesser extent for young Germans.

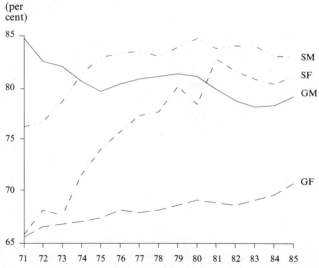

Legend: Germany (G) and Sweden (S), Females (F) and Males (M)
Source: Statistics Sweden, Labour Force Survey, various years

Figure 4.2 Labour force participation rates, 20–24-year-olds, FR Germany and Sweden, 1971–85.

Youth Unemployment

Youth unemployment has risen in recent decades in both countries mainly as a result of higher total unemployment (Table 4.8). In Sweden the youth rate tended to increase faster than the total one until a few years ago (Wadensjö, 1987a). The unemployment rate for 20–24-year-olds in both countries, as well as that for 16–19-year-olds in Sweden, has generally exceeded the rate for all ages.

Again, statistics for youth require careful interpretation, especially 16–19-year-olds. One problem is that only a part, and a decreasing part, of teenagers is in the labour force. Those in the labour force and not in apprenticeship have become an increasingly selected group, with weakening market prospects relative to those in school or apprenticeship. The treatment of trainees leads to difficulty here as well. Were apprentices excluded from the labour force along with full-time vocational students, the German youth unemployment rate and, with it, the gap relative to the Swedish rate would increase strongly.[11]

For young adults (20–24 years), the classification of participants in labour market training as outside the labour force (a status which is relatively more common in Germany) and those in subsidised employment as inside it (more common in Sweden) again distorts the comparison. Unemployment rates are thus poor indicators of the labour market situation of both teenagers and young adults.

A few decades ago most youth became established in the labour market in their teens, whereas nowadays the early twenties is the critical age. The growing importance of an initial period of unemployment and temporary work prior to acquisition of the first permanent job leads us to expect for this age group a high and increasing unemployment rate relative to the total one. We also expect the youth rate to be highly sensitive to the business cycle. In recessions, the shortage of vacancies is more problematic for recent labour market entrants than for those who have participated for longer periods. Adult workers in most cases already have a job and, if firms lay off workers, according to seniority rules they must lay off newly hired workers, among whom youths are overrepresented. However, the hypothesised tendency towards higher and more variable unemployment among youths has been counteracted by the expansion of both labour market programmes and school enrollment.

The hypothesis is assessed by regression analysis, relating the unemployment rate for young adults of both sexes to that of prime age males and a time trend (Table 4.9). The results indicate that the

Table 4.8   Unemployment rates by age category, Germany and Sweden, 1975–87

	Germany				Sweden				
	15–19[a]		20–24[b]		All	16–19		20–24		All
Year	Men	Women	Men	Women		Men	Women	Men	Women	
1975	4.3	4.5	5.9	5.8	4.7	4.2	7.1	2.1	3.5	1.6
1976	3.2	4.5	4.7	6.3	4.6	4.1	7.0	2.2	3.4	1.6
1977	3.5	5.8	4.4	6.9	4.5	5.4	8.1	2.9	3.5	1.8
1978	3.0	5.2	4.0	6.6	4.3	7.1	8.7	4.3	4.3	2.3
1979	2.1	4.0	2.8	5.8	3.8	7.0	7.9	3.6	3.8	2.1
1980	2.3	4.2	2.9	5.0	3.8	6.5	8.7	3.5	3.9	2.0
1981	4.1	5.9	4.9	6.1	5.5	8.2	10.5	4.8	4.6	2.5
1982	6.8	8.2	8.2	8.5	7.5	9.6	11.6	6.3	5.8	3.2
1983	7.9	10.0	10.3	11.1	9.1	9.9	10.8	6.7	6.9	3.5
1984	7.1	9.2	10.3	11.4	9.1	5.1	4.7	6.2	7.0	3.1
1985	6.7	9.8	9.9	10.7	9.2	4.7	4.5	6.4	6.3	2.8
1986	6.0	9.1	8.7	9.6	8.7	4.3	3.9	6.3	6.1	2.7
1987[c]	5.5	8.1	8.6	9.0	8.7	3.6	3.5	4.5	4.3	1.9

Notes
[a] 1975–76 data for May; annual averages since 1977.
[b] 1975–80 data for May, quarterly averages since 1981.
[c] The Swedish labour force survey underwent a major revision in 1987. New estimates are around 0.5 points less than those produced by previous methods.

Sources: Bundesanstalt für Arbeit data and author's calculations (Germany); Statistics Sweden, Labour force surveys.

young adult rate has exceeded the adult one for all values of the latter in Sweden and for 'realistic' ones in Germany; that the young adult rate has varied proportionally with the adult rate in Sweden but significantly less than proportionally in Germany, as indicated by the difference from unity of the estimated coefficient on the adult rate; and that the young adult rate increased significantly relative to the adult one in Sweden but not in Germany.

The rise in the ratio of young adult to adult rates in Sweden but not in Germany may reflect a more marked shift in the period of effective entry into the early twenties age group in Sweden. On the other hand, those with little or no high school education are overrepresented

Table 4.9   Regression of young adult unemployment rates on adult male rates and a time trend, Sweden and Germany, 1971–84 (Dependent variable: unemployment rate, 20–24-year-olds)

Variable	Germany	Sweden
Intercept	0.930	0.417
	(0.563)	(0.047)
Adult Rate	0.819	1.027
	(0.072)	(0.060)
Time	0.009	0.019
	(0.046)	(0.003)
$\overline{R}^2$	0.992	0.974
d	1.81	2.43

Note: Adult rate is that of 35–44-year-old males; standard errors in parentheses.

amongst unemployed 20–24-year-olds in Sweden. Many unemployed young adults had entered the labour market well before reaching the age of twenty, had had difficulty finding their first job and had already recorded several spells of unemployment (AMS, 1986b). Unemployed young adults in Sweden contain a major group with entrenched labour market problems.

The size of the youth cohorts entering the labour market will fall in both countries in the 1990s. Decreasing competition among youth entrants may reduce the youth unemployment rate, as is already apparent for the youngest workers in Germany.

Youth Wages

In both countries, pay (including apprentice allowances) is determined by collective bargaining and not subject to legal regulation, for example, through statutory minimum wages. The only exception is the prescription in Germany's Vocational Training Act that training allowances have to be increased between successive training years, although even here the actual amounts depend upon collective agreement.

In Germany, the average apprentice allowance of DM 690 per month in 1989 amounts to around one-half the average earnings of unskilled teenage employees; around one-third of that of employed 20–24-year-olds; and one quarter of full-time adult pay amongst males, one-third amongst females. Allowances vary considerably according to economic sector, ranging from DM 1100 in construction and banking to DM 440 and 250 in hairdressing and tailoring respectively (BIBB, 1990).

The fact that collective agreements differ by sector and region makes it difficult to describe youth wage patterns (Statistisches Bundesamt, 1988). Most agreements, particularly in industry, stipulate special wage rates, set as a proportion of the adult rate, for youths under 18, 19 or 20 years (for manual workers) and for young adults under age 21 or 24 (for salaried employees in service occupations). Thereafter no further wage differentiation is made by age. These special youth rates apply mostly to unskilled workers, that is, those lacking apprenticeship or equivalent training in the relevant occupation. The ratio of youth to adult rates increases with years of work experience since completion of apprenticeship or vocational training.

The trend in Sweden has been towards smaller differentials between adults and youth. For manual workers, youth relative wages increased markedly in the 1960s and the 1970s. Young salaried employees in the private sector received a large one-off relative pay raise in the mid-1970s which has since been partially eroded. The rise in relative youth pay in Sweden reflects the tendency of national collective agreements to raise the minimum wage level more rapidly for young than for adult age groups. That in turn results primarily from the solidaristic wage policy pursued by the trade union federation (LO), seeking not only equal pay for equal work but also lower wage differences for unequal work.

A comparison of youth remuneration in the collective agreements affecting manual occupations in the metalworking industries of the two countries shows that particular groups of teenagers receive rather low wage rates in each case (Tables 4.10, 4.11), depending primarily upon region in Germany and upon months of work experience in Sweden. Although in some German regions young workers receive considerably less than the adult rate over a period that stretches into their twenties, in Sweden an 18-year-old with more than six months' experience receives at least the minimum wage of an unskilled adult.[12]

The evidence suggests that the relative youth wage is generally higher in Sweden than in Germany, although for the very youngest workers, relative rates are lower in Sweden. Low youth wages may contribute to low youth unemployment in Germany.

Table 4.10 Attributes of negotiated wage rates for metalworkers in collective agreements, manual occupations, West Germany, 1988, by region

Attribute	Number of regions in which it applies
Maximum age for payment under wage for age scales	
> 21	4
19–21	1
18	1
none	6
Ratio of wage of those aged less than 18 years to adult wage rate (per cent)	
70	2
75	3
87.5	1
95	1
100	5

Source: Statistisches Bundesamt (1988).

Table 4.11   Wage rates of metalworkers in the national collective agreement by work experience and age, manual occupations, Sweden, 1987 (as percentage of minimum rate for unskilled workers)

Work experience (months)	Age		
	16	17	18
0–2	40	47	55
3–4	50	59	66
5–6	60	70	79
> 6	76	89	100

Source: Kommentar till verkstadsavtalet (1987).

Youth Employment

Youth, particularly teenagers, is naturally underrepresented in occupations which require higher education. Typical youth jobs are therefore manual ones in manufacturing and, particularly for females, the services which require neither specialised knowledge and skills nor much work experience. As many of these so-called 'everybody's jobs' have disappeared within the past two decades, so the employment prospects for unskilled 15- or 16-year-old entrants have deteriorated.

Detailed comparisons between the two countries are impeded by differences in employment classifications, reflecting the structuring of the labour market primarily by occupation in Germany and by industry in Sweden. Moreover, differing educational systems also restrict comparability of occupational distributions.

Differences in occupational patterns by age are visible within each country. The distribution of apprentices across the 360 or so apprenticeable occupations in Germany differs from that of subsequent employment. The handicraft sector, for example, trains many young people who later move to other sectors and occupations.[13] Moreover, many occupations lack apprenticeship altogether, including transportation workers, managers and professionals. The public sector usually hires employees with a completed training in other sectors or with higher education. Although Sweden has no apprenticeship system, similar occupational patterns for youths and adults appear there.

The industrial structure of youth employment is more readily comparable (Tables 4.12, 4.13). Youth employment is in each country concentrated in manufacturing, wholesale and retail trade, hotels, restaurants and personal services. The proportion of young people, especially females, in wholesale and retail trade is higher in Sweden, whereas in Germany youth employment is more slanted towards manufacturing. In Sweden youth in overrepresented in the private sector even though many work in public sector programmes. In both countries the share of youth employment accounted for by manufacturing has fallen and that in the public and service sectors has risen, particularly for 16–19-year-olds in Sweden. Youth Teams may be a factor for Sweden but trends in overall employment are clearly central.[14]

Although the evidence indicates that young people are overrepresented in particular occupations and industries, there is little evidence on the quality of youth employment.

Table 4.12   Industrial distribution of teenage employment in FR Germany and Sweden in 1973/4 and 1982/4 (percentages across sectors)

| | Sweden | | | | FR Germany | | | |
| | 1974 | | 1984 | | 1973 | | 1982 | |
	M	F	M	F	M	F	M	F
Agriculture etc.	7.4	1.9	7.8	2.3	6.5	2.8	6.7	3.2
Mining, manufacturing	48.2	22.2	35.3	12.4	49.7	34.2	46.0	29.0
Construction	10.4	1.0	11.6	1.4	13.2	1.2	15.2	0.9
Distribution	15.4	22.1	17.4	28.2	9.9	23.3	8.1	22.2
Transport, communications	6.7	2.3	6.3	4.0	5.8	3.1	4.1	3.1
Financial services	1.8	3.4	4.8	5.1	2.7	7.6	1.9	6.9
Public and other service	10.2	47.1	16.9	47.0	10.9	27.8	18.0	34.6
Total (per cent)	100	100	100	100	100	100	100	100
Total (thousands)	120	103	104	107	570	712	446	449

Note: 16–19-year-olds in Sweden, 15–19 in Germany (apprentices excluded).
Source: Mikrozensus 1973 and 1982 (FRG), Labour Force Surveys 1974, 1984 (Sweden)

Table 4.13   Industrial distribution of young adult (20–24-year-old) employment in FR Germany and Sweden in 1973/4 and 1982/4 (percentages across sectors)

| | Sweden | | | | FR Germany | | | |
| | 1974 | | 1984 | | 1973 | | 1982 | |
	M	F	M	F	M	F	M	F
Agriculture etc.	4.9	0.9	5.9	1.6	3.8	3.2	3.1	1.9
Mining, manufacturing	43.2	19.3	37.9	14.4	42.9	34.5	44.4	26.8
Construction	11.3	1.1	11.8	0.6	12.7	1.3	11.0	1.2
Distribution	12.2	16.7	14.9	18.4	9.3	17.6	8.9	18.3
Transport, communications	8.6	5.1	8.3	4.9	6.9	2.9	6.1	2.7
Financial services	4.0	6.8	5.6	5.9	4.3	9.7	3.9	10.6
Public and other service	15.8	50.2	15.6	54.2	20.2	30.7	22.5	38.6
Total (per cent)	100	100	100	100	100	100	100	100
Total (thousands)	230	193	222	205	1478	1306	1505	1376

Sources: As for Table 4.12.

4.6 CONCLUSIONS

The German and Swedish systems of youth training and employment are similar in certain key respects. Both have programmes of education, training and subsidised work which cover most teenagers, leaving only a minority to employment in the ordinary labour market. In practice people up to the age of 18 in Sweden and 19 in Germany are excluded from regular jobs in the open labour market.

The two countries differ markedly in systems of education and vocational training. Sweden has a comprehensive school for those aged 7–16 years old and an integrated upper secondary school for those aged 17–19 years with both theoretical and vocational study lines. It also undertakes an ambitious labour market policy with specific programmes for those age groups. The responsibility for programmes for 16–17-year-olds lies with the school system not with the industrial relations system. The contemporary tendency is towards an integrated school system in which everyone studies for 12 years. The rationale for that is not a myopic response to unemployment, which is at present only *circa* 1.5 per cent, but rather long-term educational objectives.

Germany, on the other hand, has a three-part school system, in which decisions concerning higher education are normally made at age 10–12 years, combined with a huge apprenticeship training system geared predominantly to those leaving compulsory or intermediate school at age 15–17 years. Around three-quarters of all 18-year-olds are nowadays covered by apprenticeship, the responsibility for which (along with other programmes for school-leavers) lies not with the school system but with the industrial relations system, predominantly with employers and trade unions.

There follows another important difference between the two systems: while Swedish vocational training in upper secondary school aims at broad occupational classifications, the German system is more directed towards particular occupations, often narrowly defined. However, the contemporary trend in Germany is towards the broadening of occupational fields in apprenticeship. Trade unions, an integral partner in the apprenticeship system, have concentrated their influence on this objective.

Despite several weaknesses and frictions, in both countries the teenage years prepare young people for the labour market, providing various forms of 'sheltered' work and work experience for the very young. Relatively low youth wage rates and training allowances may also help to integrate teenagers into mainstream employment. In both countries unemployment is consequently low amongst 16–19-year-olds, especially if it is related to all members of the age group and not only to those classified as in the labour force. In that sense Sweden and Germany provide two success stories in terms of youth education, training and employment.[15]

But the real test of institutions and policies comes when young people leave their teens. Apprenticeships come to an end in Germany and young people have to leave the youth-specific labour market programmes in Sweden. In both cases they often have to change sector and occupation. In addition, at this phase in the life-cycle, looking for a partner and starting a family influences vocational behaviour. For young men military service may interrupt career paths and require vocational reorientation. In Germany, due to the three-part school system, many (currently around 15 per cent) of those leaving apprenticeship go on to study for higher degrees. Occupational mobility and job turnover are therefore considerably higher in the early twenties than thereafter.

In both countries the unemployment rate for 20–24-year-olds has been higher than the overall rate. But either the difference between the rates (in Germany) or the absolute size of the 20–24-year-old rate (in Sweden) is still smaller than its equivalent in most European countries. This relatively favourable situation may reflect a tendency for both systems, apprenticeship and vocational school/labour market programmes, to prepare young people more effectively than do those of other countries.

Perhaps the best indicators of success are rates of labour force participation and employment. Both are considerably higher in Sweden, particularly for 20–24-year-olds (for whom the statistics are more meaningful). The large difference between the countries reflects longer university education in Germany and, amongst young adult females, differences in women's roles in the family and the greater ease of finding part-time work in Sweden.

Although young people are already integrated into the labour market by their early twenties in both countries, the labour market situation remains more favourable to young people in Sweden than in Germany. Differences in industrial relations systems contribute to this outcome but probably the important factor is the better general labour market situation in Sweden.

APPENDIX

Table 4A.1   Part-time work amongst youth by age, Sweden, 1987 (percentage of youth employees)

Age	Men			Women		
	Short part-time	Long part-time	Full-time	Short part-time	Long part-time	Full-time
16	45	8	48	57	10	33
17	37	8	55	47	15	38
18	14	10	76	23	30	47
19	9	9	82	9	30	60
20	5	5	90	5	22	73
21	3	5	92	6	20	73
22	2	3	95	5	24	71
23	3	3	94	4	24	72
24	3	5	92	4	25	71

Notes: Short part-time covers 1–19 hours per week; long part-time, 20–34; full-time, 35 plus.
Source: Statistics Sweden, Labour force surveys

Notes

1. Surveys of developments in labour markets and policy in Germany include Bundesanstalt für Arbeit (1978), Kühl (1987) and Brinkmann (1987); in Sweden, Flanagan (1987), Standing (1988) and Wadensjö (1987a).
2. This difference can be ascribed mainly to divergent experiences and traditions. The two postwar inflations may explain why the battle against inflation was given highest priority in Germany; Sweden has had no comparable experiences.
3. In 1986, 90 per cent of candidates passed their apprenticeship exams. Those who fail are allowed a second attempt after half a year.
4. Two types of higher education exist in Germany: traditional university education, which accounts for three-quarters of all those in higher education, and the technical colleges, founded in the early 1970s in order to provide a shorter and more specialised academic education in fields like engineering, commerce, business administration, social work and fine arts. Whereas university students need an Abitur, admittance to technical colleges is also possible via the Realschule, apprenticeship training or one or two years of full-time technical school. At present,

some four-fifths of those with an *Abitur* continue to higher education, either immediately or after a period of vocational training (BMBW 1987b). Because of changes in both educational behaviour and demography, the number of students increased from 850,000 in 1976 to 1,367,000 in 1986. Links between education, training and youth unemployment are discussed further in Schober (1984).

5. Almost all Swedish higher education has been integrated since 1977. Each of the six regions has one general university and several special universities (e.g. technical, medical) and colleges. Course coverage includes those for nurses and pre-school teachers. Most university students follow courses of no more than three or four years' formal duration, which is short by most European standards, and few continue to postgraduate studies. Currently around 160,000 students are enrolled in higher education.

6. Of those accepted to a course of study in the *Gymnasieskola* in 1986, 87.8 per cent were 16 years or younger, 7.5 per cent 17 years, 2.0 per cent 18 years, 0.7 per cent 19 years, 0.3 per cent 20 years and 1.7 per cent 21 years or older.

7. The inflow of students to higher education is proportionately larger in Sweden than in Germany, although the stock of students is higher in Germany than in Sweden. The difference reflects the much longer period spent at university by the average student in Germany.

8. Since 1988 the programme has been financed by the Bundesanstalt für Arbeit (Federal Employment Institute). It includes additional schooling and special instruction for apprentices whose performance is poor.

9. Employers favoured instead the extension of Youth Jobs to 18–19-year-olds (SAF, 1984).

10. The large and increasing proportion of Swedish 16–19-year-olds who work part-time, either in conjunction with full-time school attendance or on Youth Teams (Wadensjö, 1987a), is counted as in the labour force (Table 4A.1). The proportion of German youth who work part-time is as low as roughly 5 per cent (Kohler and Reyher, 1988). Military service, undertaken by most young men in both countries, is counted as outside the labour force. It thus contributes to higher participation rates for women amongst Swedish 19-year-olds, and to higher school enrolment for women amongst German 19-year-olds, given that most male high school graduates go straight into military service and resume their studies 18 months later.

11. Tessaring (1988), p. 188. If apprentices are excluded from the labour force, the unemployment rate in Germany for 18-year-olds becomes 28 per cent, as against 8 per cent on the conventional definition.

12. As the minimum rate for skilled Swedish workers exceeds that for the unskilled by 20 per cent and as adults are more commonly skilled than are young workers, youth–adult pay differentials might be expected to exceed those in Table 4.11. However, actual earnings differentials in Sweden are lower than those shown in the Table. Further wage equalisation appears to result from local agreements.

13. Thus 20 per cent of apprentices but only 7 per cent of employees are classified as mechanics. The concentration of apprenticeship in a few

occupational groups, including metalworking, construction, personal service, medical assistants and sales occupations, is visible even in relation to youth employment.

14. In Germany, the share of females in apprenticeship to 'male' occupations has increased from broadly 7 to 11 per cent despite contraction in employment in those areas.

15. Osterman (1988) provides a very favourable view of both the German and the Swedish systems of industrial relations.

5 Patterns of Public Intervention in Training and the Labour Accords in Italy and the United States

Richard C. Edwards and
Paolo Garonna

5.1 INTRODUCTION

More extensive or effective vocational training has often been seen as the most powerful remedy for both the poor employment prospects of young workers and youth joblessness. The issue of public sector support for employment-based training, especially for young workers, has once again been placed high on the policy agenda of several western countries. Both Italy and the United States, on which we focus in this chapter, have seen calls for larger and better investments in youth training. It seems likely that increased public funds and effort will be forthcoming (AFL-CIO, 1988; Grant Foundation, 1988; MIT Taskforce, 1989; Ministero del Lavoro, 1989).

Yet previous public initiatives in training have typically produced disappointing results and have not infrequently been abandoned altogether. In the US, Job Corps-type training became in the 1960s a locus of political and racial conflict. The ensuing CETA programmes of the 1970s became a favourite and fertile target for attack by Reagan conservatives. The JTPA programmes of the 1980s have been increasingly criticised by unions and other worker groups.

In Italy, the effectiveness of the Training Centres set up in the 1950s was subsequently challenged both from the left and by employers. The former argued that separate vocational education for less skilled workers reinforced class divisions and failed to recognise the emergent significance of unskilled workers in mass production industry. Employers argued that most workers found jobs independently of formal training programmes and could in any case get training 'on the job'. More recently, government promotion of special contracts for youth employment and training (*contratti di formazione e lavoro*: CFL) has been criticised for weak training content. Some have viewed them as merely a wage discount to increase the hiring of young workers. Finally, private employers and others criticise the public training system for reliance on traditional teaching methods and occupational profiles (ISFOL, 1984).

Hence we may well ask: why is there such resurgent interest in youth training programmes that in the past have seemed so faulty? What are the prospects for the initiatives proposed by this 'new interventionism'? In this chapter we discuss why training, seemingly a non-controversial 'good' favoured by all, has so frequently been at the centre of controversy. We argue that training is not a neutral activity involving simply the augmentation of labour's technical quality, but rather a vital and strategic node within the larger industrial relations system. This means, on the one side, that the articulation of training with the larger industrial relations system strongly shapes the efficacy of, and even the meaning of, training. On the other side, training often acts as a weapon in wider struggles: training controversies concern not just training but also the shaping of the industrial relations system.

An organic interconnection between training and the larger industrial relations system is not, of course, a new idea (Slichter, 1941), although it has very frequently been overlooked in recent policy debates. In this chapter, however, we have reinterpreted this connection, as traditionally understood, in the light of recent and distinct analyses of industrial relations (Gordon, Edwards and Reich, 1982; Bowles, Gordon and Weisskopf, 1983; Edwards and Podgursky, 1986; Garonna and Pisani, 1986; chapter 2, above), emphasising the breakdown of the postwar 'labour accord' and the recent crisis in industrial relations. We focus on initiatives in the public sector both because recent calls for increased training have focussed primarily upon it and because such programmes have most frequently been targeted on young workers. We use the US and Italian systems as case studies in order to illustrate that the lessons of the interconnection of training and the industrial relations system are relevant even in systems as divergent as those two.

Our approach has clear implications for the new phase of interventionism in the youth training process that many countries are now experiencing. If the effectiveness of youth training is as closely linked to the dynamics of the labour relations system as we contend, the efficacy of new training systems and public interventions depends upon the evolving nature of the current industrial relations regime. Conversely, different public training interventions will have distinct implications for the. type of industrial relations regime that does emerge. Whose interests will the new public interventions serve, and towards what new industrial relations regime will they contribute? These are the real issues at stake in the training debate.

In this chapter we define young workers as members of the labour force less than 30 years of age. We do so partly in order to focus on the entire period of transition to adult worker status and partly in order to coincide with the legal position, for instance in terms of eligibility for CFL participation in Italy.

5.2   THE PUBLIC SECTOR'S ROLE IN TRAINING ACTIVITIES

In both Italy and the US, most young workers obtain training, if any, through mechanisms other than public programmes organised explicitly for training. Of course, training in its broadest sense involves a wide variety of skills and aptitudes and incorporates general learning gained in a wide variety of private and public institutions. In this sense the formal schooling system, with compulsory attendance up to age 14 in Italy and 16 in the US, and provided in both countries primarily by public institutions, is relevant: because it teaches basic literacy, mathematics and other thinking skills, formal schooling represents the first and in many ways most important training system.

Even restricting our attention more narrowly to skills that are acquired primarily for their vocational relevance, formal schooling is still important, because it often provides vocational training together with basic education (e.g. in Italy's *Istituti Professionali* and in vocational 'tracks' in American high schools). Also in the public sector, military training involves large numbers of trainees and contributes strongly to the training of the labour force, especially in the US (Osterman, 1980; Grant Foundation, 1988).

However, both Italian and American workers have largely relied on mechanisms other than regular schooling and military training to acquire skills. Within-employment training – whether in employer training institutes, formal apprenticeship or designated learning (probationary) positions, or through informal, 'on-the-job' and 'learning-by-doing' processes – undoubtedly represents the most important post-schooling component of training. Also important are private sector training opportunities detached from current employment, such as courses offered by fee-based training institutes, private technical colleges, unions, community colleges, etc., which in Italy often receive some form of public support (Doeringer and Piore, 1971; Ryan, 1977; FGA, 1982; ISFOL, 1987).

In a 1983 survey of training in the US labour force, about 55 per cent of all employees needed specific training to qualify for their jobs. Of these, 29 per cent reported that they obtained this training through school, 10 per cent through a formal company programme, 28 per cent through informal on-the-job training, 2 per cent through the military, and 4 per cent through correspondence courses or other training not related to work, including presumably public training programmes. Similarly, for improving their skills during employment, the 35 per cent of workers who obtained such training relied largely on sources other than public programmes: 12 per cent on school, 11 per cent on formal company programmes, 14 per cent on informal on-the-job training, and 4 per cent on other sources (Carey, 1985, Tables 2, 24).[1] Thus the number of trainees enrolled in publicly organised or financed training programmes has remained a small percentage of the US labour force.

Public training programmes are somewhat more important in Italy, although they still involve relatively small numbers of youths (ISFOL, 1987, pp. 290–2). In 1985 only 20 per cent of all youth (14–19 years) attended a training course after school. The others were either still at school, or were given informal training on-the-job, or did not get any training at all. Only about 8 per cent of all youth had attended a course provided by regional government; the others got training from other sources. Remarkably, only 3 per cent of formally trained youth got their formal training within an enterprise; most of the others were instructed privately outside the firm.

The scale of apprenticeship is also comparatively small in Italy: in 1987 there were 530 000 apprentices, 10 per cent of the labour force aged 14–29 years and 4 per cent of the population of the same age. Moreover apprentice numbers have declined, from 831 000 in 1968 to 736 000 in 1980. This decline corresponds to, and is largely accounted for, by the sharp drop in youth employment. At the same time, however, the relative importance of the publicly sponsored CFL training scheme has increased: in 1987 488 000 young workers were active on CFL, constituting 7.3 per cent of the labour force and 3.5 per cent of the population of the 14–29 age group.[2] Taking the CFL and apprenticeship together, the youth labour force covered by in-firm training arrangements is somewhat higher in the 1980s than in the 1970s. However, the kind of training which young workers get through these arrangements, particularly the CFL, remains questionable.

5.3   MODELS OF STATE INTERVENTION

Public training initiatives have tended during the past three decades to follow one of three models or strategies for state intervention. We first sketch these models and then trace their connection to the industrial relations system.

The Interventionist Model

In the first strategy, the central government directly assumes responsibility for financing, stimulating or organising training activities. Although there may be cooperation with various intermediary institutions or social partners (lower levels of governmental, development agencies, etc.), the crucial feature is that the central government acts as senior partner, taking ultimate responsibility for initiating and implementing training.

In the US, the interventionist model gave shape to the first extensive public training efforts, those launched in the 1960s under Kennedy's New Frontier programme and continued under Johnson's Great Society (US President, 1966, 1968). The most important training component of these initiatives was the Manpower Training and Development Act (MTDA) of 1962. Through the MDTA and similar efforts (e.g. the Job Corps, added in 1964), the federal government assumed a direct role in providing training. Eligible individuals (residents of designated poverty areas, for instance, or disadvantaged youth) were enrolled in federally-run or federally-contracted training programmes (US GAO, 1986; MPR, 1978).

Although diverse, these programmes were administered, directly or indirectly, by federal officials, who either were or became 'experts' in the training field. Training was predominantly conceived of as a technical process organised by technocrats, even though later in the decade community groups began to gain access to funding and planning as 'community involvement' gained higher priority. The task of training was defined primarily as that of equipping workers with additional skills or knowledge (or sometimes work habits) which would raise the trainee's marginal product and hence enhance employment prospects and expected wages (Levitan and Mangum, 1984).

In Italy, the interventionist model shaped the training framework which was established early in the postwar period in the shape of training centres financed by the Ministry of Labour. The centres provided training in traditional skills and crafts for disadvantaged youth and school dropouts in working-class areas. They were public institutions but many also had a private character, for example if they were run by the Church or the trade unions. In some cases, as in construction and in printing and publishing, the centres were created by collective agreement and managed jointly by employer associations and trade unions.

Training was then institutionalised and financed by the State as an important mechanism for regulating access to and exit from employment, being seen as part of the wider public regulatory system of labour exchanges and unemployment policy. Attendance at a recognised training course became a prerequisite for eligibility for unemployment benefit or wage subsidy under the CIG (*Cassa Integrazione Guadagni*; Garonna, 1980a, 1980b). Success in qualifying examinations was an element in the allocation of redundancies and layoffs. The weaker segments of the labour force were targeted by public training, in order to remedy gaps in basic education, to integrate dropouts into the labour force and to create a queue for the rationed supply of jobs (Baussano, 1988; ISFOL, 1989).

The Devolution Model

The second form of state activity, the devolution model, provided the primary theme of the 1970s in both the US and Italy, as both governments sought to remedy the perceived shortcomings of the interventionist model. The central feature of devolution was the pushing out of responsibility for planning and organising public training programmes away from the central government to regional or other sub-units, with central government moving towards a mere financing and coordinating role.

In the US, the devolution phase was built around CETA – the Comprehensive Employment and Training Act of 1973. CETA was designed to provide 'job training and employment opportunities for economically disadvantaged, unemployed, and underemployed persons' to enable them to secure self-sustaining unsubsidised employment. CETA attempted to reverse the trend of the previous decade by offering a 'flexible, decentralised system of comprehensive and decategorised training and employment programmes, planned and operated by the states and local units of government, subject to federal oversight'. Its chief assumption was that training, while still funded at the federal level, should be administered by the states as part of President Nixon's 'creative federalism' programme. Local training efforts should be concentrated by means of bloc grants to local officials, and funding should be 'de-categorised' so that local officials could choose the mix of activities (classroom training, on-the-job training, public service employment, counselling, work experience, etc.) that was optimal 'in response to local requirements' (US President, 1976).

In Italy, devolution was introduced in 1972 when responsibility for training was transferred to regional government. The effectiveness of the public system was to be improved by introducing mechanisms for planning, coordination, and control and, above all, by realising the constitutional design that assigns responsibility for training and artisans' education to the regions. Later institutional reforms granted an important role to unions and employer organisations within the new system of labour market organisation (*Commissioni Regionali per l'Impiego, Osservatori sul Mercato del Lavoro, Istituto per lo Sviluppo della Formazione Professionale*, etc.), which became the main institutional actor in vocational training policy (*Politiche del Lavoro*, 1987).

The Flexibility Model

A third strategy of state intervention in training policy followed in the 1980s, as part of general programmes adopted by both the Italian and the American governments in pursuit of labour market flexibility. In reformulating their training policies, both governments sought to turn training activities over to the private sector, especially to private employers (ISFOL, 1988b).

In the US, flexibility was initiated in the later years of the Carter government, seeking greater employer involvement in public training programmes and introducing incentives to that end (US President, 1979). The tendency was accelerated by the Reagan government's efforts to dismantle CETA and shift subsidised training activities almost entirely to the private sector, achieved in the Job Training Partnership Act (JTPA) of 1982. JTPA introduced various innovations, including training funds for workers dislocated by business closures or permanent layoffs, but its principal thrust was to give private sector employers the central position in the management of publicly funded training programmes (US GAO, 1987a, 1987b).

In Italy the new strategy emerged in the 1980s, in line with the prevailing policy trends of deregulation and 'flexibility.' A 'reprivatisation of training' occurred, in which training was to be supported primarily at the level of the firm and under the supervision of individual employers. Youth employment and training contracts (CFL) were introduced, providing substantial labour cost discounts to employers hiring young workers. Training regulations were also revised to allow for the elimination of restrictions on apprenticeships and recruitment; for national contracts that fixed lower relative pay for apprentices, permitting greater wage dispersion; and for greater access to public funds for training by large firms, individually or in consortia (Garonna, 1986).

In both countries, then, public training policy has followed apparently similar trajectories. Despite profound differences in institutional setting (e.g. the role of unions and the legal framework) and dissimilar economic circumstances, both sets of public interventions appear to have faced similar pressures and constraints. After an ambitious vision of centralised public intervention, both governments turned first to devolution and then to flexibility.

Why did not initial visions of publicly stimulated training lead to a gradual extension of the national training systems so as to produce a comprehensive institutional framework for training? Evolution was evidently not driven in either country simply by technological or external market factors, because other societies (e.g. FR Germany, Austria, and Sweden) made different choices that strengthened comprehensive training institutions. Although, as we will see, parallel movements signified different choices within the two countries, what is striking is that neither Italy nor the US moved towards the more extensive public involvement of the kind that the new interventionism calls for nowadays. We turn next to an attempt to understand why.

5.4 THE DYNAMICS OF THE LABOUR ACCORDS

As suggested initially, we believe that the efficacy of training policies and the limits placed upon public initiatives must be understood in the context of the dynamics of the national industrial relations system. We characterise these systems for the period under consideration here in terms of a 'labour accord', that is, a set of compromise arrangements or implicit social contracts worked out between unions (and other representatives of worker interests) and major employers. Such arrangements were in part codified and shaped by law and overseen or administered by government (Edwards and Podgursky, 1986; Garonna and Pisani, 1986).

We distinguish labour accords from social partnerships, that is, the explicit social power-sharing agreements which developed in some countries (e.g. Sweden, Austria) where social democratic parties won long-term political control and the rising power of labour was accommodated through explicit power-sharing. In Italy and the US, social compromises were made, but those accommodations were necessarily incomplete, informal, implicit, and contradictory. 'Labour accord' denotes such incomplete institutional arrangements.

In the US, the postwar labour accord grew out of the militant struggles of the 1930s and the employer counter-offensive of the immediate postwar years. By the early 1950s a system had emerged with the following identifiable elements: (i) major employers accepted bargaining with unions where unions already existed, recognising their legitimacy as workers' representatives; (ii) the essential point of contact between unions and employers became the multi-year, collectively bargained contract, which both specified union gains and limited union influence to improving wages and immediate working conditions; (iii) the overall management of the business, including decisions on product price, investment and technological development, was left to 'management prerogative' (Edwards and Podgursky, 1986).

Under the US labour accord, real wages increased in proportion to the general trend in labour productivity, thereby guaranteeing real income gains to workers while eliminating intense disputes over the distribution of income. Work rights such as employment security and promotion were attached to the individual worker and based heavily on seniority. Unions for the most part did not oppose the introduction of new technologies by employers, as it tended to raise labour productivity and wages and all but junior workers would be protected from resulting job losses. During the life of a contract, the union became a junior partner in the daily management of the workplace and industrial conflict became restricted to the typically triennial bargaining for contract renewal.

These industrial relations were both shaped by and codified in the relevant federal labour legislation (the National Labour Relations Act) and the National Labour Relations Board served as an external administrator for the system. The impact of this labour accord extended far beyond the workplaces directly organised by unions, because non-union employers, the larger ones at least, tended to follow its main provisions in order to avoid unionisation. The chief omissions were those workers – lower paid workers in smaller enterprises and in the South, and especially youth, female, black, and other minority workers – whose workplaces fell outside the pale of either direct union organisation or indirect union impact.

The postwar Italian labour accord reflected the regaining of political freedom after Fascism and the defeat of the left in the 1948 elections. The new arrangements envisioned free collective bargaining with multiple unionism but without any formal mechanism for union certification or conflict regulation. However, the main element of the accord relied on the political nature of Italian unionism. Unions were given an unofficial but significant political role through centralised consultations, a free hand in union political activities such as political strikes and participation in national management of both the labour market and social security. Political divisions within the labour movement were reflected in the division of union organisations and in the subordination of union action to control by political parties (Garonna and Pisani, 1986).

Some important constitutional elements had to be suspended, such as legal regulation both of strike activities and of union organisation and action at the plant level, and the establishment of regional autonomy. Unions initially considered this arrangement an advantage, since they were still weak in the aftermath of Fascism and it provided freedom of movement and backing by political parties. Employers also looked upon it favourably because it involved weak levels of union legitimation, particularly at plant level, where union presence and activity remained weak, non-participative, and conflictual, leaving effective management of the labour process entirely in the hands of employers.

5.5 THE LABOUR ACCORDS AND THE INTERVENTIONIST MODEL

The interventionist model, although developed in the context of different labour accords, nonetheless had some basic elements in common in the two countries. Both the Italian and American accords tended to internalise training within employment.

In the US, the accord was built on two systems for training (Doeringer and Piore, 1971; Ryan, 1977, 1984a). Firstly, in the mass production industries, training was largely informal and on-the-job;

unions had little participation or interest in youth training programmes, leaving any initiatives to the employers. Most jobs only
required skills that could be learned quickly. For others, strict job
definitions and strong seniority systems provided senior workers with
sufficient job protection to induce them to participate in training
young workers who, under other circumstances, would have been their
competitors. Secondly, in the crafts, access to licences (and perhaps
skills) was strictly regulated by means of apprenticeships (Doeringer
and Piore, 1971; Thurow, 1969).

In Italy, where the job rules were much weaker, unions pressed for
employment protection (e.g. putting legal constraints on dismissals)
and for 'Institutional Exclusion' mechanisms (Garonna and Ryan,
chapter 2 above) to avoid competition from young workers. Craft
work was organised in the form of self-employment or artisans' work
or subject to strict public regulation.

The interventionist model was in both countries directly related to
the Keynesian policies and conceptions of state action which were
adopted in the 1960s. Keynesianism held out the hope that a growth
dividend could be generated to address equity issues, especially
poverty, through such means as training, without engendering social
conflict. Growth accounting associated the large unexplained residuals
with technical innovation and rising labour skills (Denison, 1967). It
was assumed that high-productivity, high-wage jobs, such as those
typically organised through the accord, were or at least could be the
norm, so that low-productivity, low-wage, and generally inferior
employment could be greatly reduced through training.

The interventionist model shaped the training activities of the
Kennedy and Johnson administrations in the US between 1960 and
1968 and accounted in Italy for much of the strengthening and central
regulation of training centres in the 1960s. In the US, public training
could be a natural complement to the organisation of training within
jobs covered by the labour accord, if only because it left such training
untouched. By focussing on the disadvantaged, including many young
workers, it neither interfered with accord-organised training nor
constituted a threat to the privileged positions of adults working
under the accord. On the other hand, because it was not integrated
into the accord structure, its potential effectiveness was highly limited
from the outset. Similarly, in Italy, training financed by the Ministry of
Labour, provided both privately and publicly for both post-school
youth and dropouts from schooling, left technical training to private
sector apprenticeships and on-the-job training.

Public training efforts in the context of the labour accords thus operated within a relatively marginal field. Training for most industrial jobs occurred through private mechanisms – and then only after a worker was hired or training obtained through the restricted supply of apprenticeships. Since the labour accord internalised to itself the training process, it precluded any central role for outside programmes. In such circumstances, central government efforts at training were reasonably directed towards – but also limited to – those workers (e.g. disadvantaged youth) left out of the industrial system. By the same token, public programmes were condemned to train for the periphery (or secondary labour market) and were largely irrelevant to the economy's industrial core.

Restricted to the training of marginal workers, public efforts never attained an essential role in the reproduction of the technical skills under the labour accord and therefore also failed to build sustaining political constituencies among the main social actors (corporate employers, unions). Having appeared as part of a social compromise required to make the labour accord politically acceptable, but lacking both an essential technical function and a mainstream sustaining constituency, public programmes were thus highly vulnerable when public priorities and private sympathies shifted elsewhere.

5.6 THE 1960S CHALLENGE TO THE LABOUR ACCORDS AND THE DEVOLUTION MODEL

Both the Italian and American labour accords were challenged in the late 1960s. In both cases the challenge came from the side of labour, with young workers playing a significant role therein. Although both challenges reshaped the labour accords, especially in Italy, they were contained and did not overturn the accords themselves. They also shaped public training interventions by pushing governments to respond and in both cases conservative governments responded with devolution. However, in another respect government responses were exactly opposite: in Italy devolution involved accommodation with the insurgent forces, whereas in the US accommodation was rejected.

The Italian Experience

The challenge to the Italian accord came from plant-level reactions to the tensions arising from the boom labour market conditions of the

1960s (Crouch and Pizzorno, 1977). Strikes, largely unofficial, and rank-and-file militancy over control of the labour process, created pressure towards the unification of the labour movement and more effective organisation of plant level actions. Activists set up Workers' Councils to supplant the *Commissioni Interne*, the bureaucratic and typically ineffective antecedent plant-level organisations. United action involving the main union organisations spread across the different sectors and became established as well at the central level. In some cases (notably the *metalmeccanici*, the most radical and unionised industrial sector) this helped to pull together the different unions and create a unified labour organisation (*Federazione Lavoratori Metalmeccanici*).

The workers' immediate demands were largely met, but with compromises that left the core of the original labour accord mostly unchanged. For example, even though after the 1960s unions acted as a unified force and often developed policy independent of the political parties, no formal mechanism was established to guarantee either the unification of union organisations or autonomy from party leadership. Unity and autonomy were still pursued largely on an *ad hoc* basis, grounded on political goodwill. Similarly, even though Workers Councils were recognised by the unions, they were not incorporated within the union structure. The political role of unions, first challenged by the radical conflicts of the 1960s, was reestablished and strengthened by the recentralisation of bargaining and incomes policies, and by deeper union involvement in the wider regulation of the labour market. Thus the original labour accord's essential trade-off was left in place: that is, the unions' role was politically recognised and exercised through wider institutional involvement; and the actual control of the labour process was left to managerial prerogative, free from union interference (Garonna and Pisani, 1986).

Two institutional reforms made the accommodation of the 1970s work. On one side, the Workers' Statute of 1970 granted privileges and rights to the main union confederations, strengthening their position *vis-à-vis* both management and the rank-and-file (Garonna and Pisani, 1986). On the other, the implementation of regional autonomy, as foreseen by the Constitution, tended to meet demands for decentralisation and political participation (Cella and Treu, 1982).

Devolution in Italy had a straightforward political meaning: it was a building block for the transformation and continuation of the labour accord during the 1970s, a response to sociopolitical pressures that broadened the consensual basis of training policy. Regional autonomy made it possible for the left to take government responsibility in some regions, which constituted in turn an important element in the broad political compromise of the period. Devolution thus actually assisted in the reassertion of political control over industrial conflict and the industrial relations system.

Young workers and the youth movement played an important role in the challenges of the 1960s and their participation influenced the effects of devolution on the training system. Under the terms of the labour accord (chapter 2, above) young workers were largely excluded from access to existing jobs in the primary sector of the economy, by both public regulation restricting access to employment and legislative constraints on dismissals and layoffs (which tended to shelter the internal labour markets of the unionised sector). Young workers, particularly the unskilled and underprivileged, were instead 'parked' in education and vocational training. However, positive net job creation during the 1960s boom opened up employment to many young workers who subsequently played leading militant roles and attained substantial bargaining power.

Young workers used their new power to question union strategies and to challenge the purposes of public training. They demanded an end to the exploitation of trainees as secondary labour; support for worker-students using their leisure time to continue basic or vocational education; and a shift in training towards the long-term interests of workers. Unions responded by taking up youth demands and by coopting their leaders into the union apparatus. Thus collective contracts, embodying the principle of 'right-to-study' introduced by the Workers' Statute, established a yearly entitlement to paid leave for training purposes, set at 150 hours. The unions organised this free time to provide basic education in literacy, law and economics, psychology, and even 'political awareness'.

The politics of devolution and the labour accord in Italy meant emphasis upon the social policy aspects of training, while its technical aspects, relation to job access, internal labour markets and turnover, became even more marginal. Demands for better pay and working conditions, greater political and union bargaining power, less work exploitation (in terms of work speeds and working hours) were decoupled from any demand for training. In fact training was feared as an individualistic solution that would threaten the collective position of the unskilled.

In the devolution model, then, training policies corresponded to a dual presumption: that technical training would take place within the plant, with skill acquisition constrained and controlled by both legislative norms and union action; and that training in school-type public institutions would be oriented towards the longer-term interests of both workers and society. In practice, however, protective regulation was widely evaded, leaving *de facto* control of technical training in the hands of individual employers. Moreover, regional governments proved by and large ineffective at steering the public training system, often using it for simple political patronage; the leading role played by the unskilled produced little interest in promoting training; and the pay policies of *egualitarismo*, in particular the reduction of differentials by age and skill, damaged economic incentives to firms and individuals to finance training. In short, the Italian training system, behind a superficial glorification of training as a source of work humanisation, suffered a serious decline.

The American Experience

In the US, the challenge to the labour accord came from those elements of the labour force who had been left out of the accord's scope and failed to share in its benefits (Bowles, Gordon and Weisskopf, 1983). The leading groups were non-whites and females, but young people also contributed.

The civil rights movement, although initially aimed at ending segregation in schools and public accommodation, quickly moved to the issue of access to and treatment in jobs. In some areas (notably industrial unions) the unions were already in the forefront of the struggle to dismantle racial barriers, but in many other cases (notably the craft unions) they represented an obstacle and struggles emerged around three particular issues: access to union-regulated craft apprenticeship; union acquiescence in unequal treatment in hiring and in the use of discriminatory job placement tests; and seniority systems, which, when combined with jobs only recently opened to minorities, worked to protect white workers and inhibit progress for black youth.

The movement for women's rights contributed a second set of challenges. The same three features – access to apprenticeships, sex-biased hiring procedures, seniority-based privileges – worked to the disadvantage of females as well. In addition, female workers increasingly came to define their interests as divergent from traditional union priorities on such issues as flexible worktime schedules, access to daycare services, occupational desegregation, affirmative action, occupational health, gender bias in pension, medical and other benefits, and comparable worth. Female workers sought to advance their interests through litigation, legislation, and political intervention, frequently directing their efforts against union leadership and the labour accord.

Finally, youth workers of all races and genders increasingly challenged an implicit *quid pro quo* of the labour accord: labour discipline at the workplace in return for a share of the increased product. The various youth movements (student power, anti-war, sexual liberation, rock and drug culture, etc.) all tended to change young workers' perceived self-interests, making such workers less accepting of authority and more demanding of freedom at work, of higher worklife quality, and of lowered career obligations. The struggles at GM's Lordstown plant and elsewhere were highly publicised, but few doubted that these exemplars represented a much broader phenomenon in which what some exaggeratedly described as a 'new working class' also challenged the legitimacy of the labour accord (Aronowitz, 1973; Gintis, 1970).

The devolution model in public training intervention represented part of a larger strategy to reduce or suppress these social conflicts that had built up around the labour accord. The reformulation of training policy was part of President Nixon's 'New Federalism' programme. As blacks, youth and other populist groups had attained considerably more power through the media and pressure on national figures than in local electoral systems, Nixon's strategy was to decentralise the control of programmes, increasing the power of (mostly conservative) local elected officials. CETA followed this pattern.

The devolution model necessarily expressed a less technocratic view of training. It reflected the souring of the initial innocent enthusiasm for training in a growth-oriented Keynesian world, as non-growth issues – social stability and inflation, in particular – came to the fore. Conservative leaders recognised the political and social attributes of training. Struggles over the control of training programmes, the connection between training and unionisation, campaigns to open jobs, apprenticeships, and training to minorities and women – all raised conservative complaints against the interventionist model. The transfer of power over training to state and local authorities, who could calibrate training to what were termed 'local needs' (in particular to the non-union customs of the South), was seen as a way of reducing social conflict.

CETA quickly became popular with big-city mayors and state politicians as they realised the political benefits of block grants subject to minimal federal oversight. It permitted local officials to hire workers, distribute subsidised jobs to various public service agencies and staff new services, all with funds neither locally raised nor locally accountable. Although the Act itself required each prime sponsor (state or city) to establish a planning council with representation from all segments of the community (including client groups and community organisations, the public employment service, education and training institutions, business and organised labour), the councils did not in most cases play a significant role in CETA operations. CETA became a public jobs and patronage vehicle for local officials.

5.7 THE CHALLENGE TO THE LABOUR ACCORDS IN THE 1970S AND THE FLEXIBILITY MODEL

At the end of the 1970s the labour accord was challenged again in both countries. This time the challenge came from different directions, mainly from employers in the US and from various sources in Italy. Unlike the outcome in the previous challenge, the structure of the accords did not survive this second set of challenges intact.

The American Experience

The confluence of stagflation and weakening union organisation made it both attractive to and possible for employers to abandon the labour accord. Stagflation contributed thereto by squeezing company profit margins, eliminating much of the surplus formerly shared with workers (Bowles, Gordon and Weisskopf, 1983). Moreover, cost-of-living clauses in collective agreements translated rapid price increases into rising nominal wages in the union sector and a growing gap between union and non-union labour costs (Edwards and Podgursky, 1986). On the other side, as union organisational strength continued to decline, partly due to the conflicts discussed in the previous section, employers could 'go non-union' without intense industrial conflict (Adams, 1985; Goldfield, 1987; Freeman, 1988b). The result was a decisive turn by employers away from the implicit understandings of the labour accord.

The employer challenge to the postwar system was quickly visible but its full consequences took longer to emerge. The labour movement's failure to obtain business support for the 1977–8 labour law reform legislation – legal changes required for the old accord-type relations to persist – signalled the new attitude. So did widespread business support for harsh actions taken by the early Reagan government, such as the destruction of the air traffic controllers' union and the appointment of bitterly anti-labour regulators to the NLRB and the Occupational Safety and Health Administration.

In the longer-term, this challenge simply accelerated the organisational decline of the unions. Unions remained strong in some sectors, of course, and, where they had sufficient strength, they were able to force employers to deal with them on something like the old terms. Even strong unions like the United Autoworkers, however, were forced into concession bargaining. Weaker unions had to accept two-tier wage systems, revised work rules, reduced worker protection and other losses. More ominously, organising lagged so far behind membership attrition that union status became virtually marginal (Dickens and Leonard, 1985; Goldfield, 1987). The devastating membership losses in the private sector during the early 1980s resulted in what has been called 'the effective de-unionisation of the American economy' (Freeman, 1988b).

Thus the understandings of the old labour accord were mostly ignored in the industrial relations of the 1980s. In this context the Reagan government was able to turn to the third strategy of public training intervention: flexibility. Its attitude was revealed in the language it used to define its goals: 'intensified efforts to reduce fraud'; the 'resolution of the backlog of unresolved audits'; a 'continued phase-down of the Young Adult Conservation programmes'; and 'an increase in efforts under the Private Sector Initiative Program' (US President, 1982).

Undoubtedly the chief novelty of the new direction was an explicit major expansion in the private sector's role in organising training activities. The principal new law, the JTPA, required the formation of state-level councils to set policy and oversee the administration of the programmes; specified that at least one-third of its members be owners, chief executives, or chief operating officers of private sector employers; and allotted, by contrast, a mere 20 per cent to the 'general population' including the general public, community-based organisations, and local education agencies and unions. JTPA also required formation of a Private Industry Council (PIC) in each service area to plan and oversee local delivery.

In practice, employer representatives dominated both state and local councils. For-profit employers provided slightly more than one third of council members and 88 per cent of chairmen (compared to 5.1 and zero per cent respectively for unions); they contributed 56.5 per cent of

PIC members, compared to 5.7 per cent for unions (US GAO, 1985, pp.7, 9, 27).

The organisation of training under JTPA was implicitly left to private sector methods, on the assumption that private industry knows best how to train workers, who need to find employment primarily in the private sector.

The Italian Experience

In Italy the collapse of the labour accord followed from two sets of difficulties. The first was the reaction to the political 'historic compromise' of the 1970s: a deepening of the political division between Socialists and Communists and the end of the 'political unity' of the union movement. The second was the tensions arising from the exclusion of particular groups from the accord, particularly young workers, but also middle managers, technicians and new entrepreneurs. These social groups openly defied unions and managed to change their policies (Garonna and Pisani, 1986).

In this new context, economic and labour policy changed direction in several respects. First, the cycle of inflation, devaluation, public deficit was broken by the adoption of rules of the European Monetary System. Secondly, industrial restructuring was effected, producing severe losses of industrial (and unionised) employment, particularly in large companies. Thirdly, labour market mechanisms, particularly job placement and employment protection, were largely 'deregulated', reintroducing the legal possibility of part-time and fixed-term employment. Fourthly, wage indexation was weakened; and most unions accepted wage moderation in collective agreements, a centralised incomes policy, and 'flexibility' in such matters as overtime, technical change, layoffs, and early retirement. However, not all unions adhered to these terms and this split further divided the union movement (Garonna, 1986).

Given the decline of private training mechanisms during the 1970s, the revaluation of apprenticeship and the introduction of the *contratti di formazione e lavoro* had a precise meaning. It added to *de facto* employer control over training at the workplace a collective, strategic influence over the training system as a whole and supported, through a particular regulation of training, the 'flexibilisation' of the labour process. Publicly supported training was associated with (i) 'deregulated' youth entry into employment, that is, hiring outside the constraints of the numerical list order; (ii) wage discounts for young hires; (iii) reduced employment protection for new recruits; and (iv) training requirements based on employer specification, dominated by short-term production interests.

Although unions were forced to accept these measures by the new industrial relations conditions, they sought with some success to turn 'flexibility' measures to their own benefit. Regulatory participation was seen as a means to enhanced union legitimacy. The unions stengthened their position on the regional bodies (*Commissioni Regionali per l'Impiego*) responsible for supervising the labour market and approving proposals for CFL projects. They also made gains at national level concerning procedures and criteria to be used in evaluating CFLs at the enterprise level. Most of all, they sought a measure of control over training within the enterprise. Finally, the unions attempted to expand their representation amongst the groups – notably youth, middle management and public sector employees – whose importance was being augmented by flexibility schemes.

In sum, devolution was abandoned in both countries because it had largely collapsed. In the US, it had produced a patronage system for local officials and its training aspects had been further overwhelmed by the transformation of CETA in the late 1970s into a counter-cyclical jobs programme. In Italy, the devolution model collapsed because it failed in its two major explicitly announced objectives: youth employment did not improve and industrial restructuring (to the extent that it was carried out) did not increase employment. The social policy objectives of training were thus exposed, and the programmes were criticised and abandoned. In the 1980s, training policy followed other areas of labour market and industrial relations policy, as both governments instituted general programmes of labour market flexibility (CEDEFOP, 1987).

5.8　CURRENT ATTITUDES TOWARDS TRAINING

By the end of the 1980s the flexibility models had themselves become the targets of growing criticism in both countries. A demand has emerged, as noted at the beginning, for a new interventionism in training. Is there a relationship between it and the old interventionism of the 1950s and 1960s? What are the prospects for the latter?

The problems created by the decline of the accord-based training system emerged clearly from a set of interviews conducted with corporate, union, and public sector training leaders in both countries. While there was considerable diversity of experiences and appraisals, some central themes echoed throughout.[3]

First, virtually all respondents agreed that current training programmes, both public and private, were inadequate. Trade union and public officials in both countries voiced this opinion most strongly but corporate opinion tended to agree.

Corporate managers were somewhat divided as to the adequacy of training in the private sector. Most felt that it was inadequate and virtually all agreed that in firms that are small or not exposed to intensive high-technology competition, training lags far behind what it should be. American corporate respondents tended to be the most positive, pointing to some companies, often including their own, which for competitive reasons maintain sophisticated training programmes. Officials associated with such programmes judged that corporate resource commitment was considerable and perhaps adequate. For the rest of the economy, however, they agreed that training was inadequate. Employers interviewed in Italy expressed stronger concerns that training was inadequate and sometimes openly voiced strong criticism, including self-criticism. One manager in a small firm noted that 'men are not growing at the same rate as enterprises'.[4]

Union officials in the US were strongly convinced of the need for more training support and were eager to be involved in organising training. This attitude appears distinctly different from that under the accord, when unionists were largely uninterested in training. The apparent explanation is that unions now see training mainly as an aid to workers whose jobs are threatened by technological change. The only dissenting union view came from a local official in charge of a massive, joint management/labour retraining programme in the automobile industry, where severe restructuring and strong bargaining by the union has, in his opinion, led to adequate support for retraining. Even so, he commented, 'it's adequate, but I won't say its enough . . .'. Most union officials, however, reported widespread membership concern about training opportunities, with JTPA and other programmes, including collectively negotiated ones, perceived as highly inadequate.

Despite different assessments of private sector training, a strong consensus existed on the need for more extensive and perhaps comprehensive public training systems. One American corporate official, responsible for all training activities in a major transportation multinational, noted:

we have to develop new models, new ways of thinking [about training]. We have to answer questions like: What are we to do with the lack of national policy, national goals and strategies in education and training? How can such a policy be developed and implemented towards a common good without destroying the gift of [our] diversity?

The main change needed – in the words of an Italian business representative – 'is essentially ideological. It means ceasing to consider training as a social buffer against the employment crisis.' According to another, 'we are going through a phase of structural shift in training from the logic of assistance to that of economic development', and 'from a social-welfare type recovery of school drop-outs' to the creation of new classes of technicians, managers and entrepreneurs. Most corporate commentators agreed that the role of training as 'social amortiser' (in the words of an Italian government official) should be phased out.

Interviewees placed especial emphasis on the need for a more active role by the public sector in basic vocational education. One union official in Italy stressed the point that

among the youth looking for a first job, 61 per cent had at the most an intermediate school diploma. Public training should be geared towards the training requirements of this 61 per cent, rather than for more specialised skills.

Private training is not considered appropriate for these tasks: as one training official in a large private Italian car factory noted, 'private initiatives often try to exploit individual room for remedial action, rather than facing up to demanding better public training programmes'. The same interviewee considered the choice of 'home-made training' by private corporations a second-best solution where adequate public programmes are not available.

Alongside their support for expanded public training, interviewees perceived many shortcomings in existing public programmes. Frequent criticisms concerned lack of evaluation and planning and teachers who were inadequate ('they look too much like professors,' said an official from the Agnelli Foundation), poorly paid and without contact with business practice. An American corporate manager noted that

vocational training (in public programmes) has a terrible problem: that problem is that they are trying to train someone for a job, but that someone does not have a job yet. Too often, people are prepared for jobs that do not exist.

Corporate officers in particular tended to be sceptical of the benefits of public programmes. The common theme was that such programmes prepared people for non-existent jobs, used old machinery, and trained for obsolete technology. One corporate executive noted that public programmes

> do not have enough money to keep capital facilities up to date with changing technology. Neither do they have the money to do development work [i.e., to develop new curricula, etc.]. Instead the focus must be on delivery [of services].

An American union official also lamented the preparation of people in public programmes for non-existent jobs. Another related much of the problem to 'lack of coordination among governmental departments', maintaining that training programmes were often conducted by different agencies from those which researched future job vacancies. Others mentioned the crucial difficulty of balancing specificity and generality in training curricula, as 'between teaching the history of informatics and explaining how to push buttons'. Firm level training was widely seen as excessively specific, public programmes as excessively general.

Managers of American public programmes, on the other hand, tended to be more positive about them, pointing to particular training schemes that, they claimed, were highly effective in providing people with basic skills, placed significant proportions of the trainees in jobs, and appeared to raise their wage levels relative to comparable workers without such training. Several lamented that many more people wanted training than could be served by current programmes; and that financial support was so skimpy, particularly as a result of the JTPA rules that prevented payment of living stipends, as well as daycare, travel and other costs of training.

Underneath issues of inefficiency, content and funding in public training programmes, however, lurks a more fundamental issue: the social dimension of training, including the control of training itself (Bulgarelli et al., 1989; NOMISMA, 1988; Garonna, 1989). At the firm level, it has been deemed essential, as one corporate manager in Italy put it, 'to train workers to work together in teams, to exchange information and advice, to be active in designing and controlling work organisation'. A training officer in an Italian region noted more succinctly: 'the role of vocational training at the plant level is all a matter of industrial relations'. An Italian trade unionist noted that bargaining over training has been badly affected by recent difficulties in plant-level bargaining (see also ISFOL, 1988a).

One difference between the two countries is that, while in the US union participation and involvement is quite minimal, in Italy unions do participate but do so ineffectively. Why unions are ineffective, however, is subject to debate. The unions 'have great influence, but it is still inadequate,' noted one union official. Unions representing cadres and technicians are significantly involved – 'too much', according to a Fiat official.

Union participation has raised two main issues in Italy. Who will exercise effective control over training activities? What risks are posed by the 'political' nature of the parties involved? The two aspects often interact in a vicious circle. Intervention by the social actors is seen as distant and somehow abstract because it is constrained by the nature of conflictual relationships. One trade union official argued that

> there are many theoretical training programmes couched in general terms, but there are far fewer practical projects inspired by concreteness, such as there would be if the convergence of interests were achieved not only at political level but also and above all at technical and economic level.

An often cited cause of inefficiency is the 'politicisation' of the social partners. The reference here obviously involves political unionism, but there is also the political role of employer organisations. Some officials stress the degeneration of political roles. Others question instead the model itself:

> frequently the conflicts (both the ideological ones and those more strictly connected with represented interests) that emerge on some occasions spill over and complicate the differences that emerge in other bargaining contests.

At times politicisation takes the form of party political interference, as when 'the task of elaborating programmes is assigned to . . . consultants nominated by the political parties'.

Conflict over control emerges differently in the US, given the extensive privatisation of public training that has already occurred through JTPA. American union officials ascribed many of the problems of public programmes to the lack of union or worker participation in the formulation of training programmes. They were very bitter about the 'sham partnership' of JTPA and insisted that a more viable training scheme was needed. One AFL-CIO official stated bluntly that what was needed was '. . . acknowledging labour as an equal partner' and that training activities should be developed jointly. This, however, appears far from current political probabilities.

The main conclusion that emerges is the conflict-dependent nature of training, above all that at the plant level. This point found clearest expression in the words of an Italian trade union training expert: 'Training reproduces the faults of the industrial relations system.'[5]

In short, the interviews revealed in both countries that some companies and, more rarely, company/union partnerships have developed programmes for training that are deemed adequate, particularly in the context of large firm size, high technology and strong unionisation. Elsewhere, training opportunities for workers were widely recognised as deficient and most interviewees saw the need for a more comprehensive system. This awareness was evident among corporate officers, whose concern is upgrading or reskilling workers who are already employed; it was more strongly felt by union officials, concerned both for workers threatened by technological change and for the unemployed; and it was strongest among managers of public training programmes, who mainly work with people without jobs.

On the other hand, public programmes receive little support as the building blocks of a new, more comprehensive system. In particular, private sector interviewees (corporate officers and, less strongly, union officials) lack confidence in the ability of such programmes to match skills training with real jobs. Moreover, the control of such programmes, especially the role of union and worker participation in their formulation, implementation, and administration, remains highly contentious.

5.9 TRAINING POLICY IN PERSPECTIVE

The debate over training has developed out of different political circumstances in Italy and the US; yet, as we have seen, these differences mask underlying similarities.

In Italy, renewed interest in training derived mainly from the problem of youth unemployment. Training has been seen, as in other European countries, as a policy antidote to the weak labour market position of young workers. It has also been supported as a response to

job losses in industries hit by restructuring, sometimes in conjunction
with income support through the CIG. Finally, training has appeared
a necessary complement to the introduction of new technologies and
the transformation of the production process.

In the US, renewed interest in training derives primarily from the
search for a route to improved international competitiveness and
secondarily from the desire to help the youth of a growing underclass
to find jobs. The Reagan government, uninterested in either project,
provided a minimalist training policy, and George Bush, despite
proclaiming himself the 'education President', has seemed unlikely to
depart from this lead. Nonetheless, wider social pressures for a more
active training policy may stimulate new initiatives.

The central underlying similarity between the two countries is that
training has become an issue because it promises a solution to the
severe economic and social problems of the early 1980s crisis and to
the late 1980s industrial restructuring; and particularly because
training appears in the flexibility model as a 'safe' intervention into
the private economy, one that leaves markets and the larger flexibility
strategies intact. This opening has been created by the demise of the
labour accords of the period 1950–80.

Yet the success of training initiatives has in the past been linked to
the dynamics of the prevailing industrial relations regime. Today these
systems are in flux in both countries, perhaps in transition to new
systems. New training initiatives are likely to succeed only if they are
consonant with the future development of industrial relations. In
particular, the flexibility model of training will work only if flexibility
is the essential feature of the wider developing system.

We doubt that 'flexibilisation' can constitute the basis for an
enduring industrial relations regime. Already stresses caused by these
policies – growing inequalities, the loss of workers' 'voice', youth
joblessness, and massive job dislocations – have produced counter-
pressures to which even conservative governments have been forced to
respond. In the democracies, workers' banners, though tattered by the
events of the past decade, still retain sufficient political appeal to
require that any industrial relations regime, to endure, must accommodate worker interests.

However, for reasons which differ between the two countries, it
appears unlikely that the old labour accords will be revived. In the US,
unions are no longer strong enough or representative enough to play
even the junior partner's role in the old labour accord. In Italy, the
unity of the labour movement, which was the aim of the 'historic

compromise' upon which the 1970s phase of the labour accord was revived, is no longer a political possibility, while new strains have arisen in association with increased European integration.

The debates over training are therefore suspended between the disappearing old relationships and the as yet imperfectly visible emergent ones. Particular hopes for training – for example, that it will relieve growing inequalities (US), resolve the youth joblessness problem (Italy), and provide a major boost for national competitiveness (both countries) – cannot be achieved without its integration into a successful industrial relations system. But that, of course, awaits determination of the form of such a system.

Whatever the character of the new industrial relations regime, in most scenarios both widespread youth access to training and public responsibility for providing youth training are likely to be essential building blocks. Debates over youth training may thus contribute to the emergence of the new industrial relations regime. The old labour accords involved workable arrangements for training young workers, and the disintegration of those accords has reduced the efficacy of that training mechanism. Employers and workers alike have suffered as a result. Employer support for increased public intervention in youth training thus involves simultaneously a recognition that purely privately arranged training (as envisioned in the flexibility model) is in practice inadequate and an appeal for public initiatives to supply the benefits available under the old accords.

The old systems, however, were based on the social compromises inherent in an accord and new training policies will likewise need to take into account the worker stake in training. For example, the emerging sense that workers have a right to training and retraining, if acknowledged and incorporated into the formal (contractual, statutory, or judicial) rules of industrial practice, could well be one way in which a new system could accommodate worker interests.

APPENDIX: SURVEY OF CURRENT ATTITUDES TOWARDS TRAINING

As part of this study, we conducted a survey of the current attitudes held by leaders within the field of employment training towards present needs, trends, and problems in employment training. We interviewed corporate executives, union officials, and public sector managers in both countries. The survey was based on an in-depth, qualitative, and open-ended questionnaire. Questionnaires identical except for language were used in the two countries; the interviews were conducted in the winter and spring of 1988. In Italy, further comparable information was drawn from interviews conducted in 1987 for CEDEFOP on the role of the social partners in the training system in Italy (CEDEFOP, 1987). By agreement, we have identified the participants only in general terms.

Notes

1. The parts sum to more than the total because some workers obtained training in more than one place.
2. The *contratti di formazione e lavoro*, introduced in 1977, were redesigned in 1983 after the effective failure of the first attempt, as part of a wider package of deregulatory measures (Garonna, 1986). Recent developments are discussed by Frey (1988).
3. See Appendix. Detailed results of the survey will be published elsewhere. By far the strongest and most consistent response is one that does not directly concern us here: that elementary and secondary education is failing to equip its graduates with the basic training, both skills and habits of learning, that are necessary. Most union officials and public sector managers interviewed agreed. The theme is strongly echoed in, for example, MIT Taskforce on Productivity (1989).
4. The reasons for the dissatisfaction are however different and sometimes inconsistent. Thus some Italian managers think that the institutional space provided by legislation or regulations for the involvement of organisations, the community, and the unions is insufficient; others think it excessive and overly formalistic. One commentator felt that there was a difficulty in translating the criticism into proposals for change, and complained about the sterility of 'a general dissatisfaction, that is expressed on all occasions when general plans are defined and discussed . . . but that offers no concrete solution nor yields practical effects'.
5. This comment also points up the difficulties in any attempt to copy training models from elsewhere. Both countries have seen calls to emulate the German model, yet, as one Italian corporate officer put it, 'to make the German model work in Italy, we would need to be in Germany'.

6 Young People and Entry Paths to Long-term Jobs in France and Great Britain[1]

David Marsden and
Jean-François Germe

6.1 AN OVERVIEW OF THE YOUTH EMPLOYMENT PROBLEM

The economies of most western industrial countries are characterised by a large proportion of long-term jobs and long-tenure occupations. In the first case, the long-term jobs are usually in enterprise internal labour markets, and in the second, the long-term relationship generally resides in the workers' ability to exercise the same skill in similar jobs in many different firms. In Britain, Main (1982) estimated that in 1968 the average completed job tenure of full-time adult males was 20 years, and that three-fifths of the workers in this group were in jobs which would last at least 10 years. Despite the impression of high labour mobility in the US, long-term jobs represent a similar proportion of those available (Hall, 1982).[2] Akerlof and Main's (1981) estimates for the US confirm these figures for males, and show that for women the comparable figure was only about a quarter lower. Akerlof and Main (1981, for the US), and Main (1981, for the UK), show that there are indeed many short-duration jobs in the economy, but that these are concentrated on a minority of the labour force who hold such jobs in succession. Apart from minority groups, young workers represent an important group holding such jobs (Osterman, 1980). Similar studies do not appear to have been done for France, but comparisons between Britain and France of current length of service and turnover in the

1970s and 1980s suggest that in France the prevalence of long-term jobs may be even more pronounced (Eyraud, Marsden and Silvestre, 1990).[3]

The entry of young workers into the jobs or occupations in which they will eventually spend much of their working lives is complex, and many young people take several jobs before finally becoming established. To the extent that young people regularly have to gain a particular qualification, and then, or as a substitute, experience a succession of jobs leading to the one they will eventually hold on a longer-term basis, one might speak of 'entry paths' into long-term employment. Hence, the concept is a descriptive one, implying a degree of statistical regularity. Such paths, we believe, are shaped by a number of factors, the most important of which include institutional rules, the organisation of training and nature of work experience required for the longer-term jobs, and relative employment costs.

The quality of working life of young people and, to some extent, the degree to which their skills are utilised are affected by the directness with which these paths lead to final jobs and occupations. A notable feature to be developed in this chapter is that the school-based vocational qualifications in France do not lead directly to skilled jobs, but that qualified young people often undergo a process of 'occupational downgrading' as they are obliged initially to accept unskilled or semi-skilled jobs, and are only upgraded into skilled jobs five to ten years later. In the US, Osterman (1980) has observed a similar 'moratorium period' during which young workers become established. This pattern contrasts with that of direct entry into skilled jobs for young workers acquiring their qualification through apprenticeship, which involves a mixture of theoretical and on-the-job learning. In terms of the classification sketched out by Garonna and Ryan (chapter 2, above), the pattern of occupational downgrading is an attribute of 'institutional exclusion' and that of more direct access associated with apprenticeship-based skills one of 'institutional inclusion'.

This chapter seeks first to analyse the evidence relating to the importance of entry paths for young workers and then to tease out some of the causes for their existence. It looks first at evidence for paths by occupation, by industry, and through small firms. It then explores some of the causes underlying their existence and their structure. It deals primarily with manual males in industry. However, it is necessary first to explore more fully the concepts underlying 'entry paths'.

6.2   ENTRY PATHS AND LABOUR MARKET STRUCTURE

To assist the exposition, it is helpful to think in terms of two different types of labour market: one based on transferable skills, which enable workers to move between firms while remaining within the same occupation, and which might be called an 'occupational labour market', and one which is based upon mobility between jobs within the same firm, but which is characterised by an absence of skill transferability between firms. This latter kind might be called an 'internal labour market'.

These two types of labour market pose rather different problems of access for young workers. To gain entry to an occupational market, it is usually necessary to gain access to the training which leads to entry into a particular occupation, such as training to become an electrician. To gain entry to an internal labour market, the more important goal for young workers is to ensure they they gain a job in a firm which offers good prospects for internal training and advancement.

The difference between these two types of labour market is illustrated in Figure 6.1.[4] The rectangular boxes represent levels of skill within individual firms. The main entry point in a strongly defined internal labour market is at the bottom where labour, which is either unskilled or has inappropriate skills, is taken on, and only reaches skilled positions within the firm after a period of in-firm or on-the-job training. In the occupational model, once a person has acquired the relevant skill for access to an occupational market, mobility between firms while retaining the same level of skill is possible, but access to skilled positions for other workers by virtue of long service is not.

These differences are reflected in training institutions in Britain and France. In British industry, the predominant form of training for skilled work is by apprenticeship: institutionalised on-the-job training with a specified theoretical content. In France, equivalent training is provided off-the-job in vocational schools, and is sanctioned by state diplomas, notably the CAP and the BEP, diplomas whose coverage expanded considerably during the 1970s. For earlier generations of skilled workers, greater reliance was placed upon acquisition of the relevant skills on-the-job, and in a relatively uninstitutionalised and informal way, the skill having currency only within the enterprise.

The differences are also reflected in the nature of pay rules. In the case of the occupational market, the transferable nature of the skills leaves employers unwilling to bear the whole cost of training. In a competitive environment with private provision of training, human

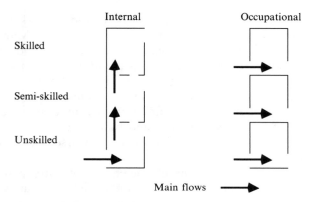

Figure 6.1   Simplified diagram of main inflows and throughflows in internal and occupational labour markets

capital theory predicts that trainees will bear the whole cost in the form of a special trainee rate of pay below the value of their output (Becker, 1975). In practice, this often breaks down because of conflict between employers and workers (Marsden, 1986a; Ryan, 1987a), and a diluted system emerges with the costs shared between trainees and employers. As a result, employees will wish to concentrate training early in their working lives in order to maximise the return on their investment, and, because of transferability, employers will have relatively little scope to offer complex pay rules thereafter. Thus, one would expect a wage-for-age rule to apply during the training period and while initial experience is gained, and then there to be a standard rate for the occupation.

In contrast, in the internal market, the lack of transferability of skills gives employers and employees much greater freedom in the design of job and pay progression. At the same time, skill is defined not in terms of training, but in terms of the demands of the particular job. Hence it is logical that pay rates should be primarily attached to jobs. Thus, plant-level bargaining tends to focus, in French internal labour markets, on where particular jobs fit into the job and pay classification system within the enterprise (Maurice et al., 1986; Eyraud et al., 1990). Typically, such classification systems disregard a worker's age and previous (external) experience or qualifications, although not length of service in the job or the enterprise.

In practice, both kinds of labour market coexist in most economies, although it is likely that one or other form will predominate within a particular sector. (The reasons for the predominance of one form or the other lie in the 'public good' nature of occupational markets, and their consequent dependence on institutional support; Marsden, 1986a). For example, the occupational model can be found in the small firm handicraft or artisan sector, and in large parts of construction, in many countries within the EEC. However, of the four major EEC industrial countries, in the manufacturing sector, Britain and West Germany are alone in the predominance of occupational markets. In both French and Italian industry, a pattern of internal markets predominates (Saunders and Marsden 1981, ch.7; Marsden, 1987b).

Ideally, one should explore the characteristics of entry paths by means of cohort and mobility studies, but these are few in number, so we have had to rely heavily upon interpretation of cross-section results for single years. These are supplemented by more direct evidence of entry paths where available from national surveys.

6.3   EVIDENCE ON YOUTH ENTRY PATHS AND VOCATIONAL TRAINING

Entry Paths and Youth Qualifications

Access to occupational labour markets requires the acquisition of a particular kind of training, and, most important, to ensure skill transferability, it requires a fairly high degree of standardisation of methods and content of training. Employers frequently bear a considerable part of the net cost of such training. (In Britain and West Germany, for apprenticeships, this is equivalent to between 1.5 and 2 years' gross pay of a skilled worker; Noll et al., 1983; IMS, 1982). The result is incentives for individual employers to cut their own training and to 'poach' skilled labour from other employers. To regulate this, and to create the means for reducing the net cost through use of a trainee discount, a strong institutional underpinning is necessary, provided by either bipartite and tripartite institutions or by the state (although it can be argued that the state is unlikely to be able to achieve this on its own).

Apprenticeships provide an institutional structure particularly well suited to meet this kind of need, as they create a readily identifiable status for young trainees and help them identify with the interests of the skilled group they will eventually join. In addition to passing on technical knowledge, the apprenticeship, conducted in part by skilled workers, initiates the apprentice into the practices of job regulation which help to maintain the occupation and its labour market. It can be argued that an important reason for the greater vitality of the system in West Germany, as compared with that in the UK, lies in the support provided by the chambers of industry and commerce and of the handicraft sector at the local level, and by the activities of the works councils in supervising training and the use of apprentice labour within the place of work.

An overview of the extent of apprentice training in different industrial sectors in France and Great Britain is given by Eurostat's Labour Cost Survey which has the merit of providing statistics on comparable sectors of the two economies, but for establishments with ten or more employees only (Table 6.1).[5]

The Labour Cost Survey shows clearly the dominant position of apprenticeship training in British industry for skilled manual workers. Among manual workers in Britain, apprenticeship training occurs heavily in some branches, such as mechanical engineering, shipbuilding, automobiles, precision instruments, printing, and construction. Below average rates of apprentice training are to be found in the process industries such as chemicals, steel, and food processing..

In France apprenticeship is not a major source of training in any of these sectors, except for construction, where there is a concentration of apprentices in small firms with less than 10 employees. However, the number of apprentices outside the industrial sector is quite large: in France it has been over 0.2m in each year since 1978, but it is mainly confined to the artisan, repair, and construction sectors (Combes, 1988). Hence it provides only a limited supply of the skills required by manufacturing, and does not provide the basis for occupational labour markets in manufacturing. In addition, within manufacturing in France, the logic of internal labour markets continues to dominate access to skilled jobs even for those with external qualifications (Maurice et al., 1986).

In fact, in France, this logic appears to prevail even over that of apprenticeship (Table 6.2) as the latter does not appear to be a major provider of skills to larger-scale manufacturing industry, unlike the situation in Britain and West Germany. Moreover, evidence from the 1972 Eurostat wage structure survey on length of service and its correlates strongly suggests that in French industry the internal labour market model predominates (Saunders and Marsden, 1981, ch. 7), which means that employers there would be ill-placed to make use of

Table 6.1   Manual apprentices and trainees[a] as a percentage of manual employment (including apprentices) in industry in Britain and France, 1981

NACE	Sector	France	UK
22	Steel	0.1	3.7
25	Chemicals	n.a.	2.2
31	Metal goods	0.4	4.2
32	Mechanical engineering	0.4	7.0
35	Automobiles	0.6	3.7
37	Instrument engineering	0.3	6.3
361	Shipbuilding	1.6	11.0
41/42	Food and drink	0.3	0.8
43	Textiles	0.1	1.6
45	Clothing and footwear	0.2	2.2
47	Paper and printing	0.2	4.2
50	Construction	1.3	10.2
1–5	Industry and construction	0.5	4.6
1–5	Absolute numbers	18 925	236 270

Notes: Includes only establishments with 10 or more employees.
[a] Corresponds to Eurostat's 'apprentice' category, defined to include all employees who do not yet fully participate in the production process and work either under a contract of apprenticeship or in conditions in which vocational training predominates over production. Employers are asked to provide apprentices' earnings and social security contributions and other related costs separately from those of other employees.
Source: Eurostat, Labour Cost Survey 1981

occupational markets, lacking the degree of job standardisation necessary, and perhaps more important, being bound by the expectations concerning internal upgrading among their existing employees.

Training Institutions, Youth Entry and Occupational Downgrading

To what extent, then, does Britain's apprenticeship system facilitate youth entry into skilled occupations, and what happens to young workers in France at a similar stage in their working lives? In Britain, apprentice-trained young workers appear to have a high probability of gaining access to skilled jobs, and this contrasts with the 'occupational downgrading' experienced by young workers in France, both those with school-based vocational qualifications and those with apprenticeships.

Table 6.2   Male employees by socioeconomic group, qualification and age,
Britain and France, 1979

| | | | Socioeconomic group | | | | |
Country	Age group	Qualification	Skilled	SSK+ USK	Other manual	All share	All number (000s)
Britain	16–24	App completed	69.5%	10.6%	2.1%	97.8%	401.2
(1984)		App in progress	72.2	13.1	0.9	100.0	253.1
		No qualification	42.2	41.5	3.9	100.0	987.8
		All	39.6	24.1	3.3	100.0	
		All (numbers)	1 163	706	96		2 940.3
	25+	App completed	50.0	11.3	1.4	100.0	2 198.8
		App in progress	39.0	24.1	1.3	100.0	56.3
		No qualification	41.6	30.6	2.4	100.0	5 325.0
		All	32.0	21.2	2.4	100.0	
		All (numbers)	3 261	2 170	246		10 205.1
France	16–24	CAP/BEP	48.9	21.6	6.7	100.0	594.7
(1982)		App in progress	13.3	71.8	1.7	100.0	135.9
		No diploma	33.2	45.7	8.6	100.0	484.3
		All	33.9	33.1	6.9	100.0	1 525.7
	25+	CAP/BEP	43.1	8.8	5.9	100.0	2 469.6
		No diploma	39.9	19.8	16.3	100.0	4 858.0
		All	29.9	12.3	10.1	100.0	10 095.7

Note: 'SSK + USK' denotes subcraft manual occupations. 'All' includes non-manual occupations. 'All' training category includes other (unreported) categories. Artisans and employers removed from French data. CAP/BEP are apprenticeship-level school-based qualifications requiring two (or three) years of study.
Source: Labour Force Surveys of Britain and France

Most of the output of apprentice training in Britain leads into skilled jobs, as around 70 per cent of young male workers aged between 16 and 24 with an apprenticeship gain access to skilled jobs. Only about one in ten are in semi-skilled or unskilled jobs (Table 6.2). Among male workers aged 25 and over, again only about one in ten of those with an apprenticeship are in semi-skilled or unskilled jobs, and these figures, relating to the whole economy, are probably lower than they would be for manufacturing only. Thus, overall, the number of apprentice-trained young workers taking jobs below their level of qualification is relatively small in Britain.

In France, cohort studies (by the CEREQ and by INSEE; Germe, 1986) suggest that certain occupations also play a key role as entry paths for young workers, but that these are often at an initially lower level of skill. There much vocational training is provided off-the-job in state schools and the acquisition of on-the-job experience is a problem. There has been widespread incidence of 'downgrading' of qualified young workers, forced to take their initial jobs in less skilled positions, often in small firms.[6] The rate of downgrading of qualified young workers in France is about double that in Britain. However, the internal labour market logic operates as these workers later achieve skilled positions.[7] The classification of apprentices in training in semi-skilled and unskilled jobs is also revealing, because, in France, apprenticeship is only recognised as a qualification if the apprentice passes the CAP or the BEP – validation is not accorded by the peer group (Table 6.2).

Evidence on occupational downgrading of new entrants in France is even sharper in the French national training survey of 1970, and again in later labour force surveys, relating more specifically to new entrants (Capdeville and Grapin, 1975, p.61).[8] This tendency has if anything been reinforced in subsequent years. In 1984 more recent young male entrants with the CAP or BEP had entered semi-skilled and unskilled than skilled jobs (14,000 as against 11,600; Table 6.3). That this process predated the rise in youth unemployment indicates that it is to some extent independent of it.

In a later analysis of the French national training survey, Pohl and Soleilhavoup (1981) show that a considerable amount of upgrading takes place as workers gain job experience. For example, over the five year periods 1965–70 and 1972–77 between 12 per cent and 13 per cent of unskilled or semi-skilled manual males were upgraded to skilled positions. More important, the study showed that the probability of upgrading for manual males from semi-skilled to skilled jobs for those with the CAP was more than twice that for those with a lower qualification or none at all. But also the probability of upgrading declined sharply after the middle twenties, all of which suggests a process of initial downgrading, and of subsequent access to upgrading during the early and middle twenties.

Such initial downgrading on labour market entry is less pervasive in Britain, but equally, subsequent upgrading to skilled positions is also less widespread in this country. One reason would seem to be the prevalence of industrial apprenticeship as a source of industrial skill, but the answer is complicated by the existence of an apprenticeship

Table 6.3   France, 1984: qualifications of young workers who had still been at school in 1983 (000s)

		Qualifications			
Sex	Occupation	Baccalauréat and higher	CAP or BEP	None or brevet des collèges	Total
Male	Skilled	3.9	11.6	5.4	21.7
Manual	SSK + USK	2.0	14.0	15.6	31.9
	All	49.0	35.0	30.0	114.0
Female	Admin	37.1	12.8	8.9	58.8
Non-manual	Other	5.1	7.5	11.9	24.2
Female	Skilled	n.a.	1.5	1.7	3.5
Manual	SSK + USK	1.4	4.9	5.9	12.1
	All	111.0	29.0	33.0	173.0

Source: Coeffic (1987), based on the Enquête sur l'Emploi.

system in France. Moreover, French apprenticeship is, as in Britain and West Germany, associated with a sizeable discount on youth employment, as the legal minimum for apprentices runs from 15 per cent of the national minimum wage (SMIC) in the first six months of apprenticeship to 45 per cent in the fourth (and usually final) six months. This percentage is raised by 10 per cent for those aged 18 and over. Even though those workers covered by the 1970 collective agreement benefit from higher rates (30 per cent of the SMIC in the first year, rising to 50 per cent in the second, and 75 per cent in the third; Camerlynck and Lyon-Caen, 1983), it is more than comparable to the discounts available in Britain. Several avenues may be explored for an explanation of the different role played by apprenticeship in France.

A first possibility is simply that French apprenticeship has been confined to skills which are little demanded in manufacturing, but this does not explain why it has not provided an attractive model which employers have sought to expand into new areas. The longstanding role of the state in assuming leadership in this area takes the explanation a bit further. Particularly in the 1970s the state has sought to promote both adult training through formation permanente and youth training through the expansion of the CAP and the introduction of the BEP, as well as by encouraging an expansion of apprentice numbers (Germe, 1986). However, despite attempts by the state to encourage a more bipartite approach by employers and worker representatives, it has been unable to get employers to take over responsibility and to maintain the institutional structures needed to run a successful apprenticeship system.

A second avenue of explanation recognises that a successful apprenticeship system provides rapid access to jobs at the appropriate level of skill, and thus is heavily dependent upon the existence of an occupational labour market. The mutual dependence between training institutions providing transferable skills and OLMs is one reason why it is difficult to establish them from scratch (Marsden, 1986a). The prevalance of internal labour market rules in enterprises imposes entry at a lower level in the skill classification, and even though many collective agreements specify that qualified workers should not be engaged at below a certain level in the classification (for example at P1, the bottom of the skilled grades), upgrading is required to reach the full skilled status (usually P3; Eyraud et al., 1990). Indeed, this example also serves to illustrate how such rules have become incorporated into, and legitimated by, industry level collective agreements. Together, these two forces did much to undermine the attempts to set up an industrial apprenticeship system in France during the 1920s and 1930s (Maurice et al., 1986, pp. 620–37).

Finally, the labour force surveys of both Britain and France reveal that a considerable proportion of those with no qualifications manage to obtain skilled jobs. If we compare skilled to semi-skilled and unskilled groups in the two age categories, it appears that the unqualified in France have a greater chance of subsequent upgrading to skilled than do their counterparts in Britain (Table 6.2). The large number of unqualified skilled workers in Britain suggests that occupational markets may be weaker in Britain than they are in Germany (chapter 4, above).

The question of quality can also be raised in connection with apprenticeship. It is only since the middle 1960s that there has been a generalised and systematic effort to raise the technical quality of apprenticeship training in Britain, notably following the 1964 Industrial Training Act. Thus, many older skilled workers in Britain have 'served their time' but gained only inadequate training. This is likely to enhance their fear of substitution by better educated teenagers, and this also suggests that the institutional rules governing access to craft occupational markets in Britain are at least as important as technical skills, and that the institutional component of job standardisation is as important as any technical or economic (cost-minimising) constraints on job design.

Trends in Vocational Training During the 1970s and 1980s

During the 1970s, the two systems of vocational training have been in a state of flux. In Britain, apprenticeship has declined, whereas in France the volume of apprenticeships and school-based vocational training has increased considerably, and it might be asked how this affects the predominance of different types of labour market in either country.

In British manufacturing, during the 1970s, male apprentices and trainees, as a percentage of male employees, fell from 6 per cent in 1970 to 4.3 per cent in 1980 (Table 6.4), this figure having fallen further since then, but, according to the Labour Force Surveys, only slightly.[9] However, these percentage declines mask a steeper decline in absolute numbers. The decline in apprentices in Britain during the 1970s was due to three main causes: the decline in manufacturing employment; a shortening of many apprenticeships from four to three years; and a reduction in the rate of training. A considerable proportion of the decline has been associated with the decline of employment in industries which have made heavy use of apprentice-based skills, such as shipbuilding, and has not been compensated by an increase in the rate of training in many branches.

In France, recent legislation, and the reform and increase in the apprenticeship levy on employers (*taxe d'apprentissage*), have boosted the number of apprentices from just over 150,000 in 1974–5 to over 220,000 in 1981–2, the rate increasing from 4 per cent to 5 per cent of the population aged between 15 and 19 (Combes, 1988). Nevertheless, as discussed earlier, apprenticeship in France remains a feature of non-manufacturing activities, notably food distribution, construction, and mechanical repairs. In addition, the rate of training, as a result largely of government-financed educational policy, has been increasing. The number of pupils in the final year of the school-based CAP and BEP vocational diplomas has increased between 1974–5 and 1982 from 111,742 to 150,566 (Table 6.5).

To conclude, the decline of apprenticeship training in Britain must cause one to ask how much longer occupational markets for skilled workers will continue to provide employers' needs. As late as 1984, around half of the existing stock of skilled male manual workers in British manufacturing were apprentice-trained (GB OPCS, 1986). As will become apparent, in France, increased state vocational training has not led to the formation of occupational markets, and the logic of internal progression continues to hold sway, although it seems likely that public training has raised the quality of skills used within ILMs.

Table 6.4   Great Britain: apprentices and trainees in manufacturing industries

Sex	Category	1965	1970	1975	1980
Numbers (000s)					
Both	Apprentices	243.3	218.6	155.3	149.5
	Trainees	145.3	202.1	135.2	90.0
Males	Apprentices	237.4	211.6	151.4	144.8
	Trainees	82.6	121.9	84.4	57.4
Share of manufacturing employment (%)					
Both	Apprentices	3.0	2.7	2.1	2.3
	Trainees	1.8	2.5	1.8	1.4
Males	Apprentices	4.3	3.8	2.9	3.1
	Trainees	1.5	2.2	1.6	1.2

Note: For figures after 1979, based on the Labour Force Surveys, see note 9.
Source: DE Gazette, September 1980, p. 947.

Table 6.5   France: number of pupils in the final year of studies for the CAP and the BEP

		1974–5	1981–2	Change (%)
CAP	Males	68 123	79 542	
	Females	11 976	14 852	
	Total	80 099	94 394	17.8
BEP	Males	30 213	51 043	
	Females	1 430	5 129	
	Total	31 643	56 172	77.5
Both	Total	111 742	150 566	34.7

Note: CAP and BEP are apprenticeship-level school-based qualifications lasting mostly two (in some cases three) years.
Source: Ministère de l'Education Nationale, quoted in Mouy (1983), tables 4, 5.

6.4 ENTRY PATHS PROVIDED BY PARTICULAR INDUSTRIES

In an industrial analysis of youth employment, Marsden and Ryan (chapter 3, above) find marked differences between countries in the degree of concentration of young workers in low paid industries, notably, that such concentration was greater in France, Italy and Belgium than in Britain, West Germany and the Netherlands. Nevertheless, there was a strong similarity between all six countries as concerns which industries were large employers of young workers. These large concentrations suggest that such industries provide initial jobs and work experience to many young workers, who subsequently move, as adults, to higher paid industries. Thus an important element of the entry paths followed by young workers would seem to involve movement between certain industries. This can be affected by the predominance of one or other type of labour market organisation in four ways.

First, one cause of such inter-industry movement of young workers appears to be that the work experience needed to complement formal school-based training is, at least partially, transferable, as concerns both the practice needed to consolidate theoretical skills and the learning of the social skills for the workplace. Some of this may be learned in many types of industry.

If the acquisition of such experience is costly and there is no compensating discount on young employment costs, then some employers may prefer to leave such familiarisation to other employers and to hire qualified young workers only when they are more mature, in their middle twenties. The segmentation effect of adult pay noted by Marsden and Ryan (1986) then represents, in part at least, a process by which qualified, but as yet inexperienced, young workers have initially to take jobs in lower paid and less sought-after industries, and so 'queue' for jobs in higher paying industries. A discount on (or a subsidy to) their employment within the higher paying industries could facilitate more direct entry into those industries, but in the absence of suitable institutional arrangements, such as a formal apprenticeship system, such discounts (and probably also such subsidies) are unacceptable to mature skilled workers who have the power to block their accession (in the last resort by not passing their knowledge to the inexperienced).

Secondly, this process is further reinforced by the internal labour market logic, as this limits the opportunities for direct access to skilled employment for qualified young workers. Between them, these two related causes (both of which may be sufficient alone) produce a complex of entry paths through lower paying industries, giving rise to a process analogous to that of 'downgrading' between occupations.

Thirdly, a predominance of occupational markets may reduce the segmentation effect via their influence both on the inter-industry dispersion of adult pay and on skill standardisation. The very transferability of skills across an occupational market introduces a degree of competitive pressure limiting the spread of earnings between firms for the same occupation.[10] This can work through wage structures within firms to create smaller inter-industry dispersion of earnings than might occur if internal labour markets predominated. This would reduce the opportunities open to young workers in lower paid industries simply because the differential between industries is smaller (it might also raise youth unemployment).

Fourthly, occupational markets might be expected to produce a more even spread of young workers between those industries using occupational markets because training and skill acquisition are more standardised than with internal labour markets.

These differences are confirmed by comparison between Britain and France. In both countries, there are distinct entry paths provided by certain industries, but the degree to which this is so is markedly greater in France than in Britain. As in other EEC countries, young male manual workers were overrepresented in branches such as footwear and wood products, and underrepresented in oil refining and chemicals (chapter 3, Table 3.3, above). These are also the branches in which adult pay was lowest. This *prima facie* evidence that these branches have continued to provide special entry paths for young male workers in the labour market is reinforced by the behaviour of many industries employing large numbers of young workers which were quite clearly employing more than could possibly expect to stay with the industry in the longer term. This movement between branches in France is also revealed in the CEREQ cohort studies (Germe, 1986; Amat and Géhin, 1987).

The similarity of the ranking of youth shares between industries between 1966, 1972 and 1978 (Table 6.6) reinforces this idea that certain industries have served as staging posts for young workers on their way to longer-term jobs in other industries, and that the distribution of youth employment between industries is not to be explained mainly by expanding or contracting employment in individual industries.

Table 6.6   Correlation coefficients between youth employment shares in 47 industries in three years, manual employees

	Males		Females	
Paired years	*France*	*UK*	*France*	*UK*
1966/1972	0.95	0.90	0.93	0.93
1972/1978	0.87	0.96	0.87	0.83
1966/1978	0.88	0.88	0.87	0.79

Source: Eurostat, Structure of Earnings Surveys.

6.5   YOUTH ENTRY AND SMALL FIRMS

In several countries, small firms,[11] and especially independent ones, play an important part in providing young workers with their first jobs (Germe, 1986). In some cases, they provide training places, as in West Germany, but they may also use young workers as a source of cheap labour (Garonna, 1986). It is also true that many youth-intensive industries also have a concentration of small firms (e.g. construction, textiles and clothing).

A number of studies by CEREQ (Germe, 1986; Maréchal and Viney, 1983) have highlighted the important role of small French firms in offering a special point of entry to young workers. The same appears to be true of Britain (Table 6.7), as establishments with less than 25 employees have a disproportionate number of workers under 21.

One factor behind this may be the faster rate of job creation among small firms, but accompanying this also is a shorter average life span of such firms as compared with larger ones. In Britain, the share of jobs in small firms may also have increased between 1979 and 1982 as this was a time during which large establishments were shedding labour very fast.

However, underlying mechanisms may also differ between the two countries. Germe (1986) has argued that employment in small firms enabled young French workers to gain the element of work experience missing from the school-based CAP and BEP qualifications, although such employment has been mainly in semi-skilled and unskilled jobs (Table 6.2). Larger establishments, which in France pay a sizable wage differential over small ones, are able to be more choosy about the workers they hire.

The position in Britain and FR Germany contains some of these elements but is complicated by the predominance of occupational labour markets. These make upgrading to skilled positions a less common occurrence than in France. There is some tendency for young workers in Britain to serve their apprenticeships in independent small firms, and then use the access that this gives them to occupational markets to move later to larger firms,[12] although this appears to be much less developed than in West Germany, where the small firm handicraft sector regularly trains apprentices in excess of its needs (Casey, 1986; Noll et al., 1983).

Table 6.7   UK, 1984: small firms and young people's employment

Sex	Sector	Plant size (employees)	Employment by age (000s)		
			< 21	20–30	All
Male	Manufacturing	< 25	101.4	141.4	610.3
		25 +	255.6	688.1	3 336.6
	Construction	< 25	86.5	101.3	415.7
		25 +	76.0	154.6	699.0
	Services	< 25	326.0	454.9	1 961.1
		25 +	294.0	921.6	3 909.6
Female	Manufacturing	< 21	43.3	59.6	315.0
		25 +	190.0	339.9	1 297.6
	Construction	< 25	5.9	14.0	78.8
		25 +	13.7	15.2	65.1
	Services	< 25	475.4	611.8	3 425.9
		25 +	398.0	896.1	3 738.0

Note: Includes full-time and part-time employees of all ages.
Source: Labour Force Survey, 1984.

The attractiveness of youth to small firms is in part a matter of their lower employment cost. In both Britain and France, small establishments offer lower earnings, for a given level of skill, than larger establishments. In both countries, wages in large establishments are higher than in small ones. In 1984, average monthly earnings of all employees in manufacturing establishments with 1,000 or more employees, compared to those with between 10 and 49 employees, were 13 and 28 per cent higher in France and in the UK respectively (Eurostat, 1986). These wage differences by plant size can also be found among skilled workers.[13] This suggests that small firms are not able to compete with large ones for the best qualified, and most efficient workers (although some workers may prefer the less impersonal relations of small firms). Thus, to some extent, small establishments and, by extension, small firms may be in an analogous position to low paying industries in relation to workers 'queuing' for the more rewarding jobs.

Thus in both countries small firms play an important part in providing training and experience for young labour market entrants. In France they provide experience to complement school-based vocational training, and in Britain they also provide a more than proportionate amount of apprenticeship training.

6.6 CONCLUSIONS

This chapter has analysed youth entry paths to long-term jobs in Britain and France, exploring in greater detail one country from each of two categories within the EEC, as classified by labour market (chapter 3, above). In Britain, a combination of apprentice pay rules, occupational markets and lesser segmentation of industries in terms of adult pay have facilitated more direct access for young workers – which in turn would give rise to a smaller inter-industry dispersion of manual male youth employment. In France, the absence of industrial apprenticeships, the lesser influence of wage-for-age rules, the importance of internal labour markets and a larger degree of segmentation have worked to produce a greater degree of occupational downgrading, and concentration of young entrants in low pay industries.

The complex nature of entry paths and, in particular, the elements of downgrading by occupation and their equivalent between industries and between establishments of different sizes, are to a great extent all manifestations of labour market disequilibrium, and notably a prevalence of non-compensating wage differentials which make pure free market solutions impractical. The existence of apprenticeship institutions in FR Germany and in Britain provides one support for more direct youth access to long-term jobs, but the industrial and small firm concentration of youth employment even in Britain reveals the prevalence of segmentation.

The usefulness or otherwise of the period of transition between labour market entry and arrival in long-term jobs and occupations is hard to assess. It has perhaps a clearer economic function in France, where there appears to be a need to complement school-based vocational training, and there is a problem of integrating general qualifications into a structure of internal labour markets which make extensive use of internal upgrading, especially where the upgrading takes place within individual firms or industries. But it is less clear where it involves movement between industries and into larger establishments, where it is questionable how much of the experience is of use to other employers.

This aspect of the problem is equally relevant to Britain. In this case, the 'downgrading' process seems to be more akin to the 'moratorium period' young workers pass through while they seek entry into internal labour markets as described by Piore (1972) and Osterman (1980). There remains also the attendant risk that many young workers will not manage the transition to long-term jobs.

Finally, although this chapter has focussed mainly on the characteristics of entry paths used in the 1970s and early 1980s, it has to be recognised that changes in the factors underlying them may cause the paths to change and possibly to break down. The crisis of apprenticeship training in Britain is one such factor, and the increased government intervention in youth labour markets in both countries with special training and employment schemes is another.

APPENDIX: COMPARISON OF ALTERNATIVE SOURCES ON APPRENTICE NUMBERS

This appendix checks Labour Cost Survey (LCS) estimates of apprenticeship numbers against information from other sources.

Britain

Three other sources of data on apprenticeships are available (Table 6A.1): the Department of Employment's annual survey of apprentices and trainees in manufacturing (DE/App); the Engineering Industry Training Board/DE's survey of occupations in engineering (DE/ EITB); and the Labour Force Survey (LFS). Both the Labour Cost Survey and the DE apprenticeship surveys cover only manufacturing establishments with 10 or more employees.

Table 6A.1   Number of apprentices and trainees in Britain according to different sources, 1978

Source	Scope	Sectors	Estab size	Month	Sex	Type of trainee	Numbers	% of all workers
LCS	UK	Manf	⩾10	Oct	M + F	App + trnee	216 928	3.2
DE/App	GB	Manf	⩾10	May	M + F	App	156 200	2.2
						Trnee	116 300	1.7
						App + trnee	272 500	3.9
DE/EITB	GB	Engineering	All	May	M + F	App	89 780	2.9
						Trnee	17 640	0.6
						App + trnee	107 420	3.4
LFS[a]	GB	All	All	Year	M	App	997 356	20.4
					F	App	105 226	2.2

Note: a. LFS estimates cover workers aged 16–59 with apprenticeship training (including incomplete).

France

The French Ministry of Education estimated the number of apprentices at 168,000 in 1975–6, against the slightly lower figure of 143,000 based on the 1975 population census (Table 6A.2). According to Mouy (1983, Table 1), among apprentices preparing for an industrial qualification in 1978–79, 34% were in construction, 30% in food preparation and retailing, and 29% in mechanical repair trades.

Table 6A.2   Apprentice numbers in France since 1954

Population census	1954	255 000
	1968	363 000
	1975	143 000
Ministry of Education	1975–6	168 000
	1980–1	215 000
	1985–6	213 000

Note: Ministry estimates derived from survey by the Centre de Formation d'Apprentis.
Source: Combes (1988).

Notes

1. The authors would like to thank Paul Ryan and the other participants at the Palermo conference for extensive comments on earlier drafts of this paper. Thanks are also due to the Joseph Rowntree Memorial Trust, the ESRC and the CNRS for financial support.

2. Hall (1982) estimated that, among male and female workers aged 30 and over, 40 per cent are in jobs which will eventually last for 20 years or more and 75 per cent are in jobs which can be expected to last for five years or more. Akerlof and Main (1981) estimated mean completed job tenures for semi-skilled and skilled manual males in the US of between 16 and 20 years and, for women in similar grades, of between 13 and 14 years.

3. For the six original EEC member countries, the 1972 Eurostat SEI provides figures on current job tenures, which for manual males aged 30–44 in manufacturing range between median values of 6.8 years in FR Germany and 8.2 years in Belgium and, for manual women, between 3.1 years in the Netherlands and 6.1 years in Belgium. If one assumes that the employed population in manufacturing is in roughly steady state, that is neither expanding nor contracting, then completed job tenures can be shown to be roughly double current values and these figures suggest median completed job tenures of between 13 and 16 years for manual males and between 6 and 12 years for manual females. Comparing Britain and France, Eyraud, Marsden and Silvestre (1990) calculate that in 1978 the proportion of manual males in industry with five or more years' service in Britain was 54 per cent, against 66 per cent in France.

4. The original idea for this kind of diagrammatic presentation can be found in Robinson (1970).

5. As apprenticeship training is not a central concern of the survey, its reliability is checked in the appendix against data from various national sources. When account is taken of differences in coverage, it is broadly consistent with other sources.

6. Unlike the situation in Britain, the percentage of qualified workers in semi-skilled and unskilled jobs declines in France as workers advance through their twenties and gain promotion.

7. A first reaction would be to ask whether a higher proportion of jobs classified as skilled in Britain could create a smaller probability of downgrading than in France. However, the LFS data underlying Table 6.2 show similar proportions of workers classified as skilled in both countries, at 33.7 per cent in Britain, and 30.4 per cent in France.

8. More than half (54 per cent) of males entering work between 1965 and 1970 with the CAP or BEP diplomas took up unskilled or semi-skilled manual jobs. The quality of work experience differed between qualified and unqualified young male entrants, those with no diploma being more frequently assigned jobs involving only simple repetitive tasks (Capdeville and Grapin, 1975, p. 67).

9. Labour Force Survey estimates of apprentices as a percentage of all employees of working age, for males and females respectively, stood at

2.6 per cent and 0.4 per cent in 1979, and at 2.3 per cent and 0.7 per cent in 1986 (*Employment Gazette*, March 1988, Table 8, p.140). However, over the same period, the number of male employees fell markedly, and the percentages mask a decline in male apprentice numbers from 333,000 in 1979 to 258,000 in 1986.

10. Nevertheless, Mackay et al. (1971) observed that considerable differences in pay rates could persist between firms in the same local labour market and for the same occupation. Thus, although inter-firm competitive pressures on wages may be greater in occupational than in internal labour markets, in practice, occupational markets may diverge considerably from the rather simple model used in this chapter.

11. In this discussion, because most small establishments are also small enterprises, we use the word 'firm' where the distinction is unimportant, and we use the terms 'enterprise' and 'establishment' where precision is necessary.

12. In Britain, among those aged 16–24 in establishments with under 25 employees, 18 per cent were apprentice-trained, against 23 per cent in those with 25 or more employees. In contrast, 15 per cent of those in the small establishments were still serving apprenticeships against 14 per cent in the larger ones (1984 LFS tapes). As most manufacturing apprenticeships are of similar length and commence at 16 years of age, this suggests that, on completion, a number of young workers may be changing jobs to larger establishments. The point receives some corroboration from the 1978 Eurostat Labour Cost Survey, which showed that small establishments (with 10–49 employees) spent a higher proportion of their total labour costs on vocational training than did larger establishments (50 or more employees), the figures being respectively 2.5 per cent and 1.8 per cent (Marsden, 1986b, 1990b). These figures include only direct costs plus trainee wages and because in Britain apprentice wages represent about 70 per cent of total apprentice training costs (Jones, 1986) they should give a rough indication of the relative number of apprentices in small establishments.

13. In British engineering plants in 1980, skilled production workers in establishments with 500 or more employees earned about 10 per cent more than those in establishments with between 25 and 99 employees (DEG, 1980). According to the same survey, in 1970, the difference had been about 18 per cent. In French industry in 1972, skilled workers in plants with 500 or more employees earned about 15 per cent more than those in plants with between 10 and 49 employees (Eurostat, 1972).

Part III
Youth and Trade Unions

7 The Alienation of Young Workers from Trade Unions: the Case of the Netherlands[1]

Tinie Akkermans, Albert J. A. Felling and Jan Peters

7.1 INTRODUCTION: THE PROBLEM

This chapter focuses on young workers as a declining membership category in Dutch trade unions. Union membership of young people has fallen dramatically in the Netherlands, in contrast to that in some countries, notably Sweden (LO-Statistik, 1986). While overall union membership has recently stabilised, after a dramatic reduction during the 1980s, and while women are joining unions in increasing numbers, young people appear increasingly uninterested.

Overall union membership in the Netherlands, never high compared to that in other countries, declined absolutely after 1979 and relatively (i.e. in terms of membership density) after 1977, making the 1980s the crisis period of Dutch unionism (Table 7.1). Whereas membership density had since the Second World War remained consistently above 35 per cent, in 1983 it fell to 32 per cent and has since declined below 30 per cent (Table 7.1). Dutch unions fall nowadays into the lowest of Koepke's three categories of membership density in Europe (density less than 25 per cent).[2]

Recently women have constituted the great majority of new members of Dutch trade unions: for example, in 1987, 85 per cent of new members of the Social Democratic Federation, FNV. Nevertheless the female share of total membership is still very small, at only 15 per cent in 1985. In terms of female unionisation, Dutch unions also join the lowest European category, along with FR Germany, Switzerland and Luxemburg (Koepke, 1987, p.12).

Table 7.1   Trade union membership by federation, 1977–89

| | Absolute numbers | | | | | Membership density total (%) |
	FNV	CNV	MHP	Other	Total	
1977	1 067 500	258 800	113 700	329 400	1 769 400	41
1978	1 070 300	293 900	114 100	307 400	1 785 700	40
1979	1 077 900	300 700	117 400	295 900	1 791 900	40
1980	1 077 800	304 300	118 500	289 100	1 789 600	39
1981	1 042 400	297 300	114 800	282 300	1 736 900	38
1982	1 015 000	342 400	113 400	253 000	1 724 500	37
1983	978 900	331 800	111 500	223 800	1 646 000	32
1984	932 800	311 300	110 200	229 100	1 583 300	30
1985	898 500	300 000	108 100	234 300	1 540 900	29
1986	890 000	295 800	109 400	240 800	1 536 000	29
1987	902 000	290 600	110 700	246 500	1 549 800	27
1988	912 000	291 600	112 000	253 000	1 568 600	26
1989	937 400	295 000	121 800	260 300	1 614 500	24

Notes: Federation details in Table 7A.1.
Sources: *Pocket yearbook*, 1985, p. 133; *Trade Union Statistics*, 1985, p. 13; *Studienotitie*, 1986, p. 2.

At the same time, the Dutch union movement has grown greyer. The membership share of those aged more than 25 years rose between 1977 and 1985 in all three union federations: in the (Social Democratic) FNV from 85 to 92 per cent, in the (Christian) CNV from 87 to 92 per cent and in the (white collar) MHP from 94 to 98 per cent.

The greying of Dutch unions reflects the fact that youth membership has become the greatest area of difficulty, with young people heavily underrepresented in unions. Defining youth broadly as embracing 18 to 29 years of age,[3] youth membership declined relatively as well as absolutely during the first half of the 1980s amongst both males and females (Tables 7.2, 7.3). Recent figures seem to indicate the end of the trend, but recent membership growth amongst young males is explained by an exceptional surge of unionism amongst military conscripts. Female membership has grown recently only amongst workers aged more than 25 years (Table 7.4).

This chapter concentrates upon the difficulties which Dutch unions face in recruiting young workers, setting aside such other recruitment

Table 7.2   Union members aged less than 25 years: numbers and membership density, by federation, 1977–1985

| | Membership (numbers, % share of total membership) | | | | Youth membership density (%) |
	FNV	CNV	MHP	Other	Total	
1977	162 300 (15)	34 40 (13)	6 600 (6)	74 100 (22)	277 400 (16)	26
1979	147 900 (14)	45 900 (16)	2 200 (2)	74 500 (25)	270 500 (15)	25
1981	135 100 (13)	43 100 (14)	3 200 (3)	66 800 (24)	248 200 (14)	22
1983	100 700 (10)	41 600 (12)	3 100 (3)	43 400 (19)	188 800 (12)	16
1985	73 700 (8)	24 600 (8)	2 300 (2)	45 500 (19)	146 100 (10)	13

Source: Trade union statistical records.

Table 7.3   Trade union membership of workers aged less than 25 years, by sex, 1979–87

| | Males | | Females | | Both |
	Numbers	Density	Numbers	Density	Density
1979	168 800	35%	54 900	14%	25%
1985	109 900	19%	36 200	7%	13%
1987	116 600	22%	36 500	7%	15%

Source: Trade union statistical records.

problems as those posed by the expansion of service employment and the position of women and minorities (Maiwald, 1985). Section 7.2 outlines the problem which faces the unions and distinguishes five different lines of explanation, four of which have already received extensive attention. The fifth theoretical approach stresses the emergence of a new type of worker, a worker with a totally different culture than that of traditional union members. The cultural profile of this new worker is described empirically in section 7.3. Existing union policies towards young people are considered in section 7.4. Our analysis leads to the conclusion that the prospects for organising among these workers are bleak. Unions will have to reconsider their choice of recruitment target categories.

Table 7.4   Trade union membership growth in 1987 by sex and age (000s)

Age	Male	Female	Both
< 25	+ 7	0	+ 7
25–64	− 18	+ 15	− 3
> 64	+ 6	+ 3	+ 9
All	− 5	+ 18	+ 13

Source: Trade union statistical records

7.2   THEORETICAL APPROACHES

Dutch industrial relations have long been characterised by heterogeneous representation. In contrast to the unitarist characteristic (*Einheitsgewerkschaften*) of the German system, in the Netherlands each social partner is represented at every level by at least two actors. This internal plurality reflects to some extent religious divisions (*verzuiling*), to some extent other factors, including the separate organisation of higher employees since the early 1970s.

Despite such decentralising tendencies, the multiple actors still possess rather centralised structures. Such internal centralisation has long been recognised as a factor facilitating neocorporatism, which many authors see as almost synonymous with Dutch industrial relations (Wilensky, 1981). The theoretical value and empirical relevance of the neocorporatist model has received considerable attention (Akkermans and Grootings, 1978; Akkermans and Nobelen, 1983; Zimmermann, 1984; Geul, Nobelen and Slomp, 1985; Albeda and Ten Hove, 1986; Reynaerts and Nagelkerke, 1986).

Neocorporatism is fostered in the Netherlands by centralisation and, on the other side of the coin, the striking weakness of unions at company level. Another important factor is the tendency, found amongst all the players in the system, towards consultation and negotiation, associated with a low incidence of industrial disputes. Foreign observers and practitioners accustomed to thinking of trade unions as 'wage machines', that is, prosecutors of an active wage policy, formulating and arguing wage claims and backing them up with threats of strike action, find it difficult to understand the extreme wage moderation practised by Dutch unions.[4] To put the point strongly: Dutch union leaders always appear embarrassed to have to put wage claims. They immediately provide escape routes to employers and government, offering continued moderation in return for particular benefits. Wage moderation is the continuous factor, though its rationale varies over time (Akkermans, 1985).

The membership problem of Dutch unions must be seen against this background. The wide range of factors which influence individual decisions to join or leave unions can be grouped into five categories.[5] The first involves the sociology of unionism, looking to union structure as the key issue and seeing in centralised bureaucracy a deterrent to the recruitment and retention of members. Secondly, the sociology of labour emphasises changes in the objective position of labour. Thirdly, political economy focuses upon the part played by government and employer policies. Fourthly, consumer economics points to union policies and products which are unsatisfactory to potential and actual members. Finally, the sociology of culture seeks an explanation in changing worker values and postulates the emergence of the 'new worker'. These five theoretical approaches to union membership difficulties are now considered in turn.

Inhospitable Union Structures

Since Robert Michels and Max Weber, bureaucratic and distant structures have provided a classic theme in the sociology of unionism. Indeed, as a leading factor behind the inability of unions to maintain membership, bureaucratic centralisation has been proved highly relevant (Van de Vall, 1967). Since Dutch unions are hardly present at the workplace, workers are not able to 'meet them in person' (Windmuller, 1969, pp. 182–207). The emergence of fewer and bigger unions during the last two decades as a result of mergers has also contributed to increased distance between the rank and file and the leadership.

Within the two main trade union federations (FNV and CNV) separate youth organisations exist and possess rather more autonomy than their counterparts abroad. Youth organisations in German and English unions are more confined to propaganda and training. The relative autonomy of Dutch youth organisations gives free rein for politicisation and even opposition to official union policies of wage moderation. For a while, especially in the 1960s, this option attracted young people to unions. However, the influence of this attribute may be reversed at present, in that scope for political action no longer attracts young members. At the same time, the relationship between youth organisations and their federations has considerably worsened, which has in turn adversely affected their image.

The Fragmentation of the Working Class

Both social scientists and union officials (Visser, 1985) have in recent years noted that the old working class has been 'quartered' by several social developments. High unemployment has divided workers and caused direct loss of members (Visser, D., 1984); marginal employment creation occurs in union-hostile sectors; changing work patterns, for example greater flexibility of work, impede unionisation; the qualification structure of employment has changed in favour of less unionised strata (Kern and Schumann, 1984; Buitelaar, 1988).

The Political–economic Context: the Mangling of Unions

The fragmentation of the working class has been furthered by important political–economic developments, especially youth-related policies on the part of the state and the employers (Ygnace, 1987). A decline in the importance of unions is linked to greater initiative on the part of management (Ammassari, 1986). Declining trade union strength in industrial countries is also linked to the growth of deregulation. The inability or unwillingness of the state to guarantee social welfare and stability, combined with high unemployment, creates a vacuum in legal–political bargaining power that employers exploit in an effort to roll back social policies (Lecher, 1987).

The deregulatory trend contrasts with the pluralism which prevailed in the 1960s, and the corporatism of the 1970s.[6] A few exceptions to the trend must be noted: Sweden, of course, and, in some respects, France, with the Auroux laws (Erbes-Seguin 1986). However, in the Netherlands, particularly in the youth context, the trend can be observed at full strength. Dutch government and employers are pursuing policies to reduce the earnings of young people. The rationale is similar to that advanced in Britain by the Thatcher government: the level of youth wages is depicted as one of the two leading causes of youth unemployment (Ryan, 1987a). The post-1982 Lubbers government has accordingly cut the youth minimum wage.

The other factor to which youth unemployment is attributed is insufficient education and work experience. To combat youth unemployment, the Dutch government has developed a number of job creation programmes, amongst which especially the Youth Employment Guarantee Scheme stands out. It aims ambitiously to find jobs, or at least useful activities, for all unemployed youngsters (up to 25), in return for which they continue to receive social allowances. Another example is a proposal for 'city watches' in the biggest cities, serving the multiple function of policeman, meter reader and rubbish collector. An experiment along these lines will be financed from funds raised in the context of youth employment schemes (Van Dijk, Akkermans and Hövels, 1988).

In the public sector, the Home Minister has reached an agreement with the civil service unions about the spending of the resources freed by the reduction of youth salaries. Union suggestions include special assistance for ethnic minorities and childcare, together with special activities for youth working in the Department of Defence. The resulting suggestions are passed to the various departments for implementation.

Unemployment has already declined thanks to these programmes (OECD, 1988b) although the Central Planning Office ascribes the result to job creation based on economic growth. In any case, unemployment has been falling even faster amongst the younger than amongst the older age groups. During the last four years roughly 90 per cent of school-leavers have found a job within one year. These changes have been accompanied by a considerable reduction in the purchasing power of youngsters, which is especially relevant to their perception of union policies.

Unsatisfactory Union Policies

Attractive products attract buyers and vice versa. In this approach, trade unions are viewed, and define themselves, as 'companies' exploring consumer markets, developing products, competing with other 'companies' to sell their products. Politicisation gives way to marketing. The apparent implication is that unions should pay more attention to young people as a target category. Youth has indeed been chosen as the most important target category and Dutch unions have attempted, albeit weakly, to make their products and themselves more attractive to young people.

However, the unions have not managed to develop successful policies – at least not policies robust enough to stem attacks by competitors, the employers and the state. The underlying difficulty is that the price of union services is obvious to the buyer, in that the cost is felt, whereas the product is either not an individual good or is not visible as such. Wage improvements may thus not be attributed to union efforts, particularly under the Dutch system of making collective agreements generally binding. Under such conditions, improvements in employment are attributed to government policy and to the hiring practices of individual employers, whereas unions are blamed for not preventing cuts in salaries and social security.

The 'New Worker'

In contrast to the extensive research which has been devoted to the four preceding lines of explanation, the possibility that trade unionism is not part of the reference framework of youth, as part of the broader culture of the 'new worker', has received little attention.

The fourth factor considered above, unsuitable union policies, implied a utilitarian approach to unionism (Van Ham, Paauwe and Williams, 1985). Assuming a pragmatic rather than an ideological stance, people join (or leave) unions because of their satisfaction (or dissatisfaction) with union policies. The present approach focusses in addition upon the criteria which workers use when evaluating union policies.

This chapter pays special attention to the question of worker criteria because of its relative unfamiliarity. Evidence of its importance is widespread (Akkermans, 1986, pp. 184–5), notably in the rise of consumerism, or even hedonism, which some researchers believe to have become an increasingly important reason for seeking work (Godschalk, 1986; Guffens, 1985). According to research conducted at the CNV federation,

> Potential members can have different motives for joining trade unions. For example, ideological reasons, or because of a desire for solidarity with a particular social group. In the past these kind of motives were predominant. In contrast individuals now seem to join for more materialistic and pragmatic reasons. Until 1985 Dutch trade unions were not really able to respond adequately to these changing motives. They still tried to attract members on the base of moral and ideological arguments. (Paauwe, 1987, p.2)

Awareness of changing cultural factors is widespread, but values and motives are often mixed up. Three examples illustrate a general but vague awareness. Firstly, the Director of the European Trade Union

Institute sees a new view of work amongst young people, reflecting a new way of life and resistant to the traditional pattern of the trade unions. Training and education play an important role in young people's expectations of the future. They give high moral and political importance to peace and disarmament, environmental protection and opposition to racism and xenophobia (Koepke, 1987, p.13).

Secondly, young people (age less than 27 years) questioned about employment and unemployment, trade unions and social problems showed different attitudes according to age and union membership. For example, the percentage agreeing with the statement that 'we must solve unemployment together and foreigners must therefore not be ordered to leave the country' amounted to 56 per cent amongst school-leavers, 67 per cent amongst the young unemployed, as against 73–4 per cent amongst both members of the CNV youth section and young non-members in employment (De Graaf and Paauwe, 1984, Appendix V).

Thirdly, a survey sponsored by the youth organisation of a major union (AbvaKabo) proves almost devoid of awareness of a cultural factor. Three categories of young worker are distinguished: school-leavers who are in need of information about unions; employed non-members who 'do not feel at home' in unions; and members whose main explanation of their membership is 'social pressure' by their family, friends and colleagues (*Jongeren en de Vakbond*, 1986).[7]

The concept of the 'new worker' clearly requires clarification. To explain why workers do or do not join a union and why interest in unions is on the decrease amongst young people we will take the hypothesis of the new worker as a starting point. As indicated above, the literature characterises the new worker in terms of a hedonistically coloured individualism which pushes into the background any interest in the classical labour problem of inequality in society and which replaces it with attention to more 'modern' problems, such as environmental ones. Because new workers are mostly young, we can expect this generation of youngsters, who grew up in relative wealth, to be characterised by a so-called post-materialistic value orientation (Inglehart, 1977). This orientation places particular value upon the environment, co-determination and free speech.

At the same time, the individualism of the new worker implies a low interest in everything to do with conventional politics and even goes hand in hand with a rather traditional and conservative attitude. This traditionalism and conservatism shows itself in the political sphere; in opinions about such socioeconomic issues as income redistribution and such sociocultural topics as euthanasia, abortion, gender-based roles, education and teaching. The CNV research project cited above also suggests that the new worker also has a rather negative and intolerant attitude towards strangers and foreigners, an attribute which is becoming an important issue in Dutch public debate.

Such a combination of hedonistic individualism, lack of political interest and conservative opinions is unfavourable to interest in membership of trade unions, which try to organise workers on the basis of such values as solidarity, progressive politics and social reform.

To see how far the new worker in the Netherlands *anno* 1985 exists and explains the lack of interest in unions amongst young workers, we contrast the cultural profiles of the following categories: (i) younger workers vis-à-vis older workers; (ii) union members vis-à-vis non-members, both in general and separately for younger and older sub-categories. The cultural profile of the new worker, as sketched above, should then emerge amongst the younger rather than the older workers and amongst the younger non-members rather than amongst their contemporaries who are members of unions.

7.3   DATA AND RESULTS

Our analysis is based upon a national survey of 3003 Dutch people aged between 18 and 70 years.[8] The present sample is restricted to persons employed for at least 15 hours per week, excluding therefore, *inter alia*, the self-employed, the unemployed, pensioners, the disabled, persons engaged mostly in housework, students and part-timers on short hours. In order to compare age groups we select further, limiting the sample to 18–29-year-olds on the one hand and 45–64-year-olds on the other. The result is a sample of 647 employed respondents, divided into young and old groups, and into union members and non-members. Union density is estimated at 23 per cent amongst younger workers, as opposed to 35 per cent amongst older workers and 26 per cent overall (Table 7.5, Table 7A.1, below).

For the empirical delineation of the 'ideal type' new worker, as sketched in the preceding section, we use indicators of economic and cultural conservatism; opinions on work; political party preference; political participation, interest and alienation; materialism and post materialism; localism; authoritarianism, anomy and ethnocentrism; and finally opinions about education and the environment. The

Table 7.5   Sample size by age and union membership

Age	Members	Non-members	Total
18–29	61	295	356
45–64	101	190	291
Total	162	485	647

Notes: Further breakdowns in Table 7A.1.
Source: SOCON.

survey unfortunately provides no direct evidence of attitudes to trade unionism. The questions from which the data derive are provided in Appendix B.

Four paired categories are contrasted:

(a) union members, 18–29 years, and non-members of the same age group;
(b) union members, 45–64 years, and non-members of the same age group;
(c) all union members and all non-members;
(d) all 18–29 years olds with all 45–64-year-olds.

Some tabular comparisons of paired groups make use of percentages, others mean factor scores. In the former case, the size of the differences is indicated by Cramer's V, in which case we also mention if the coefficient concerned is significant at the 5 per cent level (alpha equals 0.05). In the latter case, factor scores are standardised around a mean of 500 and a standard deviation of 100 and the significance of the differences in mean scores is indicated by the eta coefficient, again at the 5 per cent level.[9]

Cultural and Economic Conservatism

In the Netherlands, conservatism has two distinct forms: economic and cultural (Felling and Peters, 1986). Economic conservatism expresses itself in resistance to the equalisation of incomes, government intervention and militant trade unionism. Cultural conservatism resists unrestricted freedom of expression; rejects such life-affecting interventions as euthanasia, abortion and suicide; and favours a traditional differentation between the roles of men and women.

We compare the various groups in terms of these six distinct dimensions, which when scaled and integrated yield two combined scales, measuring economic and cultural conservatism respectively (Table 7.6). Taking cultural conservatism first, it appears that all four comparisons yield significant differences on the total scale. Non-members are more conservative than members, both as a whole and within the two age groups; older workers are more conservative than younger ones.

Closer inspection of the three sub-scales reveals differences in cultural conservatism by group. Differences in cultural conservatism are more marked by age than by membership, with the difference most marked in terms of attitude to life-affecting interventions (Table 7.6, columns 10–13). Differences by membership status prove significant in only two areas. The first involves freedom of expression, where older members prove significantly less conservative than their non-member contemporaries: only 23 per cent of the former group is strongly opposed, as against 35 per cent of the latter group. Differences between members and non-members amongst young workers are however much smaller on this issue, with 15 and 20 per cent respectively strongly opposing.

The second area of significant differences by membership status concerns attitudes to the differentiation of gender roles. Here a significant difference emerges only amongst the young, with union members again significantly less conservative than non-members (mean scores 457 and 487 respectively, as against 499 and 512 respectively amongst older workers).

Differences in economic conservatism are smaller than expected in terms of issues as central to unions as income redistribution and union militancy. In terms of income levelling and government intervention, older workers are significantly more conservative than younger workers, the proportions of respondents who were at most weakly opposed to income redistribution amounting to 60 and 49 per cent respectively and, for government intervention in pursuit of that end, 69 and 57 per cent.

However a further difference is that young union members take the lead in both areas. A much higher proportion of members than of non-members amongst the young expresses a progressive standpoint on both income redistribution (74 against 57 per cent) and public intervention (82 against 66 per cent).

In sum, inter-generational differences dominate in patterns of conservatism, even on such issues of vital interest to unions and their members as income levelling and union militancy. The cultural profile of the new worker is particularly visible amongst young non-members, who prove, at least on the cultural issues, more conservative than young members.

Bourgeois Mentality, Individualism, Social Criticism and the Work Ethic

We now investigate whether the cultural profile of the new worker is further characterised by individualism, bourgeois values, rejection of the traditional work ethic and low interest in the classic labour movement problem of social inequality. All are measured by factor scores (Table 7.7).

We interpret a bourgeois value orientation in terms of two aspects, namely familial and economic mentality (Felling, Peters and Schreuder, 1983). A familial bourgeois mentality is one strongly oriented to the family, marriage and children, whereas its economic counterpart attaches high importance to profession, career and financial security.

Hedonistically coloured individualism is measured in two ways. The first is a hedonistic value orientation, in which enjoying life and *carpe diem* are central. The second involves an autonomous attitude to life which rejects subjection to rules and dependence on others, seeking to decide for oneself what can and what may be done. A social–critical value orientation expresses political and economic egalitarianism, in attaching importance to breaking down existing power relations and building a truly democratic society, as well as seeking less social and economic inequality. Finally, rejection of the work ethic is measured by the extent to which one sees work as a natural duty of man.

The data indicate that social criticism (and the linked issue of interest in social inequality) is present to similar extent amongst all categories, old and young, members and non-members alike (Table 7.7). Differences emerge however on the other criteria, particularly bourgeois attitudes and the work ethic. Older workers are much more bourgeois, especially on familial issues, than younger workers (scores of 522 and 460 respectively). The opinion that work is a natural duty of man is also held more widely amongst older workers (516 versus 473).

There is also a significant difference within the youth category between members and non-members. Young non-members are more strongly oriented than young members to marriage and the family (respective scores of 467 and 428) and to the traditional work ethic (479 and 445).

Table 7.6 Cultural and economic conservatism by union membership and age (percentages and factor scores)

Criterion	Statement	Group responses (percentages or mean scores)									Test statistics for intergroup differences			
		(1)	(2)	(3)	(4)	(5)	(6)	(7)	(8)	(9)	(10)	(11)	(12)	(13)
Against full freedom of expression	Weak	54	43	46	25	49	36	45	32	39	0.09	0.21*	0.12*	0.15*
	Medium	31	37	31	40	31	38	36	37	36				
	Strong	15	20	23	35	20	26	19	31	25				
Against life-affecting interventions	Weak	43	31	31	25	35	29	33	27	30	0.10	0.10	0.07	0.11*
	Medium	51	57	56	55	54	56	56	55	56				
	Strong	7	12	13	20	11	15	11	18	14				
Traditional view of women[+]		457	487	499	512	484	497	482	507	494	0.13*	0.06	0.06	0.13*
Cultural conservatism[+]		446	484	491	524	475	499	476	512	493	0.16*	0.16*	0.11*	0.19*
Resistance to income levelling	Weak	74	57	55	45	62	52	60	49	55	0.14*	0.10	0.09*	0.12*
	Medium	20	38	37	45	30	41	35	42	38				
	Strong	7	5	8	10	7	7	5	9	7				
Resistance to government intervention	Weak	82	66	55	57	65	63	69	57	63	0.14*	0.04	0.04	0.19*
	Medium	7	7	2	3	4	6	7	3	5				
	Strong	11	27	43	40	31	32	24	41	32				
Resistance to union militancy	Weak	35	39	32	34	33	37	39	33	36	0.09	0.04	0.05	0.11*
	Medium	44	33	33	29	37	32	35	30	33				
	Strong	21	28	35	37	30	31	26	36	31				

	(1)	(2)	(3)	(4)	(5)	(6)	(7)	(8)	(9)	(10)	(11)	(12)	(13)
Economic conservatism[+]	471	490	504	519	491	502	487	514	499	0.08	0.07	0.05	0.14*
N (sample size) Min	59	289	101	187	160	476	348	288	636				
Max	61	295	101	190	162	485	356	291	647				

Notes: Asterisk denotes significantly different from zero (p = 0.05). [+] mean standardised factor scores (percentages otherwise).

Columns: (1)–(9) give group percentages and scores –
(1) Union members 18–29 years
(2) Non-members 18–29 years
(3) Union members 45–64 years
(4) Non-members 45–64 years
(5) Union members, both age groups
(6) Non-members, both age groups
(7) All 18–29-year-olds
(8) All 45–64-year-olds
(9) All 18–29 and 45–64-year-olds

(10)–(13) give test statistics (Eta/V) for intergroup differences –
(10) between members and non-members amongst 18–29-year-olds
(11) between members and non-members amongst 45–64-year-olds
(12) between members and non-members amongst both age groups
(13) between 18–29-year-olds and 45–64-year-olds

Source: SOCON.

Table 7.7   Value orientations and traditional work ethic by membership and age (mean standardised factor scores)

Criterion	Group responses									Test statistic for intergroup differences			
	(1)	(2)	(3)	(4)	(5)	(6)	(7)	(8)	(9)	(10)	(11)	(12)	(13)
Bourgeois, familial	428	467	528	519	490	487	460	522	488	0.14*	0.05	0.01	0.30*
Bourgeois, economic	457	520	496	491	481	508	509	493	502	0.25*	0.03	0.13*	0.09*
Autonomy	489	503	469	493	477	499	500	485	493	0.06	0.11*	0.10*	0.09*
Hedonism	515	535	479	468	493	509	531	472	505	0.08	0.05	0.07	0.29*
Socially critical	505	497	505	493	505	496	499	497	498	0.03	0.06	0.04	0.01
Pro work ethic	445	479	520	514	489	493	473	516	492	0.14*	0.03	0.01	0.22*
N1	61	290	100	181	161	471	351	281	632				
N2	39	182	56	109	95	291	221	165	386				

Notes: N2 is sample size for work ethic responses, N1 for all others; asterisk denotes significantly different from zero (p = 0.05)

Columns: (1)–(9) give group mean factor scores –
(1)   Union members 18–29 years
(2)   Non-members 18–29 years
(3)   Union members 45–64 years
(4)   Non-members 45–64 years
(9)   All 18–29 and 45–64-year-olds
(5)   Union members, both age groups
(6)   Non-members, both age groups
(7)   All 18–29-year-olds
(8)   All 45–64-year-olds

(10)–(13) give test statistics (Eta/V) for intergroup differences –
(10)   between members and non-members amongst 18–29-year-olds
(11)   between members and non-members amongst 45–64-year-olds
(12)   between members and non-members amongst both age groups
(13)   between 18–29-year-olds and 45–64-year-olds

Source: SOCON.

The difference between the two groups with respect to the economic side of bourgeois mentality follows the same pattern but proves stronger still (520 versus 457) and dominates inter-group differences on that issue. What may be termed a 'yuppie' mentality is thus most extensive amongst non-member young workers.

Autonomy and especially hedonism are by contrast differentiated mainly by age. A hedonistic orientation to life provides the leading difference between young and older workers (mean scores 531 and 472 respectively). Differences in autonomy (500 and 485) follow the same pattern but are considerably smaller. Membership is not however irrelevant to these criteria. Although differences between the mean scores of members and non-members in terms of autonomy and hedonism are not great, they do point systematically in a single direction, viz. that non-members are more attached to autonomy and hedonistic values than are members.

In summary, as in the case of cultural and economic conservatism, differences between age groups dominate in terms of bourgeois mentality and individualism (including autonomy and enjoyment of life). In addition, it appears possible to detect a type of young worker with a noticeably traditional-bourgeois and individualistic inclination. This new worker is to be found mostly amongst non-members. Young members of unions exhibit such values much less frequently. Finally, the anticipated differences between worker categories in interest in social inequality do not emerge in practice: scores are highly similar on this criterion across all categories of worker.

Political Attitudes and Party Preferences

Several indicators permit comparison of political attitudes by age and union membership:

(a) Party preference: the party for which the respondent would vote in elections for the Second Chamber of Parliament. Amongst young workers, considerable differences emerge according to union membership status (Table 7.8). Young union members are more prone than are non-members to vote for the PvdA (social democratic, 40 and 37 per cent respectively), small left-wing parties (21 and 5 per cent) and D66 (progressive liberal; 8 and 4 per cent), and less inclined towards the CDA (christian democrats; 17 and 21 per cent respectively) and the

VVD (conservative liberal; 9 and 28 per cent). The differences between these preferences for the small left parties and for the right-wing VVD are both particularly striking. Differences in party preference are also visible between younger and older workers, particularly in terms of preference for the CDA (20 and 39 per cent respectively) and the PvdA (38 and 30 per cent). It is also noteworthy that younger workers are more widely inclined than are older ones to prefer the right-wing VVD (24 and 18 per cent), reflecting the exceptionally high support for that party amongst young non-unionists.

(b) Political self-rating, where the respondent rates himself as left to right on a 10 point scale. Young union members consider themselves outspokenly left-wing far more frequently than do their non-union contemporaries (45 per cent as against 22 per cent). Age differences are however insignificant.

(c) Political participation, conventional and unconventional (Elsinga, 1984). Conventional participation denotes involvement in such political activities as political discussions, attending political meetings and activity on behalf of a political party. Such activities relate to the institutionalised political process. By contrast, unconventional participation stands outside mainstream channels of political activity, involving *inter alia* petitions, boycotts, demonstrations and the occupation of buildings, generally in protest against government policy.

Older workers are more likely than are young workers to participate strongly in conventional political activities (45 and 27 per cent respectively) whereas younger workers are the more active in terms of unconventional political activities (29 and 46 per cent). The difference by union membership is striking for both types of political participation amongst young workers. Amongst those who are unionists, 48 and 73 per cent participate strongly in conventional and in unconventional activities respectively, whereas only 24 and 40 per cent of young non-unionists do the same.

(d) Materialistic and post-materialistic value orientation: following Inglehart (1979), the importance attached to such issues as a stable economy, economic growth, the maintenance of public order and a strong army; and to such so-called post-materialistic matters as political participation, freedom of expression and a less impersonal society.

The contrast between the greater materialism (and lesser post-materialism) of the older relative to the younger workers is striking, but not as much as that between members and non-members amongst older workers. If the growth of post-materialism is seen as a generational phenomenon, differences by age should be the most marked of all. In fact, although age-based differences are significant and in the expected direction, those between (older) members and non-members are far greater. Amongst the former 23 per cent are outspokenly post-materialistic, as against only 11 per cent amongst older non-members; similarly, 35 per cent of older non-members are outspokenly materialistic, as against only 19 per cent of union members belonging to the same generation.

(e) Political interest: the extent of the respondent's knowledge of politics and his perception of politics as important enough to keep himself well informed. It is striking to find that older workers show more interest in politics than do young workers (scores of 533 and 489 respectively). Furthermore there is a strong difference within the younger age group, between the much greater interest in politics of union members than of non-members (543 and 479 respectively).

(f) Political alienation, which reflects the respondent's self-perceived influence on politics, the perceived complexity of politics and the degree to which he or she thinks that politicians and political parties are really concerned with voters' interests. As was the case for materialist values, differences between members and non-members amongst older workers prove the most marked, with older members much less alienated from politics than are their non-member contemporaries (mean scores 465 and 507 respectively). Differences by age are however insignificant on this criterion.

(g) Ethnocentrism and the environment. Younger workers prove less nationalistic than older workers (scores of 472 and 504 respectively) and union members, both older and younger, are less ethnocentric than non-members. However, differences in ecological awareness and commitment are visible only amongst young workers, where they are strongly associated with union membership.

In summary, in contrast to finding conservatism and social values, inter-group differences in political attitudes pivot more around union membership than around age. Left-wing political preferences and self-image, intensive political participation, both conventional and unconventional, as well as strong political interest all clearly distinguish union members from non-members within the youth cohort. Insofar as the new worker has to be sought amongst the young non-members, there is evidence in that category of widespread lack of political interest and apathy. Non-membership of unions amongst young workers is itself clearly associated with such attitudes.

Table 7.8 Political attitudes by union membership and age group

Criterion	Statement	Group responses (percentages or mean scores)									Test statistics for intergroup differences			
		(1)	(2)	(3)	(4)	(5)	(6)	(7)	(8)	(9)	(10)	(11)	(12)	(13)
Political party preference	Small left	21	5	4	3	10	4	8	3	6	0.28*	0.12	0.17*	0.22*
	PvdA	40	37	31	29	34	34	38	30	34				
	D66	8	4	6	7	7	5	5	6	6				
	CDA	17	21	43	36	33	27	20	39	29				
	VVD	9	28	15	20	13	24	24	18	21				
	Small right	6	5	1	5	3	5	5	4	4				
Political self-rating	Left	45	22	27	19	33	21	25	22	24	0.21*	0.10	0.13	0.04
	Centre	23	46	40	46	35	46	43	44	43				
	Right	32	32	33	36	32	33	32	35	33				
Political participation: conventional	Weak	3	22	6	16	5	20	20	12	16	0.23*	0.19*	0.24*	0.19*
	Medium	48	54	39	45	42	51	53	43	49				
	Strong	48	24	55	39	53	29	27	45	35				
Political participation: non-conventional	Weak	3	14	18	29	13	20	12	25	19	0.24*	0.13	0.11	0.19*
	Medium	24	46	49	44	42	45	42	46	44				
	Strong	73	40	33	27	45	35	46	29	37				
Materialistic	Very	23	19	19	35	20	25	20	28	24	0.09	0.23*	0.09	0.13*
	Ordinary	26	37	36	27	33	33	35	31	33				
Post-materialistic	Very	29	21	23	11	25	27	22	16	19				
	Ordinary	23	23	22	27	22	25	23	25	24				

	(1)	(2)	(3)	(4)	(5)	(6)	(7)	(8)	(9)	(10)	(11)	(12)	(13)
Political interest	543	479	550	522	548	496	489	533	509	0.24*	0.13	0.23*	0.22*
Political alienation	462	492	465	507	464	498	488	490	489	0.12	0.18*	0.15*	0.01
Ethnocentrism	444	477	469	527	461	496	472	504	487	0.14*	0.28*	0.16*	0.17*
Environment: activism	557	495	517	492	529	494	504	502	503	0.23*	0.12	0.16*	0.01
Environment: sacrifice	538	492	532	506	534	498	499	516	507	0.17*	0.14	0.17*	0.09

Notes: Asterisk denotes significantly different from zero ($p = 0.05$); sample sizes in Table 7A.2.

Columns: (1)–(9) give group percentages and scores –
(1) Union members 18–29 years
(2) Non-members 18–29 years
(3) Union members 45–64 years
(4) Non-members 45–64 years
(5) Union members, both age groups
(6) Non-members, both age groups
(7) All 18–29-year-olds
(8) All 45–64-year-olds
(9) All 18–29 and 45–64-year-olds

(10)–(13) give test statistics (Eta/V) for intergroup differences –
(10) between members and non-members amongst 18–29-year-olds
(11) between members and non-members amongst 45–64-year-olds
(12) between members and non-members amongst both age groups
(13) between 18–29-year-olds and 45–64-year-olds

Source: SOCON.

7.4   DISCUSSION AND CONCLUSIONS

We have sketched above the cultural profile of different categories of male employees in the Netherlands in 1985, comparing older and younger workers, union members and non-members. Special attention has been given to the postulated concept of the new worker, who is expected to show up primarily amongst young workers who are not union members.

Clear differences have emerged between younger and older workers on the large majority of criteria, corresponding in most cases to conventional expectation. One result is somewhat surprising: the economic aspects of bourgeois mentality, that is, orientation towards profession, career and financial security, which more often characterise younger than older workers.

The most distinctive contrast between young and old involves the extent of hedonistic attitudes amongst the young. We have not found, as might be expected, a widespread tendency amongst youth towards social criticism, but rather a *carpe diem* attitude geared to the enjoyment of life. This mentality is in the Netherlands *anno* 1985 the most important trade mark of workers between 18 and 29 years of age. In politics we have found that it is not the older but the younger workers who favour most frequently the conservative liberal party (VVD). Furthermore, older workers proved to be the more active where conventional political activities are concerned, although younger workers show more extensive unconventional political participation. Finally, younger workers are generally less interested in politics than older workers.

We expect the cultural profile of the new worker to manifest itself most clearly amongst unorganised young workers and we have found that the empirical properties of the latter category correspond broadly to the 'ideal type' cultural profile. We do find amongst 18–29-year-old workers who do not belong to a trade union the common occurrence of a distinctive combination of hedonistic individualism, lack of political interest and traditional and conservative opinions in a number of areas.

The most important departure from the 'ideal type' is the finding that amongst the new workers interest in more 'modern' social problems such as the ecological problem does not replace interest in the classical labour problem of social inequality. On this issue, as indeed on others, young non-members are less interested and involved than are young unionists. All in all, we have observed that the new worker has a rather traditional and conservative attitude, tending towards living on one's own and for oneself, mainly oriented towards career and financial security and, consequently, with little inclination towards political or social involvement.

Although the scope of our study is limited – in particular we cannot establish definitively a structural shift from such a snapshot – the new worker who emerges from our analyses constitutes a difficult category, one even scarcely approachable, for the recruitment activities of Dutch trade unions. Insofar as unions present themselves on the basis of the values of solidarity, progressiveness and social reform, the new worker will not find them attractive at all. In combination with the other factors which contribute to the decline of union membership, unions face almost no prospect of creating interest within this category of worker. On the other hand, were unions to adapt their recruitment policies to the cultural profile of the new worker, the result would probably involve a fundamental loss of identity, which might in the longer term endanger the survival of the unions. The upshot might appear to be that trade unions can best write off the new worker as a potential member because the cultural crevasse between them is too broad to be bridged.

The importance of cultural change does not rule out a role for the other explanations discussed in section 7.2 above. The environment in which unions operate is changing in other respects as well. Although unemployment, especially long term unemployment, remains high in the Netherlands, youth unemployment is on the decline. The baby boom has worked itself out and more young people remain longer in school. More young workers have a less favourable opinion of the union movement *qua* individual and collective products and *qua* social appeal, as a friendly society. Indeed, evidence of widespread trainee expectations that a union will be of use for getting a job is consistent with this utilitarian cultural pattern (Hughes and Brinkley, 1979; Baethge et al., 1988).

We conclude therefore that the future of unions is less than rosy. It remains to be seen whether attempts to develop new products for new markets and to improve cooperation between unions will suffice to alter the course of events. Evidence of adaptation in union strategies can already be seen in increasing concentration on interest representation instead of broader political action; in 'one issue' work, for example, on vocational education; in sector-specific programmes; and in better public relations.

However, as long as the Dutch union movement retains an identity and an image in terms of a broad social movement, or particularly a worker movement, we must predict that it will remain small. Any opening towards growth must depend upon meeting the aspirations of the new workers. This however would require some sacrifice of identity. The strategic problem is most difficult for the FNV, which still claims to represent the whole spectrum of employment. The CNV federation has at least the safety of its 'own' recruitment ground: workers who desire an organisation based on Christian principles. The higher cadre grouping, MHP, has as its recruitment category people who more commonly prefer a utilitarian approach. But the FNV in particular must face tough choices as it seeks an optimal balance between few and new.

APPENDIX A: SOCON DATA ON UNIONISM

Estimates of the extent of unionisation at the end of 1985:

(a)   C.B.S. (including people looking for work): 29.0 per cent.
(b)   SOCON (in employment for at least 35 hours per week): 26.3 per cent.

Table 7A.1   Union membership by age in SOCON data

| | Age category | | | | |
	18–29	*30–39*	*40–49*	*50–64*	*All*
Overall density (%)	17.1	26.6	32.7	34.2	26.3
Absolute numbers (000s)					
Members					
FNV	43	81	49	33	206
CNV	12	9	20	14	55
MHP	1	9	10	8	28
Other[a]	5	8	9	8	30
All unions	61	107	88	63	319
Non-members	295	296	181	121	893
Total	356	403	269	184	1 212

Notes to Table 7A.1

a Including AbvaKabo.

FNV: Federatie Nederlandse Vakbeweging (Federation of Dutch Trade Unions) (Social-Democratic)

CNV: Christelijk Nationaal Vakverbond (Christian National Trade Union Federation)

MHP: Vakcentrale voor Middelbaar en Hoger Personeel (Trade Union Federation of Cadre and Higher Personnel)

AbvaKabo: Algemene Bond Van Ambtenaren/Katholieke Ambtenaren Bond (Amalgamated General and Catholic Union of Public Employees).

Table 7A.2 Numbers of respondents to political preference questions by question and respondent category

Question	*Respondent Category*								
	(1)	*(2)*	*(3)*	*(4)*	*(5)*	*(6)*	*(7)*	*(8)*	*(9)*
Party preference	53	205	84	152	137	357	258	236	494
Self-rating	31	171	67	101	98	272	202	168	370
Participation, conventional	31	179	71	113	102	292	210	184	394
Participation, non-conventional	29	148	67	107	96	255	177	174	351
Materialism	31	174	69	107	100	281	205	176	381
Interest, alienation	31	172	71	108	102	280	203	179	382
Ethnocentrism	30	167	66	102	96	269	197	168	365
Environment (both)	30	164	65	105	95	269	194	170	364

Note: Questions and groups as in Table 7.8.

Source: SOCON.

APPENDIX B: SOCON QUESTIONS USED IN THIS ANALYSIS

Cultural and Economic Conservatism (Table 7.6)

Cultural conservatism (total; alpha = 0.57)

a. Against freedom of expression (H = 0.47; Rho = 0.74)

Do you think that everybody in our country ought to be free to do X, or do you think that this freedom should be restricted?

Where X is:

1. Say whatever he/she wants to in public,

2. Write whatever he/she wants to in public,

3. Demonstrate in favour of or against a cause,
4. Criticise the royal house in public,
5. Refuse military service,
6. Occupy buildings such as schools, factories or universities in order to enforce justified demands.

b. Against interference in life (H = 0.52; Rho = 0.72)
1. A married couple chooses to have no children even though there is no medical reason why they shouldn't. Can you accept such an attitude or do you find it unacceptable?
2. Do you think it should be possible for a woman to have an abortion without further discussion if she wants to?
3. Imagine a doctor can put a person out of his pains at his own request by administering an injection. According to you, should he do it or not?
4. According to you, are there circumstances in which abortion should be permitted?
5. Do you think people should have the right to kill themselves if they want to, or do you think this should be prevented?

c. Traditional image of women (alpha = 0.67)
1. A woman is better suited to raise small children than is a man.
2. It isn't really as important for a girl to get a good education as it is for a boy.
3. It cannot be helped, but boys can be brought up freer than girls.
4. It is unnatural if women give guidance to men in industry.

Economic conservatism (total; alpha = 0.71)

a. Resistance to levelling of incomes and status (H = 0.54; Rho = 0.74)
1. Workers still have to struggle for an equal position in society.
2. The differences between classes ought to be smaller than they are at present.
3. Would you like the differences between high and low incomes to become greater or smaller? Or would you like them to remain the same?

b. Resistance to government intervention concerning income levelling (alpha = 0.48)
1. Are you in favour of or against government intervention to reduce income differences, for example?

c. Resistance to militant union policy (alpha = 0.58)
1. The trade unions have to adopt a much harder line if they are to promote workers' interests.
2. The trade unions have to advise their members to vote for the parties that promote workers' interests best.

Value Orientations and Traditional Work Ethic (Table 7.7)

a. Familial bourgeois mentality (alpha = 0.82)
1. The importance of being married
2. The importance of having children and raising them
3. The importance of living for your family
4. The importance of a future for your children
5. The importance of a happy family life

b. Economic bourgeois mentality (alpha = 0.69)
1. The importance of getting on in life
2. The importance of being in a good financial position
3. The importance of social security
4. The importance of the sense of having accomplished something in life

c. Autonomy (alpha = 0.73)
1. The importance of being able to do whatever you like
2. The importance of the possibility of deciding for oneself what is allowed and what is not
3. The importance of not being tied to rules
4. The importance of being independent of anyone

d. Hedonism (alpha = 0.68)
1. The importance of enjoying life
2. The importance of having fun

e. Social criticism (alpha = 0.75)
1. The importance of contributing to the reduction of existing income diferences
2. The importance of promoting greater equality in society
3. The importance of breaking through the existing power relations
4. The importance of an active commitment to a society in which everyone has a voice

f. Traditional work ethic, work as a duty (alpha = 0.82)
1. I feel happiest after having worked hard.
2. If someone wants to enjoy life he ought to be prepared to work hard for it.
3. You can only do what you like after you have done your duty.
4. Work should always come first, even if this means less leisure time.
5. It is an obligation for every citizen who is able to, to contribute to society by working.

Political Party Preference and Political Opinions (Table 7.8)

a. Conventional political participation (H = 0.55; Rho = 0.77)
1. How often do you read about politics in the newspapers?
2. How often do you discuss politics with other people?
3. How often do you try to convince friends to vote the same as you?
4. How often do you work with other people in this community to try to solve some local problem?
5. How often do you attend a political meeting or rally?
6. How often do you contact public officials or politicians?
7. How often do you spend time working for a political party or candidate?

b. Non-conventional political participation (H = 0.54; Rho = 0.81)
Participation in:
1. Petitions
2. Boycotts
3. Lawful demonstration
4. Refusal to pay rent, tax or premiums
5. Unofficial strikes
6. Occupation of buildings
7. Blocking traffic
8. Damaging things
9. Personal violence

c. Materialism
Desirability of:
1. Maintaining order in this country
2. Fighting rising prices
3. High rate of economic growth
4. Strong Dutch army
5. Stable economy
6. Fight against crime

d. Post-materialism

Desirability of:
1. Giving people more say in the decisions of government
2. Protecting freedom of speech
3. Giving people more say in decisions at work and in the community
4. Making cities and countryside more beautiful
5. Striving for a friendlier society
6. Striving for a society in which ideas are more important than money

e. Political interest (alpha = 0.85)
1. I wouldn't know what the political future of our country should look like.
2. It is important for everyone to engage in politics.
3. Most political problems are so complicated that I cannot understand them.
4. I always make thorough enquiries into political developments.
5. I have explicit ideas about the political future of this country.
6. I have little knowledge of politics.

f. Political alienation (alpha = 0.82)
1. People like me have no say at all in what the government does.
2. Sometimes politics and what the government does seem so complicated that a person like me cannot really understand what is going on.
3. I don't think that public officials care much about what people like me think.
4. Those whom we elect as members of parliament lose touch with the people pretty quickly.
5. Parties are only interested in people's votes, not in their opinions.

g. Ethnocentrism (alpha = 0.81)
1. Everywhere in the world Dutch people are beloved.
2. We, the Dutch people, are always ready to put our shoulders to the wheel.
3. Generally speaking, Holland is a better country than most others.
4. We, the Dutch, have reason to be proud of our history.
5. Other countries can learn a lot of good things from our country.

h. Willingness to act over environmental problems (alpha = 0.77)
1. I would take part in a demonstration against more and more industrialisation.
2. I am prepared to support strict public controls on cars and lorries.

3. I would not join a demonstration against felling trees.
4. I wouldn't dream of writing a letter to the papers to protest against an ugly block of flats.
5. If there was a protest meeting against the start of a polluting factory in the neighbourhood, you could expect to find me there.
6. I shall join in with a protest which tries to do something about acid rain.

i. Willingness to make sacrifices for the environment (alpha = 0.69)
1. I am prepared to give up something for a cleaner environment.
2. I would be prepared to pay higher prices if that would mean less industrial pollution.
3. It is a good thing that the government wants to combat water pollution but it must not cost me a penny.

Notes

1.   Earlier versions of this chapter were presented at seminars in Trento (Akkermans and Hövels, 1987) and Palermo. We thank Caspar Hoppe for his contribution to the completion of this chapter.
2.   The three categories by membership density are (Koepke, 1987, p.6):
      (a) 60–90 per cent – Sweden, Denmark, Finland, Norway, Belgium, Luxembourg
      (b) 40–60 per cent – Austria, Great Britain, Ireland, Italy, FR Germany
      (c) 0–40 per cent – France, the Netherlands, Switzerland, Spain, Portugal, Greece.
3.   Although union statistics classify young members variously as those aged less than 25 or 28 years, we adopt 18–29 years as the range of the youth category and 45–64 as that of the old category. We also follow Becker's distinction between four successive generations: (i) 'prewar': born 1910–30; (ii) 'silent': born 1930–40; (iii) 'protest': born 1940–55; (iv) 'lost': born after 1955 (Becker, 1985, 1987). At the time of our study (1985), therefore, our 'old' category combines Becker's first two generations and our 'young' category is identical to his fourth generation. (See also Appendix A.)
4.   An enduringly valuable description of postwar developments in Dutch industrial relations can be found in Windmuller (1969).
5.   Jaap Paauwe distinguishes eleven 'causes of the decline of membership', five related to the socioeconomic context and six internal to unions: (a) contextual: high unemployment; shifting sectoral employment; changing work patterns; regulation of unemployment benefits (with no role for unions); changes in workers' values; (b) internal: union mergers; cost of living allowances; lack of market research; lack of cooperation between unions; lack of 'exclusive' benefits for trade union members; exposure in the mass media (Paauwe, 1987, pp. 1–4).

6. Lecher considers Britain, the US, Japan and France and emphasises four factors: (i) state and private campaigns to weaken unions; (ii) the push for flexibility of labour; (iii) the dismantling of the social state; (iv) the privatization of state functions.

7. For further evidence of the growing awareness within the trade unions see Aaneen (1985), Kranenburg (1985) and Visser, J. (1984).

8. The survey is a part of the research programme 'Social and cultural developments in the Netherlands' (SOCON), a joint project involving Nijmegen and Tilburg Universities. A number of the questions, including those concerning value orientations and conservatism, were put to the full sample of 3,003 respondents. Others, including those on politics and ethnocentrism, were put to only half the sample. The actual response counts are reported in Table 7A.2. However, these two sub-samples, to which different blocks of questions have been put, are constructed in such a way that the groups of 1,500 respondents also form a representative sample of the male Dutch population aged between 18 and 70 years. Fuller documentation of the research base is provided in Felling, Peters and Schreuder (1987).

9. The analysis of SOCON data in this chapter utilises factor analysis (Nie, 1983) and Mokken scale analysis (Mokken, 1971). In the factor analysis, only factors accounting for variances greater than unity were retained. Factor scores were obtained (after recoding negatively formulated variables) using the default regression method in the SPSS-X statistical analysis package, fixing the mean regression factor score for each construct at 500 and the standard deviation at 100. Missing factor scores were left blank. Cronbach's alpha was used as the reliability coefficient. Mokken scale analysis is a stochastic cumulative scaling model which identifies the underlying dimension of a group of variables. Scores on the original variables were combined where appropriate into a single score by counting the number of positive responses to the original variables. The symbol H is the scalability coefficient of the set of variables, the symbol Rho the reliability coefficient.

8 Trade Union Policies towards the Youth Training Scheme in Great Britain: the Arguments[1]
Paul Ryan

. . . you can, friends, even with government, with the MSC and with your own people at times, get tired of arguing (Bill Keys, General Council; TUC, 1985, p. 435).

8.1 INTRODUCTION

The rapid rise of youth unemployment in Britain in the first half of the 1970s (Table 1.1, above) led to a succession of ameliorative policies. The Youth Training Scheme (YTS) stands in the centre of this line of policy development. Introduced in 1983 as direct successor to the Work Experience Programme (1976–8) and the Youth Opportunities Programme (1978–83), YTS was extended in 1986 from a one- to a two-year programme, and reconstituted in 1990 as (New) Youth Training. YTS has also inspired parallel schemes for older workers, primarily young adults, including the Job Training Scheme of 1986–7 (JTS) and Employment Training (ET, 1988–).

YTS has proved the largest and most durable of a wide range of schemes aimed at young people (section 2.4, above). At its peak in the late 1980s, most early school-leavers entered the scheme, spending the bulk of their time in work experience placements with mainstream employers who incurred no immediate payroll costs on their behalf. The resulting threat to trade unions is that the pay and job security of established employees are undermined if employers respond by using YTS trainees for work or training which would otherwise have been performed by regular employees, that is, for 'job substitution'.[2]

Unions have had to decide how to respond to the threat. The simplest reaction is outright rejection, refusing to cooperate with YTS

234

within the union's area of organisation. The alternative is the strategy promoted by the Trades Union Congress (TUC), the collective body to which most unions are affiliated: to accept YTS on condition that its content be open to union regulation and to negotiate safeguards for union interests. These alternatives may be interpreted as variants of exclusion and inclusion under Institutional Regulation (chapter 2, above).

The choice between cooperation and rejection has since 1983 proved a leading area of conflict in the policy-making bodies of both the TUC and many of its affiliates. Although TUC strategy has prevailed at its own annual conferences, the policy-making bodies of one-half of its 40 largest affiliates, accounting for two thirds of the membership, adopted at some point during 1983–8 oppositional stances of varying severity towards it. Those espousing a total boycott of YTS accounted on their own for more than one-fifth of the membership (Ryan, 1991b).

Oppositional policies were rarely adopted continuously throughout the period and were often evaded or ignored when the union's Executive favoured TUC strategy. Nevertheless, they constituted a major obstacle to the success of both TUC strategy and YTS itself, as well as contributing to the collapse of TUC strategy when the government extended YTS principles to the adult unemployed in 1987–8.

This chapter outlines and assesses the arguments advanced within the union movement concerning TUC strategy on YTS. Section 8.2 discusses the threat posed by YTS to union interests. Section 8.3 outlines the content of TUC strategy. The arguments presented by trade unionists for and against it are presented in sections 8.4 and 8.5 respectively and discussed in section 8.6, followed by the conclusions in section 8.7.[3]

Evidence is derived largely from published documents, primarily conference proceedings and union newspapers. The verbatim proceedings of the annual conferences of both the TUC ('Congress') and the public services manual union NUPE, which saw endemic conflict over YTS, have been drawn upon extensively.

Consideration of published materials alone has two drawbacks. Firstly, the formal record is incomplete: several unions reveal little or nothing about their policies in their publications. Secondly, the informal record is absent, in that public pronouncements often exclude sensitive but important considerations, particularly those of a personal and political nature. These two attributes clearly debar any full coverage of the issues raised by YTS. However, the issues raised in public debate range wide and the public stances of trade unionists are of sufficient importance to warrant study in themselves.

8.2 THE YOUTH TRAINING SCHEME: DESIGN AND OPERATION

YTS has provided unemployed young school-leavers with guaranteed access to limited duration, low paid traineeships based primarily upon work experience. The maximum duration of a traineeship rose from one to two years in 1986 with the transition to the two-year scheme (YTS2). The YTS trainee is entitled to a structured programme of training and work experience. At least 25 per cent of trainee time (13 weeks) had to be spent in off-the-job training under YTS1, 21 per cent (20 weeks) under YTS2.[4]

Four characteristics of YTS have been particularly relevant to trade union interests: its emphasis on work experience, its financial attributes, its constituency and its size.

The centrality of work experience to youth intervention goes back to YTS's predecessors, WEP and YOP. Work experience accounted under YTS2 for more than two-thirds of the time spent by trainees in mainstream schemes. The share has fallen over time, as the proportion of trainee time spent in off-the-job training has risen relative to both YOP and the early days of YTS.[5] Nevertheless, the great majority of YTS trainees have spent most of their time on YTS in actual work assignments with participating employers.

Financial Attributes

All YTS participants effectively receive a weekly training allowance paid out of public funds. The first year trainee allowance of £29.50 (£35 in the second year) amounted in April 1989 to around 30 per cent of the average gross pay of 16–17-year-old employees. The allowance had been more generous at the outset: the 1989 figure represented a decline from more than 40 per cent in 1983, or a fall 23 per cent.[6]

YTS places are provided by Managing Agents, most of whom contract out the provision of at least some work experience to external employers.[7] Managing Agents receive a management fee (£110 in 1987/8) and a training grant (£438 and £100 for first and second years respectively) for each trainee year.[8] Wages need not be paid to, nor social security contributions made on behalf of, trainees. Although trade unions have indeed negotiated 'top up' payments and even employee status for a minority, the key point is that most trainees still impose no direct payroll cost upon work experience sponsors.[9]

Managing Agents are required in return to provide trainees with an integrated programme of training and work experience. They must meet the costs of required off-the-job training but against that they can set the remainder of the training grant and – prospectively more important – the value of whatever output trainees produce during work experience, whether provided directly to them or to subcontracting sponsors.

The key to the problem posed by YTS to unions lies here. If employers are required to provide high quality training in costly skills, they will undoubtedly have to subsidise their YTS operations. If however they are permitted to provide low quality training for jobs which require little skill, they will be able to profit from YTS by using trainees as cheap labour.

The rhetoric of YTS suggests the former. A formal regulatory apparatus, including standard setting and enforcement, has been developed to enforce quality standards in YTS training. However, the practice of YTS has only too often indicated the latter. What employers do with trainee work experience has remained largely their own business, reflecting the slow, patchy and even illusory growth of public quality control (Lee, Marsden, Rickman and Duncombe, 1990; Marsden and Ryan, 1991). The bulk of training places have involved low level skills for which training costs are relatively low (Begg, Blake, Deakin and Pratten, 1990). Most work experience placements have been provided in a single location by small employers whose lack of interest in subsidising training is well known (GB TA, 1989b, p. 11).

YTS has thus in practice permitted employers considerable leeway to use work experience not only to offset training costs but even to cut costs and make money. Such activity generally involves the substitution of trainee labour for that of ordinary employees, whether young or adult.

An attempt was made in the initial design of YTS to prevent youth–youth substitution by including an 'additionality' provision: employers who engaged YTS trainees over and above their normal recruitment of young people were to be provided with additional full grants (including trainee allowances) on behalf of two youth employees for every three YTS places offered.[10] The goal was to make YTS a supplement to rather than a substitute for normal youth recruitment.

However, additionality subsidies were soon dropped. Moreover, the importance attached by all interested parties to high levels of trainee transition to employment at the end of YTS projects has encouraged the substitution of YTS for normal youth recruitment and training. The threat of job substitution thus became central to YTS, once hopes of curbing it through additionality subsidies and public quality control had been proved illusory.

Constituency and Size

YTS's target group has comprised almost exclusively the early (16- and 17-year-old) school-leavers who remain so much more numerous in the British labour force than in those of other advanced economies. The unemployment rate of that age group rose to unprecedented heights in the early 1980s. Even in the presence of YTS's predecessor, YOP, the 16–17-year-old unemployment rate exceeded one-third in the early 1980s (Figure 1.1, above).

The fact that almost all participants have entered YTS at 16 or 17 years of age affects its threat to trade union interests. The low experience and skill of 16–17-year-olds makes them technically limited substitutes for many other workers in jobs which require more than minimal levels of skill and responsibility (Ryan, 1987a). Substitution threats are thus likely to focus upon less skilled adult employment and upon entry jobs and apprenticeships for young workers themselves.

The final attribute of YTS of relevance to trade unions is its scale of operation. A mix of incentives and compulsion combined with enduringly high youth joblessness to produce large-scale participation in YTS after its first year of operation.

All unemployed 16-year-olds have since 1980 been guaranteed a place on YOP/YTS by the Christmas after leaving school. In 1987 the guarantee was extended to 17-year-olds under YTS2. Employer use of YTS as a recruitment and screening device for permanent employment encouraged young people to participate (Raffe, 1988). An element of compulsion crept in at an early stage, with 'YTS refusers' made liable to reduction of their social security benefits. It was extended in 1988 by the denial of benefit to 16- and 17-year-olds, who were henceforth to be referred to YTS for placement.

YTS rapidly became the largest single manpower programme in the country. By its peak in 1988/9 more than two million young people had passed through it and three-fifths of all 16–17-year-old school-leavers – one-third of the age cohort – were enrolling in it annually (GB TA, 1989b, Table 1).

The operational attributes of YTS reflect the situation at the end of the 1980s. At its inception in 1982/3, the shape of the scheme was less well defined and more open to optimistic interpretation than it had become by, say, 1986. In particular, the power of additionality subsidies and public quality control as curbs on substitution remained to be tested. However, the centrality of work experience and the low level of employer payroll costs were key features of YTS from the outset. YOP had already provided trade unions with a sense of the difficulties which faced them under YTS. The problem was partly to understand those difficulties, but, more important, to determine how to respond to them.

8.3 TUC STRATEGY

The strategy which the TUC's General Council developed in the early 1980s to counter YTS's threat to union interests was disseminated in a series of publications and meetings during 1982/3 (TUC, 1982, 1983b).[11] Unions were encouraged to accept YTS, subject to regulation of the terms on which trainees function, particularly at the workplace. Union regulation of YTS was to be pursued at two levels: indirectly, through union involvement in the design and operation of special measures such as YTS; directly, through negotiating the content of particular YTS schemes (Ryan, 1989, section II; Keep, 1986).

Taking indirect regulation first, the design and operation of most manpower schemes was undertaken at that time by a set of semi-autonomous multipartite public bodies, on which government, employers, unions, and educators were represented. Organised within the Manpower Services Commission (MSC), the structure comprised the Youth Training Group, which oversaw YTS, the Area Manpower Boards, charged with approving YTS proposals in each locality, and the Programme Review Teams for particular YTS schemes.[12]

The change to YTS2 in 1986 was accompanied by a further elaboration of tripartite structures within the MSC, notably to develop quality control and certification in YTS. The entire panoply of bodies was however swept away in 1988 when the government reacted to the TUC conference's rejection of Employment Training by absorbing these functions into the newly created Training Agency, a vertically administered sub-unit of its Employment Department. YTS has since then been administered and reshaped without union involvement.

Direct regulation of YTS was to be complementary to its indirect counterpart. Unions were to use their newly won decentralised bargaining rights to negotiate improvements in particular YTS schemes. A union faced by proposals for a YTS scheme was urged to ensure that (i) a proper training plan be drawn up and enforced and (ii) the YTS grant be spent wholly on trainees, either as training expenditures or, particularly where training costs were low, as 'top up' payments or employee status for trainees. The TUC encouraged unionists to press non-participating unionised employers to introduce YTS schemes, in order to move YTS activity away from the non-union sector, previously dominant under YOP, where direct regulation of YTS was clearly impossible (TUC, 1982; 1983b; 1984, p. 46).

The TUC strategy towards youth schemes shows similarities to its recently emerged preference for combining legal regulation with collective bargaining instead of relying on collective bargaining alone. The TUC's support for employment protection legislation in the 1970s and a national minimum wage in the 1980s both involved a role for legislation in providing national minimum terms and conditions above which collective bargaining may seek to rise. TUC strategy for YTS also combined national minima, embodied in MSC regulations, with scope for decentralised bargaining of improvements, embodied in union rights to negotiate particular YTS schemes. The YTS strategy had, however, been reached from the opposite direction: its point of departure, YOP, had determined the terms and conditions of its participants solely by national regulation, without provision for the decentralised negotiation of particular schemes.

8.4   ARGUMENTS ADVANCED IN SUPPORT OF TUC STRATEGY

The TUC's strategy has been supported by two main lines of argument, one positive, the other negative. Positive arguments emphasise the scope for successful regulation of YTS along the lines sought by unions. Negative ones concede the failings of YTS but hold that its rejection by unions would only worsen both the scheme and the damage done by it to union interests.

Positive Arguments

The TUC's approach registered early successes in 1982. A long line of union leaders spoke at Congress in favour of YTS, some with enthusiasm and most urging the scope which the scheme offered for implementing TUC strategy and adapting it to union interests – in particular to curb job substitution and to improve terms and conditions for its participants (TUC, 1983a, pp. 477–87).

A key early argument for TUC strategy involved the introduction of YTS itself. It concerned the adjustment of an existing scheme, YOP, in directions sought by the TUC – notably by requiring some training content; by including 'additionality' subsidies and increasing the involvement of unions in quality control; and by requiring unionised YTS sponsors to win the approval of 'recognised and appropriate' trade unions before proposed schemes could proceed. Last but not least, unions won the right to negotiate with particular YTS sponsors terms and conditions for trainees superior to the nationally required minima.

This set of attributes harmonised with the TUC's regulatory aspirations, differentiating YTS from YOP and permitting the presentation of YTS as a clean break from its discredited predecessor: 'a fundamental improvement on the YOP scheme' and 'one area where the TUC can rightly claim that it has made positive progress over the past year'.

An element of uncertainty characterised even early claims on behalf of YTS, in that some supporters of TUC strategy at the 1982 and 1983 Congresses cited the scheme's long-term rather than short-term potential, arguing that, if it were not yet the national training system which unions sought, at least it 'could offer the basis for a permanent two-year scheme of vocational preparation for young people aged 16–19 . . .' (TUC, 1983a, pp. 467, 598; 1984, p. 431).

Regulatory successes

Continuing advocacy of TUC strategy against rejectionist alternatives was helped by evidence of its success. The TUC hoped that increased allowances, employee status (or at least a job offer at the end of the scheme), low substitution and trainee union membership would be won in a wide range of schemes. Evidence of achievements in any or all of these areas could be cited in support of its strategy.

Evidence of successful regulation of YTS was advanced by, for example, the tax officials (IRSF) and construction workers (UCATT) at the 1984 Congress. According to the UCATT speaker, the suggestion has been made that nothing has been accomplished. I would like to tell you what we have achieved in the construction industry. We have welded the YTS onto our scheme of training . . . and of the 20,000 places which are assured each year we have a 97 per cent take-up. It is just not on to say that we must come out of YTS. (TUC, 1985, p. 481)

Two years later, the college lecturers' union, NATFHE, in an otherwise unflattering assessment of union achievements under YTS, praised the YTS agreements secured by USDAW in distribution, involving increased compensation and employee status for trainees, as a 'great step forward' (TUC, 1987, p. 537).

Similarly, the electricians' union (EETPU) pointed out to the 1987 Congress the quadrupling of apprentice-type training volume in electrical contracting since the 1983 joint agreement which re-based its first year upon YTS principles. The electricians challenged unions in other sectors to do similarly but gave YTS itself little credit for the achievement (TUC, 1988, p. 505). Finally, POEU, the telecommunications union, supported YTS at 1983 Congress on the grounds that it had been used in telecommunications to develop a good training scheme which protected existing apprenticeship schemes (TUC, 1984, p. 431).

Successful regulation of YTS was also claimed in intra-union debates. For example, the IRSF Executive pointed out to advocates of a boycott the high training quality of a YTS scheme negotiated at a Telford computing facility, reinforcing the point by quoting a trainee as saying 'I don't feel exploited . . . and there's always someone to turn to if you do' (*Assessment*, Sept 1985; March 1986, p. 5). A delegate to the 1985 APEX conference praised the success of the YTS scheme negotiated by her branch with a major airline (*Apex*, July 1985, p. 15). The 1986 annual report of the Executive of the pottery workers' union, CATU, praised the efforts of the TUC over YTS and claimed that training standards and trainee continuation into employment were both high under YTS in that sector (*Potter*, June 1986).

Evidence of successful recruitment of trainees into unions was also used to support cooperation with YTS. The IRSF Executive's extensive publicity in favour of its YTS scheme at Telford noted that all of the trainees had joined the union (*Assessment*, October 1985). A generally favourable survey of YTS in the steel industry by the steelworkers' journal emphasised high rates of both union membership and transition to employment, amongst trainees in some local schemes (*Phoenix*, August 1988, pp. 14–15).[13]

Achievements other than those on the TUC's immediate agenda were sometimes credited to YTS by supporters of TUC policy. A speaker to the 1985 NATFHE conference claimed that, presumably as a result of YTS, 'more young people from the working class were coming into the Further Education colleges now than ever did before' (*NATFHE Journal*, July 1985, p. 28). The willingness of young people to participate in YTS – 'takeup in 1984 doubled over that in 1983' – was also advanced by the General Council in support of its strategy at the 1984 Congress (TUC, 1985, p. 483).

When no particular regulatory successes could be cited, the argument might fall back upon the potential achievements of YTS and TUC regulation, particularly if a change of government was in prospect. A delegate put it to the public services union NUPE conference in 1983 that

> we are going to have a Labour government returned on 9 June, which completely alters the situation . . . what we need to be arguing for, under a new Labour government, is not a simplistic case for withdrawal [from YTS] . . . we need to convert YTS into something positive and meaningful. (NUPE, 1983, p. 212)

The poor electoral fortunes of the Labour Party throughout the 1980s undoubtedly accounted for the rarity and wishfulness of the appeal.

Procedural arguments
Procedural issues also cropped up in arguments for TUC strategy. Negotiation and bargaining were presented as the natural activity of trade unions. The case for negotiation was usually made primarily in substantive terms: what it can deliver. However, procedural preferences were usually present as well, albeit only implicitly.

General procedural justifications for TUC strategy were suggested by an editorial observation that a CPSA Executive motion to CPSA's 1983 conference, accepting YTS in principle, reflected the committee 'naturally wanting to carry out its traditional trade union role' (*Red Tape*, 1983, May, 2, p. 7). The argument can also be inferred from a delegate's appeal to the 1984 NUPE conference:

> We are stuck with it [YTS]. Get stuck in there, take your coats off and fight the employers round their own table, not outside on a public platform (NUPE, 1984, p. 126),

and by the leader of the Labour Party at the 1988 Congress with reference to proposals to boycott another training scheme:

. . . the question which must be addressed by this Movement – and it is the classic trade union question – is: do you achieve those ends best from outside or from inside? . . . outside you make demands, inside you make the case. (TUC 1989a, p. 480)

The language used in such defences of negotiation suggests the importance of procedural considerations and intrinsic conceptions of the role of trade unions, and not simply instrumental ones.

Arguments in favour of negotiating the content of YTS overlapped with those for TUC involvement in tripartite bodies such as the MSC. According to a speaker from an admittedly interested public sector union (CSU), the MSC

is one of the few bodies over which the trade union movement can exercise some control . . . the involvement of both sides of industry, plus educational interests, in the determination of this policy is a great strength. (TUC, 1983a, p. 480)

The General Council's response to the controversy over YTS at the 1983 Congress started similarly:

the MSC was the concept of this Congress and, indeed, we fought for it and we got it. (TUC, 1984, p. 435)

The fact that youth schemes more unpalatable still from the union standpoint had already been developed, under the aegis of the Department of Employment rather that of the MSC, was also advanced in favour of union involvement in YTS and MSC. According to the CSU speaker to the following Congress,

if we pull out of YTS . . . we shall be opening the way for the government's alternative to the YTS, which is there and in place and is the real slave labour scheme. It is the scheme with no training . . . called the Young Workers' Scheme. (TUC, 1985, p. 482)

Particular procedural successes were cited in support of TUC strategy. The 1984 NUPE conference heard a delegate claim that in his town

all the trade union officials in the borough can look at every single job [i.e. YTS proposal] and thus ensure high training quality and avoid job substitution (NUPE, 1984, p. 120).

A final procedurally oriented argument for TUC strategy was its pragmatic, case-by-case approach to regulating YTS, which permitted boycotts where appropriate. Unions which found particular schemes unacceptable had the power to veto them, either directly at the workplace or indirectly through MSC Area Manpower Boards. Such procedures had the substantive merit of not 'ditching the good schemes . . . as well as the bad schemes' (ibid.) and the procedural one of giving a role to the trade unionists affected. Thus a delegate to the 1984 NUPE conference stated in support of cooperation with YTS,

> I am confident that we can leave it to the branches to decide which are the schemes that will exploit young people and which will provide some useful training. (NUPE, 1984, p. 124)

From Positive to Negative Arguments

By the time YTS began operations in 1983, the support shown for TUC strategy at the 1982 Congress had dwindled rapidly, largely as a result of the increasingly visible discrepancy between government and union aspirations for YTS.[14]

Official support for TUC strategy went rapidly on the defensive. The General Council representative stated early in his opening speech that

> we know the weakness in the YTS as well as anyone else and maybe better than most

and emphasised in his winding up speech that

> the General Council are not suggesting for one moment to any of you that YTS is the millenium. My God, it is far from it!

Of the many speeches favouring TUC strategy on that occasion, only that of the telecommunications union (POEU) advanced positive arguments, outlining the advantages of YTS over YOP from the union standpoint, though that speech too recognised the 'shortcomings of the YTS scheme' (TUC, 1984, pp. 404, 431, 435). The protracted defensive effort to contain opposition to YTS had begun.

A vivid example of defensive support of TUC strategy is provided by the distribution workers' union, USDAW, whose President defended it against widespread discontent at the union's 1984 conference, describing YTS as

> a cheap ploy to take people off the [unemployment] register . . . a
> choice between being flattened by a steamroller or having your head
> screwed up in a vice

before explaining anticlimactically

> we choose what we think we can survive with (*Dawn*, May 1984).[15]

The convergence of trade unionists' perceptions of YTS was
particularly evident at the 1986 Congress, when only UCATT spoke
favourably of YTS and when the General Council's speaker demurred
from its critics only in degree and in his hopes for the future:

> we are well aware of the weaknesses of the YTS: the poor level of the
> allowance . . . the need to ensure that many more young people in
> YTS secure jobs with the employer who is training them, the need to
> avoid job substitution . . . But the criticisms of YTS go a little over
> the top. Some of the problems referred to are being rectified in the
> two-year YTS. (TUC, 1987, p. 541)

The Defensive Case

Defensive arguments for TUC strategy towards YTS have contained
several strands. The most widely invoked postulates union weakness,
insisting that unions cannot stop YTS. As the General Secretary of
USDAW insisted to opponents of YTS at the union's 1986 conference,
'you don't have a choice whether there is to be a YTS scheme or not'
(*Dawn*, June 1986).

The argument is supported by noting that, were unions to try to stop
YTS, the scheme would still operate, but only in unorganised workplaces, on minimal terms and conditions. The winding-up speaker for
the General Council urged the 1983 TUC conference:

> friends, the alternative is this. If you reject what I am saying, YTS
> will go on . . . It will go on in non-union establishments with no
> monitoring, no control by us within the movement.

The final stage of the argument holds that young workers would
then be worse off than had they been protected by union negotiation
and it would be wrong for the unions, in two often used images, to
'turn their backs on' and 'walk away from' young people (TUC, 1984,
pp. 404, 435). Youth is in a vulnerable position and no other party can
be relied upon to look after its interests. As the UCATT defence of
TUC strategy to the 1984 Congress argued,

if we pull out of the YTS . . . who will then represent the real interests of the young people? We are the anchor line. (TUC, 1985, p. 480)

The argument that unions were powerless to stop YTS proved especially influential in particular unions, in conjunction with recent membership losses and competition with other unions to recruit members.[16] Calls for opposition to YTS were then often met by urging that a single-union boycott would be ineffective, as other unions were prepared to cooperate with the scheme. The danger that such a policy would lose potential members to rival unions might also be suggested discreetly.

For example, a further attempt to reverse COHSE's standing boycott of YTS was justified primarily in terms of its inefficacy. The General Secretary urged:

if our present policy was successful, YTS wouldn't be in hospitals today but they are there, in outpatient departments, on wards . . . YTS will expand because other trade unions support it. (*Health Services*, August 1987, p. 8)

The President of the hosiery workers' union (NUHKW), opposing at the union's 1986 conference a proposal to require normal pay rates and job guarantees for YTS trainees in the industry, insisted that

nobody in the union could sanction a YTS scheme. All they could do was to say whether they support the scheme or not. If we don't there are other avenues and other unions. (*Hosiery and Knitwear News*, July 1986)[17]

Industrial interests
A second defensive argument in favour of TUC strategy urged the undesirability of losing the jobs of union members by opposing schemes. Such arguments were presented at Congress in 1983 and 1984 by an interested and loyal civil service union, the CSU. The point was made only indirectly in 1983, when the CSU claimed that

we are in agreement with the criticism [of YTS] because we feel that we are better placed than most to be critical ourselves. Many of our members are employed by the MSC as technical and instructional staff. (TUC, 1984, p. 430)

The point was made explicitly a year later, when the CSU speaker noted that the amendment by the local government officials' union NALGO, which envisaged withdrawal from YTS

> would destroy thousands of jobs that are now involved in the running of YTS. (TUC, 1985, p. 482)

The argument was deployed more frequently within unions with such direct interests. The NATFHE Executive's attempt to defeat a 1985 conference motion opposing YTS in principle made extensive reference to the interests of affected members.

> Passing the motion was going to kick our YTS supervisor members in the teeth,

asserted one speaker, while another asked which opponents of YTS would go and tell

> the good number of YTS supervisors we had recruited that we had voted to oppose the scheme they have worked hard to improve and which employs them and pays their wages.

A YTS supervisor spoke in support of the leadership (*NATFHE Journal*, July 1985, p. 28).[18]

In a similar context, the CPSA Executive defended its involvement with YTS in defiance of conference policy to the union's 1984 conference primarily in terms of the 'some 4,000 MSC members who were employed to administer the scheme', and the danger that 'if there were continued union opposition the jobs of those members would be put at risk' (*Red Tape*, July 1984, p. 9).

A final twist to the support given to TUC policy by industrial interests concerned YTS trainees themselves. A delegate to the 1988 APEX conference advanced the need to look after the union's YTS members as a reason for opposing a motion calling for withdrawal from YTS (*Apex*, June 1988, p. 14).

Reputation

A further, sometimes a last ditch, defensive argument emerged more slowly, as calls for a boycott of YTS became more widespread. It held that rejection of YTS would prove a public relations disaster for trade unions, in that it would allow their enemies, notably the Conservative government and the press, to scapegoat them as enemies of youth and training. The argument was first advanced mildly in TUC debate on behalf of the General Council after a second year of divisions over policy towards YTS:

> if we were to walk away from the scheme there would be many who would be ready to say that we were not interested, that we do not care, that there is no interest in the future. (TUC, 1985, p. 483)

The argument had even been used at a NUPE conference by a delegate favouring policies towards YTS similar to those of Militant, an influential Trotskyite group. Supporting a policy of attaching strict conditions to YTS schemes rather than rejecting them entirely, he expressed the desire to

> nail the lie . . . that the members of NUPE are opposed to youth training. We are not opposed to youth training and let the press print that . . . (NUPE, 1984, p. 119)

A variant had arisen earlier at the 1983 NATFHE conference, when an Executive speaker asked delegates to 'consider the implications of opposing TUC policy', including 'the reaction of the MSC and others who have accused teachers of inflexibility and remoteness from industry' (*NATFHE Journal*, June 1983, p. 20).[19]

Loss of reputation was also cited in individual unions which had boycotted YTS, with supporters of TUC strategy arguing that the boycott had isolated the union. Resolutions seeking to overturn COHSE's boycott of YTS at its 1986 and 1987 conferences both claimed that 'COHSE is the only TUC affiliate against involvement with YTS's (*Health Services*, July 1987, p. 28). The same claim was made by the General Secretary of CPSA at the 1988 Congress (TUC, 1989, p. 518). Such claims implied a loss of reputation for the union as a result of opposing TUC policy and boycotting YTS.[20]

Procedural issues
Defenders of TUC strategy have also used procedural arguments to criticise the opposition's alternatives, particularly boycotts and political campaigns, as less desirable than negotiation. Again, criticism is couched primarily in terms of effectiveness, with intrinsic procedural preferences suggested in the terminology.

A critic of a boycott motion urged its supporters at the 1984 NUPE conference to get yourselves back in the real world. Do not live in cloud-cuckoo land by believing that we, as a union, can take government on and defeat them. (NUPE, 1984, p. 125)

The CPSA General Secretary criticised retrospectively his union's prolonged boycott of YTS:

the union was pitched into a black hole of damaging negativeness . . . the recent change of direction is proving to my membership how much unions can achieve when they concentrate upon their real job rather than, for political reasons that have nothing to do with the members' or workers' interests, refuse to do anything but oppose. (TUC, 1989a, p. 518)

A NATFHE speaker described rejectionism as the 'politics of futile gestures' (TUC, 1985, p. 424) and a delegate to the 1984 NALGO conference said

. . . the scheme is here and our members' jobs are bound up in it .. we no longer have the luxury of being able to adopt a principled stand, as it is called. (*Public Service*, July 1984)

These speakers' choice of terminology (cloud-cuckoo land, black holes, etc.) again suggests a distinct procedural – even a moral – aversion to boycotts and political campaigns.

8.5   ARGUMENTS ADVANCED AGAINST TUC STRATEGY

TUC strategy encountered strong opposition throughout the life of YTS, notwithstanding the 1987 shift in the focus of opposition to similar schemes for unemployed adults. A variety of oppositional stances emerged, including: acceptance of YTS in principle but requiring such terms and conditions as to make its operation unlikely; rejection of YTS in principle but informal cooperation with it in practice; and outright rejection of YTS in both principle and practice. This discussion reflects primarily the arguments of the last group, those calling for outright rejection of YTS and TUC strategy towards it.[21]

Threat to Established Terms and Conditions

The principal line of attack on TUC strategy asserted the unacceptable and dangerous nature of the terms and conditions provided to young people by YTS. The replacement of established terms and conditions of employment for young workers by insecure and low paid YTS traineeships was depicted as involving both the exploitation of young people and the undermining of union achievments for young and adult workers alike.

The NGA motion criticising YTS at Congress in 1983 described the MSC as

> an agency to create low paid work, often under general conditions unacceptable to organised labour, in order to distort the unemployment figures. (TUC, 1984, p. 427)

A year later, a NALGO speaker linked YTS to wider issues of flexibility and deregulation in arguing that the government wanted

> a flexible, pliant, adaptable non-union workforce in this country, grateful to receive a job at any price, and they are going to use the YTS to get it. (TUC, 1985, p. 479)

Some dramatic threats were attributed to YTS in the early days. The 1983 NGA speech cited the interest shown by the Secretary of State for Employment in a proposal to set up factories to use YTS trainees to produce components more cheaply than Far Eastern producers.[22] She even raised the prospect of indirect undercutting and strike-breaking through YTS: unemployed ex-trainees being

> available to undertake employment in the event of disputes and to work in conditions that are inferior to those that have already been established. (TUC, 1984, pp. 427, 8)

Criticism of the terms and conditions provided to young people by YTS often focussed on health and safety. Such criticism emerged under YOP and became intense during the second year of YTS, when rejectionist speeches to Congress from CPSA and NGA attacked the accident rate under YTS, citing it as evidence of

> the lack of supervision, training and protection for young people on the scheme. (TUC, 1985, p. 481)

Instances of Regulatory Failure

Such criticisms implicitly assumed that the TUC's regulatory strategy had not worked and could not work. The goals of widespread 'topping up', employee status, job guarantees, etc., were seen as generally unattainable, and YTS as incapable of proving an acceptable training scheme.

Pessimism concerning the regulation of YTS by unions focussed primarily upon its indirect channel, viz. the MSC committees which approve and monitor YTS schemes. The effectiveness of such curbs on low quality training, job substitution and trainee exploitation has been denied repeatedly by opponents of TUC strategy.

A delegate calling on the public services union NUPE to reconsider its cooperation with YTS stated that

> schemes which we [our branch] have rejected outright . . . have gone through on the approval of MSC officers, bypassing the Area Board. (NUPE, 1984, p. 127)

An opponent of YTS alleged a year later that 45 per cent of proposals for schemes evaded Area Manpower Boards entirely, thereby preventing union regulation (NUPE, 1985, p. 244). Similarly, a delegate opposing his union's involvement with YTS at the 1984 APEX conference 'mentioned 54 different schemes in Lancashire, only two of which were operating above a minimum standard, and there had been only one instance of a trade union complaint being heard' (*Apex*, May 1984, p. 10).

Much of the fire concentrated on the MSC. The NGA concluded from its criticism of the YTS health and safety record that

> the MSC are clearly not ensuring that the placements are being provided with proper training . . . they are taken on for cheap labour . . . the MSC employs no full-time safety staff'. (TUC, 1985, p. 481)

The MSC was attacked at the 1983 NATFHE conference for conducting quality control inspections by telephone (*NATFHE Journal*, June 1983, p. 21). The union's 1985 switch to rejection of YTS in principle was explained to Congress in terms of the scheme's failings. The NATFHE delegate spoke from personal experience of the

> in-built limitations on trade union monitoring and control that every TUC nominee on every Area Manpower Board has experienced at first hand . . . the serious abuses of the scheme in the areas of job substitution and health and safety. (TUC 1986, p. 505)

The other regulatory channel envisaged by TUC strategy, viz. negotiation of the content of schemes at unionised workplaces, came in for surprisingly little criticism, notwithstanding evidence that topping up and employee status remained exceptional and that employers and the MSC had made creative use of inter-union competition to circumvent opposition to particular proposals.

The main criticism belittled the scope for applying direct regulation. The speaker who criticised Area Board procedures to the 1984 NUPE conference also stated that although

> 75 per cent of our [branch] membership . . . are directly employed on MSC schemes . . . about 4 per cent of the membership is covered by union recognition agreements . . . let alone having grievance and disciplinary procedures . . . we are not in a position to negotiate improvements in their conditions. (Ibid.)

Opponents of YTS also cited the government's preference for private provision and competition in the delivery of both work experience places and off-the-job training. Such arguments were made most forcefully in the college lecturers' union, NATFHE, whose 'conditions of service and training were coming under pressure', according to a 1983 conference delegate who advocated opposition to YTS, as a result of being forced to compete with 'private organisations out to make a profit' which 'cut corners by employing untrained staff on low wages, working long hours, in inadequate conditions, using inadequate materials and resources' (*NATFHE Journal*, June 1983, p. 21).

The more sophisticated proponents of regulatory failure accepted evidence of the success of particular YTS schemes, as advanced by supporters of TUC strategy, but denied their generalisability. The Executive member who spoke for the opposition to YTS at the 1985 NATFHE conference said that

> there were good YTS schemes, no doubt, but they were run by organisations that had always done good training . . . for every good YTS scheme there is a lousy rip-off scheme. (*NATFHE Journal*, July 1985, p. 28)

Similarly, the IRSF leadership's use of the Telford YTS scheme to win support for cooperation with YTS was deflected by arguing that Telford funding levels could not be reproduced throughout the country and that the substitution of YTS for clerical assistantships elsewhere could not be prevented, particularly as it only took five weeks to learn the job (*Assessment*, February 1987).

Opponents of TUC strategy also cited cutbacks in YTS provision for disadvantaged youth. A 1984 motion to the GMBATU conference which claimed that 28,000 Mode B places had been closed down on government instructions was instrumental in a rare defeat for cooperation with YTS by that union (GMBATU, 1985, pp. 529–31).

Alternatives to YTS: Training

The issue of alternatives has been central to the rejectionist as well as to the pro-TUC position. Opponents of TUC strategy in occupational unions proposed alternative systems of vocational preparation.

At the 1983 Congress the NGA contrasted YTS unfavourably to apprenticeship training, describing the scheme as

> totally inadequate in quality . . . [it] will create a reservoir of state-funded, partly trained and barely-trained labour. (TUC, 1984, pp. 427–8)

TASS seconded the NGA motion in less uncompromising terms but saw in training quality the 'poisonous side of the YTS package':

> YTS may reduce the unemployment statistics and it might even be useful for some of the kids to go on it but it will not provide any of the skills of which the economy is so short . . . skilled craftsmen, technicians, technologists and the supervisors of non-technical staff . . . the £1 billion that will be used to fund the scheme is being financed at the expense of real occupational training. (TUC 1984, p. 429)

The metalworking union AUEW, which held out until 1988 against any link between YTS principles and apprenticeship, told the 1986 Congress that

> YTS is artificial. It does not address the real issues. Even though some programmes offer reasonable training . . . in the main the standard is not high . . . the question of exploitation and cheap labour in YTS still remains. YTS is no substitute at all for a good apprenticeship. (TUC, 1987, p. 535)

Similar concerns were expressed by the opponents of YTS in the teaching unions, notably the Scottish teachers (EIS) whose boycott motions in 1984 and 1985 called for the replacement of YTS by

> a comprehensive system of education and training based on further education colleges, secondary schools and trade-union activities. (*Scottish Educational Journal*, 22 June 1984, p. 8; 21 June 1985, p. 9)

A radically different training alternative featured amongst rejection-ist motions during 1983–5. It called upon the unions to establish their own training centres for unemployed young people, using unemployed adults to provide the training. That alternative was identified with a Trotskyite group, the Workers' Revolutionary Party (WRP). The political orientation of its sponsors limited the appeal of this alternative to YTS. It was discussed, denounced by the platform and rejected at the 1983 and 1984 NUPE conferences, but it did get composited into the rejectionist motion which carried the 1985 COHSE conference (NUPE, 1983, 1984; *Health Services*, July 1985).

Alternatives to YTS: Employment

Outside the occupational unions YTS has more commonly been viewed primarily as an employment scheme and the alternatives to it have been conceived on a broader scale.

Opposition to YTS has often presented high youth unemployment as the result of political choice by the Conservative government and, as such, potentially reversible by political campaigns. According to the NGA at the 1983 Congress,

> in the absence of a reversal of the government's economic policy there is no hope for young people. (TUC, 1984, p. 428)

However, Marxist opponents of YTS and TUC strategy evinced less optimism about or interest in immediate political alternatives. The solitary 1982 opposition on the part of the furniture workers' union, FTATU, concluded that

> there has been a deliberate political act that is causing youth unemployment and adult unemployment . . ., we have to analyse this situation and realise that it is the development of the capitalist system in this country that has brought this about. Until we have tackled the political basis of this social system that will not be overcome. (TUC, 1983a, p. 487)

Similarly, a motion calling for 'the abolition of the exploitative YOPs', carried by the 1983 conference of the actors' union and couched in Marxist terminology, appeared unaware that YOP was about to give way to YTS (*Equity Journal*, June 1983, motion 40).

Such critics naturally denied claims that the election of a Labour goverment would lead to the acceptability of a revamped YTS. A delegate to the 1983 NUPE conference argued that youth training and YOP schemes were actually in existence under a Labour government and they were still cheap labour then . . . no doubt they will continue to be cheap labour whichever government is returned on 9 June. (NUPE, 1983, p. 213)

However, the existence of superior alternatives to YTS was argued frequently in the public sector in connection with cutbacks in public employment. The sponsor of a motion to the 1984 CPSA conference which described YTS in the civil service as a 'cynical publicity stunt' noted the predicted loss of 160,000 jobs in the civil service between 1979 and 1989 and asserted that

> if the government was really concerned about the plight of the young unemployed they could provide 165,000 real jobs tomorrow. (*Red Tape*, July 1984, p. 9)

An Executive member spoke similarly to the 1987 conference:

> the government is trying to cut corners in office staffing costs. If YTS jobs exist why cannot these youngsters be employed as Administrative Assistants? (*Red Tape*, July 1987, p. 14)

However, the appeal of immediate political alternatives to YTS declined with the successive 1983 and 1987 reelections of the Conservative government and the defeat of the 1984–5 miners' strike. Such possibilities featured rarely thereafter in the oppositionist case, leaving rejectionists increasingly vulnerable to the charge that they offered no alternative. As a supporter of TUC strategy said to the 1985 college lecturers' conference which voted to oppose YTS, 'I haven't heard anything so far on the alternatives' (*NATFHE Journal*, p. 28).

Youth Interests

Opponents of YTS countered assertions that to reject YTS would be to hurt young people not by denying the importance of youth interests but by urging that they would be better served by rejecting YTS.

The NGA's attack on YTS in 1983 denounced it for raising 'false expectations for the young unemployed' who would only have to return to unemployment once their time was up (TUC, 1984, p. 427). The possibility that YTS might at least do something for young people while they were active on it could also be denied by asserting that substitution was rife, as YTS replaced regular youth employment. COHSE justified its opposition to YTS at the 1985 Congress on these grounds:

> by our endorsement of YTS schemes and by their extension [to two years] we are denying trade union benefits to the young people of this country for another period. (TUC, 1986, p. 508)

Rejectionists often went on to argue that young people would blame rather than thank trade unions if they cooperated with YTS. The 1983 NGA broadside asserted that

> if we continue to support the YTS we shall rightly be condemned by our children for being parties to a fraud. (TUC, 1984, p. 429)

The recruitment of young people into unions would accordingly be promoted by rejecting rather than by endorsing TUC strategy. According to a NUPE delegate,

> future recruitment will be made more difficult. People will say, 'if the trade union accepts that . . . what is the point of joining a trade union in the first place?' (NUPE, 1983, p. 209)

Opponents of YTS sometimes also looked for evidence to the actions of young people themselves. The low take-up of places in the first year of YTS was cited by the NGA at the 1984 Congress, along with the government's move towards compulsion, as evidence

> that unemployed youngsters are highly aware that YTS is offering them little by way of proper training. (TUC, 1985, p. 481)

A delegate to the 1984 NUPE conference claimed that one-quarter of YTS trainees had left the scheme early, concluding that they preferred to risk a 40 per cent cut in their benefits than to take what the scheme offered (NUPE, 1984, p. 121). A year later, a rejectionist referred to recent strikes by schoolchildren against YTS as proof that 'youth today are rejecting the schemes out of hand' (NUPE, 1985, p 245).

However, the actions and views of young people faded from oppositional arguments, presumably reflecting the increase in YTS take-up after 1983/4 and the lack of further strikes by secondary school students.

Union Reputation and Industrial Interests

The TUC's argument that rejection of its strategy would allow the enemies of trade unionism to damage the reputation of the trade union movement also encountered a rejectionist counterpart.

The local government officials' union, NALGO, sponsored at the 1984 Congress a move towards TUC withdrawal from YTS after six months. It argued that the 'credibility of the trade union movement' was at stake as a result of participating in YTS as it stood (TUC, 1985, p. 479). Separate moves to force TUC withdrawal from tripartite bodies such as MSC during the period were justified in similar terms.

Industrial interests placed opponents of YTS in the affected unions in a delicate position. Arguments that the jobs of union members would be lost as a result of a boycott were typically ignored in rejectionist speeches to Congress, even when it was the affected union itself which was directly involved, as with CPSA in 1984 and NATFHE in 1985.

Within such unions, however, the argument about job losses for the members was less easily evaded. Oppositionists in NATFHE responded to the issue by claiming that YTS was already taking away members' jobs by fostering private off-the-job training, more precarious funding and a 'candyfloss education system' in general. Supporters of a 1983 motion calling for a campaign against YTS asserted that 'teaching jobs are not secured by grovelling to the MSC for pennies' and that

> those who expected jobs to be created by YTS would be disappointed. Redundancies were expected and privatisation would take work away from the FE colleges. (*NATFHE Journal*, July 1983, p. 20)

An alternative response occurred two years later when a leading opponent of TUC strategy appeared willing to accept such losses in return for the more important goal of opposing YTS. According to the union's newspaper, the speaker

> would not attack the proposers [of an amendment to delete the words 'oppose YTS'] on grounds of vested interest but would simply say 'don't be too near the trees to see the wood, . . . he was surprised the General Secretary had come in on this . . .'

The sensitivity of the issue was clear. Moreover, once the union's opposition to YTS had been officially established, the victors' unwillingness to seek a full-scale boycott was explained in terms of job loss:

not that we were going to withdraw or fail to cooperate: we could not do that because our members' jobs were at stake. (*NATFHE Journal*, July 1985, p. 28; June 1986, p. 34)

In CPSA, another union to oppose YTS despite the dependence of many of its members upon YTS funding, arguments in favour of participating in YTS in order to protect jobs were apparently raised only at the 1983 and 1984 annual conferences and ignored by the rejectionist majority on each occasion (*Red Tape*, July 1983, *passim*). The opponents of TUC strategy thus found no effective answer to the charge that their policy endangered the jobs of members.

Procedural Issues

A central rejectionist argument involved the intentions of the government towards both youth and trade unions. Its opponents often depicted YTS as a trick played upon unions by a hostile government, simultaneously concealing youth unemployment and undermining trade unionism. It was variously termed a

Trojan horse introduced by this government with a deliberate intention of attacking the trade union movement from within (STUC, 1983)

and, at the 1983 TUC conference, a 'conspiracy against an entire generation of youngsters', 'nothing more than a sophisticated and cynical rerun of YOP', a 'con trick' and a 'fraud' (TUC, 1984, p. 434).

The rhetoric was underpinned by the perception that the Conservative government would not permit YTS to function along the lines sought by unions. A delegate to NUPE's 1984 conference asked:

does anyone really think that the government are going to allow continued and developing improvements . . . on these schemes when the whole intention of the schemes is to destroy wages and conditions? (NUPE, 1984, p. 126)

NALGO argued at Congress in 1984 that the government had 'totally distorted the original aims of the scheme', referring in particular to the low level of the allowance and moves to compel the young unemployed to participate (TUC, 1985, p. 479).

Opponents of TUC strategy also challenged the proposition that unions were powerless to curb YTS, urging that a hostile government must have found the unions useful in continuing their role in the MSC. A speaker to the 1985 NUPE conference asserted that

> we are legitimising these schemes by staying in them . . . the TUC legitimise them. (NUPE, 1985, p. 247)

A speaker to the previous year's conference had cited the remarks of a government minister, to the effect that

> the participation of the TUC was essential to the functioning of these schemes,

as evidence that a boycott would indeed affect the government and therefore might improve what was on offer (NUPE, 1984, p. 121).

The implication of these views was that the government was manipulating the TUC representatives on the MSC and that the importance attached by the General Council to its MSC role was mistaken. The TASS speaker to 1983 Congress asserted that

> the MSC was once a genuinely tripartite and independent body but it is now seemingly a creature of government. (TUC, 1984, p. 430)

However, an opponent of YTS in NUPE urged that the TUC's usefulness to the government would not last long. Once the government had defeated the miners' strike,

> they are really going to go to town on YTS and you will see all positions held by trade unionists on the MSC swept away at a moment's notice. (NUPE, 1984, p. 126)

The suggestion that TUC participation in MSC and the YTS involved gullibility, if not collaboration with the enemy, led to angry exchanges at the normally over-managed annual TUC conference when, in 1983, Bill Keys' angry response on behalf of the General Council indicated that a nerve had been struck (TUC, 1984, p. 435).

Some opponents of YTS have shown little interest in the virtues of negotiation *per se* and have even displayed aversion to making any concessions from their list of goals. The 1989 CPSA annual conference 'severely censured' its Executive for recommending an agreement on YTS in the civil service which did not embody all the demands voted at conference in 1988. Little need for compromise was seen by these critics of YTS, even though further strike action against the introduction of YTS was unlikely and the government enjoyed as a result freedom to impose YTS on terms more to its liking (*Red Tape*, August 1989).[23]

8.6 DISCUSSION

The issues raised in union debates over YTS ranged wide, reflecting the heterogeneous and complex nature of the scheme itself. Disagreement was promoted by the heterogeneity and complexity of YTS, as different observers attached particular importance to different attributes of the scheme.

Positive Support for TUC Strategy

Manual craft unions provided most of the positive arguments advanced in favour of YTS and TUC strategy. UCATT, EETPU and POEU – craft unions which had blended YTS with apprenticeship training – were amongst the few to speak in that vein in early Congress debates on YTS (section 8.4, above).[24] It appears that an ideal of 'proper' craft training, identified with apprenticeship, informed many unionists' evaluations of YTS. The NATFHE Executive appealed to such values when it asked conference delegates

> to consider the implications of opposing TUC policy, of campaigning against the apprenticeships that some unions had negotiated through YTS. (*NATFHE Journal*, June 1983, p. 20)

The other side of the craft coin was the low profile adopted by supporters of TUC strategy which had negotiated significant variations in trainee terms and conditions – notably the 'top up' payments and employee status secured by the banking and distribution unions, BIFU and USDAW. Their achievements were not widely cited in support of TUC strategy, either within those unions or at Congress itself – a lacuna which may reflect not simply the reservations of the leaders of the two unions concerning YTS itself but also the low status of training for the many less skilled jobs in their sectors. In any event, their reticence contributed to the defensive stance of pro-TUC argumentation.[25]

A notable absentee in positive arguments for TUC strategy was the proposition, implicit in the EETPU's praise of its training scheme to Congress in 1987 and popular with both government and economists, that the low allowances and low payroll costs of YTS trainees provided valuable training incentives. The General Council had implicitly accepted the argument in advising unions to press harder for 'topping up' when the employer's training costs were low (TUC, 1984, p. 46). Otherwise the argument never appears in defences of YTS or TUC strategy, indicating further the low credibility in union circles of YTS as a training scheme.[26]

The Role of Evidence

The degree to which the debate was informed by the evidence varied considerably. Experience on YTS's operations was cited widely by both sides, notably in unions like APEX and NATFHE with open conference traditions and small numerical differences at annual conference between the two camps.

Fresh evidence of unfavourable outcomes was cited by NATFHE to explain its newly established opposition to YTS at the 1985 Congress:

> the experience of the last year has radically increased the criticism of the scheme, and the calls from teachers and other trade unionists (including unions like my own) for outright opposition are stronger and stronger. (TUC, 1986, p. 505)

Examples of low quality YTS schemes cited at successive APEX conferences between 1983 and 1988 far outnumbered those of acceptable ones, thereby contributing to the rising voting strength of the rejectionist minority, which almost won in 1986 (*Apex*, May 1986, p. 11).

At the same time, the more sensational arguments used against YTS fell out of circulation as the evidence proved inconsistent. Factories using only trainee labour to make import-competing goods, ex-trainees being used as strike-breakers and a worse health and safety record in YTS than in regular youth employment – the failure of such dire predictions to materialise helped narrow the range of dispute.

However, the evidence remained incomplete, notably on job substitution. On a rare occasion when evidence was cited on substitution, its inaccuracy went unchallenged. Contrasting YTS favourably to its adult counterpart, JTS, an ASTMS speaker made the remarkable understatement that YTS,

> with its much more rigorous monitoring and approval arrangements, is identified already with a 17 per cent job substitution effect. (TUC, 1988, p. 507)

The MSC's estimate of job substitution rates under YTS had been one-third in its early days, rising to one-half by 1987 – and those figures were undoubtedly underestimates (Ryan, 1989, p. 189). The debate proceeded largely uninformed by evidence on the basic issue of substitution.

More generally, the systemic assessment of net gains under YTS which might have helped to focus the discussion remained conspicuously absent.[27] The General Council limited itself to listing YTS developments in its annual reports, emphasising procedural matters such as TUC representation on MSC bodies and innovations in quality control. The substantive outcomes which it mentioned were at best mixed, with gains on health and safety coverage, duration of off-the-job training and union recruitment to be set against losses on funding levels, the trainee allowance, provision of modes not relying on work experience, and compulsory participation. The issue of job substitution was avoided entirely.[28]

However, for many protagonists on both sides of the debate the evidence was of secondary importance. For some, particularly on the right wing and amongst some union leaderships, the primary requirement was adherence to the TUC, however impoverished the situation of YTS on the ground; for others, particularly on the left wing and amongst union activists, what mattered was opposition to government policy and class collaboration, however well TUC strategy worked. To the extent that evidence provided a useful ingredient in their arguments, the sheer heterogeneity of YTS provided ample scope for both sides to pull out attractive or unattractive evidence to suit their cases. But the balance of the evidence was not a matter of much interest to either side.

In any event, as evidence about the operation of YTS became available it also became less important for the key issues in dispute. The failings of YTS were acknowledged by most supporters of TUC strategy, as evidenced by the predominance of defensive arguments after 1982 (section 8.4, above). The key area of disagreement concerned then the tactics to adopt towards the widely criticised scheme. As a NATFHE speaker had said towards the end of the controversy over YTS at the 1983 Congress:

> The issue is not disagreement on the basic problems of YTS. It has its deficiencies and there are problems of quality and of job substitution and of depressing wages. The issue is not . . . are we or are we not fighting for real jobs? . . . it is something on which we are not divided. But the issue is in respect of the YTS as it is administered at the present time: should we give up, should we opt out . . .? (TUC, 1984, p. 436)

Arguments Against a Boycott

The defensive arguments which predominated in support for TUC strategy involve assumptions which are open to criticism, as well as showing some inconsistency amongst themselves.

The leading defensive charge – that YTS would proceed anyway, but on worse terms and conditions, if unions opposed it, leaving trainees worse off – contained two implicit assumptions. The first was that the interests of young people matter to trade unions. If not, the deterioration in trainee conditions resulting from a boycott would not matter to unions. The second is that unions are strong enough to improve trainees' terms and conditions. If not, there would be no advantage for young people in union involvement in YTS.

The importance of youth interests in the formation of wider union objectives is low or zero in economic models which treat trade unions as democratic aggregates of rationally self-interested individuals. Young people are too few and too junior for their interests to matter in the formation of a majority coalition. Only if leadership interests count and are dependent on union size are the interests of young people, as marginal members, likely to matter (Oswald, 1985; Pemberton, 1988; Ryan, 1987a).

The role of youth interests in the formation of union policies cannot be inferred from public declarations, as all participants in union debates on YTS paid at least lip service to helping young people. Effective priorities might however be indicated by the popularity of YTS boycotts. Exclusion of YTS trainees from unionised plants would serve the interests of the relevant adult employees by preventing the direct substitution of trainee labour for their own. As long as indirect substitution (losing work to non-union YTS sponsors)[29] was not a significant threat, as in highly unionised sectors, a wholly adult-centred union might therefore be expected to favour a boycott.

A significant minority of unions did boycott YTS, but as their actions were influenced by a wide range of factors, including employer attitudes, that policy alone does not indicate conclusively a low effective orientation on their part to youth interests (Ryan, 1990b). Along with other evidence, however, it points in that direction. The lack of union interest in reducing overtime work in order to increase employment was cited by the UCW and FBU speakers to Congress in 1982 as evidence of the low effective priority which most unions gave to youth interests (TUC, 1983a, pp. 483–4).[30]

The second requirement for the argument 'YTS can't be blocked' to have force is that direct union regulation register significant successes, either by raising the national minimum terms and conditions set for YTS trainees by the MSC or by negotiating in unionised firms significant improvements over those minima. Were union presence ineffective in both spheres, withdrawal from YTS would leave trainees no worse off than before.

The argument is particularly vulnerable at this point. The defensive slant of most support for TUC strategy implicitly admitted that the results of regulation had been unimpressive. National minimum terms and conditions provided to trainees by MSC not only continued to be unsatisfactory to trade unions, but also deteriorated in such key areas as the value of the trainee allowance and voluntary participation. The latter change was particularly embarrassing for the TUC, which had strenuously opposed it and even suggested that its introduction would lead to withdrawal of support for YTS.[31] Finally, improvements on the MSC's national minima had been negotiated for only for a small minority of trainees until YTS2 made inroads into mainstream employment for 17-year-olds.

Thus the limited importance of youth interests to most unions and the poor achievements of union regulation together undermine the leading defensive argument for TUC strategy. However, as long as outcomes would have been still worse for trainees in the absence of union involvement – and few could deny that possibility – the argument retained some force.[32]

Similarly, the argument which sought to protect the political reputation of the union movement by avoiding boycotts involved some inconsistency, in seeking to protect a political reputation while insisting that it not be used in political campaigns against the widely perceived inadequacies of YTS. However, the TUC's emphasis upon the political costs of rejecting government training schemes was affirmed in 1988, for the short term at least, when the unions suffered extensive adverse publicity after Congress voted to boycott Employment Training.

The various defensive arguments marshalled in favour of TUC strategy were not always mutually consistent. In particular, a boycott of YTS would not affect the jobs of unionised MSC employees, were boycotts indeed ineffective against YTS. The boycott would then simply shift YTS takeup entirely into the non-union sector. MSC employees would find that the identity of their YTS sponsors had changed but they would not be out of a job.

Finally, arguments against boycotting YTS were weakened when the TUC refused in 1987 to cooperate with a similar training scheme for adults, the Job Training Scheme (TUC, 1988, pp. 154ff). The marked parallels between YTS and JTS made it difficult to defend cooperating with the one and boycotting the other by painting YTS as a greatly superior scheme – although some tried to do just that, including the ASTMS speaker to the 1987 Congress (TUC, 1988, p. 507). JTS had little effect on union strategy towards YTS at the TUC level as Congress was preoccupied during 1987–8 with the furore over adult training. However, many unions saw at that time a resurgence, and even the emergence, of internal opposition to TUC strategy towards YTS, most notably in NUPE, whose 1988 conference passed for the first time a motion to boycott it.[33]

At the same time, the TUC's refusal to cooperate with JTS rendered hollow many of the arguments which it had previously deployed against boycotts *per se*, particularly as the early demise of JTS was widely claimed as a victory for union opposition.

Opposition to TUC Strategy

The role of wider political conflict in fuelling opposition to YTS is clear. The hostility of the post-1979 Conservative government to trade unions, together with its willingness to alter statistical methods and social security rules in order to reduce registered youth unemployment, lent credence to interpretations of YTS as deceptive and abusive. Bitterness towards the government after its 1983 reelection undoubtedly fostered opposition to YTS and TUC strategy at the 1983 Congress. The exaggeraged claims subsequently made by the government on behalf of YTS rankled with many union critics. The growing influence amongst union activists of revolutionary left-wing groups, particularly Militant and the Workers' Revolutionary Party (WRP), during the early 1980s led to further emphasis upon the wider political context of YTS.

The arguments advanced by the opponents of TUC strategy were less elaborate and less prone to internal inconsistency than those of its supporters. Outright opposition to an enemy is easier to justify than are cautious dealings with her.

The importance of wider politics in argument in the opposition camp points to a fundamental divergence of views over the function and potential of trade unionism. Left-wing politics has long looked to unions as potential mobilisers of political opinion for revolutionary objectives, while criticising union practice for its concentration upon immediate industrial objectives. The opponents of TUC strategy pressed for a wider and more vigorous role in the political battle with a hostile government than union leaders were generally interested in playing.

However, the lack of a constructive alternative to YTS as long as the Conservative government retained power proved the most damaging argument against the opponents of TUC strategy. The remarkable isolation of the unions which rejected YTS, failing even to rebut allegations that each stood alone in rejecting the scheme, confirmed the essentially negative nature of their cause under the political conditions of the time.

8.7 CONCLUSIONS

The importance of the arguments used for and against TUC strategy in debates within the union movement might be doubted, particularly during a period when the public standing and political influence of trade unions was at their lowest ebb since the inter-war period. Nevertheless, union debates over YTS are important for the understanding of at least two issues: national training policy and trade unions themselves.

Concerning training policy, the unions' debates indicate the degree to which both the supporters and the critics of TUC policy agreed early on that the quality of YTS as a whole was indefensibly low. YTS's lack of legitimacy in the eyes of organised labour was undoubtedly fostered by political conflict with a deregulatory government but the failings of the scheme itself were central. The supporters of TUC strategy would have welcomed the better resourced and better run YTS which would have allowed them to sing its praises to the critics instead of defensively arguing that it could be worse.

The contribution of the 1981 New Training Initiative to the reform of initial training has as a result been handicapped, particularly in the highly unionised, traded goods sector, where inadequate skill supplies and utilisation contribute strongly to poor economic performance.

Concerning unions themselves, the heated debates and contested votes which marked many conference discussions of YTS and TUC strategy brought internal democracy to the fore and showed its power to affect union policy and government alike. Many union leaders inclined to support TUC policy found themselves prevented from doing so by hostile conference majorities. Existing controversies over the roles of top officials, the Executive and conference in representing the views of the membership were intensified by YTS, notably in CPSA, IRSF and EQUITY. The weakness of internal democracy in some other unions permitted leadership control over policy towards YTS.

The government's wish to 'talk up' the achievements of YTS would have had an easier run had not annual conferences been in a position in most unions to reflect members' views and to discuss and decide policy. The Conservative government found itself facing a difficulty over its employment and training schemes not wholly unlike the one its Labour predecessor had faced over incomes policy: most union leaders were prepared to cooperate with its plans but internal union democracy made it difficult for many of them to do so.

Debates on YTS indicate also the complexity of the the balance between youth and adult interests in union policy. The evidence is broadly consistent with interpretations of the kind favoured by modern economic analyses of trade union goals, though it points also to the importance of both wider politics and internal organisation in setting union goals.

Finally, there is the question of who was right, the TUC or its opponents. Even with the benefit of hindsight the question is not easily answered, given the variety of issues on which an assessment must hinge. The strongest rejectionist argument is that the substantive gains of union cooperation proved small and that the union movement would have been better placed to publicise that fact and influence the policy had it not been involved in running YTS. The government's rapid improvement of its plans for adult training during 1987–8 in response to the threat of a union boycott favours such a view. No government could accept with equanimity the exclusion from unionised employment of its vaunted schemes to improve training.

At the same time, the advantage of cooperation with YTS was simply that it gave unions something to do in the area where they do best: negotiation. The disappointing nature of the results certainly sheds doubt upon the value of the unions' seats at a table where the menu was set by a government with radically different tastes. However, outcomes under YTS might well have been even worse for trainees and trade unions under a general boycott, while involvement in it and the MSC provided some continuity and sense of purpose to union officials who had otherwise been marginalised and demoralised by the abrupt reversal of their political fortunes in 1979.

The relative importance of the two categories of benefit is not easily established and hinges partly upon the role which trade unions are seen as playing best: political campaigning or negotiating. The two functions are to some extent complementary and a greater willingness to consider withdrawing support from YTS during 1982–4 might have forced a better training scheme out of the government. However such threats cannot be deployed indefinitely. The difficulties which NATFHE and NALGO faced in simultaneously opposing YTS or ET and continuing to work with it suggest that a choice had ultimately to be made.

However, from another standpoint, the choice between the alternatives was not so important. The two sides to the debate shared a perception that the union movement lacked the power to permit their opponent's strategy to succeed, even if they denied the same for their own policies. On that issue they were both close to the truth: neither strategy offered much of a dividend, to either trade unions or youth training, under the political and economic circumstances of the time.

APPENDIX

Initials, full titles and 1983 membership (thousands) of trade unions cited:

APEX	Association of Professional, Clerical and Computer Staff; 100
ASTMS	Association of Scientific, Technical and Managerial Staffs; 410
AUEW	Amalgamated Union of Engineering Workers (Engineering Section); 1,005
BIFU	Banking, Insurance and Finance Union; 157
CATU	Ceramics and Allied Trades Union; 29
COHSE	Confederation of Health Service Employees; 223
CPSA	Civil and Public Services Association; 199
CSU	Civil Service Union; 40
EETPU	Electrical, Electronic, Telecommunications and Plumbing Union; 365
EIS	Educational Institute of Scotland; 46
EQUITY	British Actors' Equity Association; 32
FBU	Fire Brigades' Union; 43

FTATU Furniture, Timber and Allied Trades Union; 58
GMBATU General, Municipal, Boilermakers and Allied Trade Union; 875
IPCS Institute of Professional Civil Servants; 93
IRSF Inland Revenue Staff Federation; 57
ISTC Iron and Steel Trades Confederation; 91
NALGO National and Local Government Officers' Association; 784
NATFHE National Association of Teachers in Further and Higher Education; 71
NGA National Graphical Association 1982; 129
NUHKW National Union of Hosiery and Knitwear Workers; 57
NUJ National Union of Journalists; 33
NUPE National Union of Public Employees; 689
POEU Post Office Engineering Union; 130
TASS Technical, Administrative and Supervisory Section (AUEW); 215
TGWU Transport and General Workers' Union; 1547
UCATT Union of Construction, Allied Trades and Technicians; 260
UCW Union of Communications Workers; 196
USDAW Union of Shop, Distributive and Allied Workers; 403

Sources: Maksymiw, Eaton and Gill (1990); *TUC Bulletin*, various issues.

Notes

1. Comments, suggestions and assistance provided by William Brown, John Dunn, John Gennard, Colin Gill, John Kelly, Roger Moore, Helen Rainbird, Paul Willman and participants at the 1988 Palermo conference are gratefully acknowledged.
2. The terminology of substitution is confusing. The economic literature distinguishes between the 'deadweight' and 'substitution' effects of schemes such as YTS, referring to the replacement of ordinary employment or apprenticeship contracts for 16–17-year-olds and 18–64-year-olds respectively (Deakin and Pratten, 1987). The term 'job substitution' which is commonly used in union discussions denotes both forms of displacement.
3. An earlier assessment of TUC strategy is provided by Ryan (1989). Union policies towards youth schemes are discussed by Eversley (1986) and Rainbird (1988).

4. YTS also requires that trainees receive a four-week holiday each year and provides for coverage by health and safety law.

5. The ratio of actual to minimum required trainee time spent in off-the-job training rose from 1.09 in 1983/4 to 1.55 in 1986/7 (bases of 13 and 20 weeks under YTS1 and YTS2 respectively; GB DE, 1985; TUC, 1989b, p. 72). YTS also includes delivery modes not involving work experience (Mode B1 to 1986, premium places since) in order to make provision for trainees with little or no prospect of finding a work experience placement, but the importance of such provision fell from 23 per cent in 1983/4 to 15 per cent in 1987/8 (GB MSC, 1984, Table 3.1; GB TA, 1989b, Table 2).

6. Department of Employment, *New Earnings Survey*, 1983 and 1989.

7. In 1987/8, 62 per cent of Managing Agents contracted out at least some work experience (GB TA, 1989b, p. 11).

8. Recognising the role of Managing Agents as channels for government payment of trainee allowances, these estimates deduct the trainee allowance from the basic grant of £1,920 per trainee year paid by the Treasury.

9. The proportion of YTS trainees receiving additional payments or employee status rose rapidly after 1986. By 1989, 23 per cent enjoyed employee status – and, by implication, substantial 'top up' payments from their employers (TUC, 1989b, p. 72). Nevertheless, most trainees still did not receive supplements and the growth of 'topping up' after 1986 was easy for employers who substituted second-year YTS for ordinary 17-year-old employment. Work experience sponsors have also been required to pay modest amounts to Managing Agents for the services of their trainees in cases where the two roles are distinct.

10. Were YTS trainees additional to normal staffing levels (youth and adult combined), no plant-level substitution could be inferred from employer use of work experience, but economy-wide substitution would still be involved to the extent that employment was displaced in other organisations.

11. The 48–member General Council, comprising representatives of the affiliated unions, is formally responsible for the execution of policies decided by Congress. In practice the General Council exerts considerable influence over policy formulation and the proceedings of Congress. The vigorous disputes seen at Congress during the 1980s over YTS and ET have been the exception rather than the rule in this respect (Maksymiw, Eaton and Gill, 1990, pp. 11–13).

12. The activities of the MSC are outlined in its annual reports (e.g. GB MSC 1984) and discussed in Lindley (1983), Raffe (1984), St John-Brooks (1985), Benn and Fairley (1986) and Finn (1987).

13. Arguments in favour of YTS generally neglected the curbs on substitution, such as the vetos on YTS placements when staffing was below establishment levels which were negotiated in banking, the civil service and the Inland Revenue.

14. A major factor was the government's priority to volume rather than training quality. All that remained of a list of proposed training requirements in YTS was 13 weeks' off-the-job training – and the

quality of even that was in the eyes of unions jeopardised by privatisation (Ryan, 1984b; Keep, 1986). As the leader of the banking union, BIFU, said 'we must recognise that there is political pressure to secure as many places as possible . . . and it is clear that standards will be reduced, if necessary, to get those places' (TUC, 1984, p. 427).

15. Similarly, the President of the college lecturers' union, a key supporter of TUC policy during 1983–5, described YTS as a 'total and utter shambles' and 'bucket-shop training' (*NATFHE Journal*, June, 1983, July 1984). A report on the 1983 conference of the white collar union APEX, whose leaders also supported TUC policy, noted that 'those who supported the composite [motion in favour of TUC strategy] had few good things to say about the scheme' (*Apex*, July 1983). The leadership of the health service union COHSE, supporting a motion to reverse a policy of boycotting YTS, could come up with no warmer description of the introduction of YTS2 in 1986 than a 'ray of hope' (*Health Services*, July 1986).

16. The combined membership of the largest 40 unions affiliated to the TUC in 1983 was 13.4 per cent less than it had been in 1979 (Ryan, 1991b).

17. Competitive recruitment also assisted TUC strategy by weakening the opposition of the three unions – NGA, TASS and NUJ – which sponsored criticism of TUC strategy at the 1983 Congress (Ryan, 1991b).

18. A similar plea came in 1985 from the FE lecturers' section of the Scottish teachers' union, EIS: 'if the [conference] approved non-cooperation with the scheme, it would be saying to FE lecturers that they were going to have to ignore 20–40 per cent of their work' (*Scottish Educational Journal*, 21 June 1985).

19. The issue climaxed in the 1988 controversy over Employment Training. The leader of the Labour Party insisted to the 1988 TUC conference that, were a boycott adopted, 'while none of the deficiencies . . . of Employment Training will be the fault of the trade union movement, you will get the blame . . . you will be the whipping boy . . . you will be the excuse for everything that goes wrong' (TUC, 1989a, p. 480).

20. The inconsistency of the two claims is underlined by the fact that at least seven unions adopted policies of boycotting YTS at some point during 1983–8 (Ryan, 1991b).

21. Examples of the three oppositional stances are provided by the AEU (1983–7), NATFHE (1985–) and CPSA (1983–7) respectively (Ryan, 1991b).

22. The minister was quoted as not anticipating union opposition to the proposal as 'it will not displace British jobs' (*The Sunday Times*, 12 September 1982). It was also cited by a critic of YTS at the 1983 NUPE conference (NUPE, 1983, p. 210).

23. An element of revenge may be inferred in the 1989 CPSA censure vote, punishing the General Secretary in particular for his 'black hole' denunciation to the 1988 Congress of his union's history of boycotting YTS.

24. POEU soon thereafter changed sides, voting to boycott YTS and denouncing the collapse of apprenticeship (*POEU Journal*, November 1983; TUC, 1987, p. 538).

25. Industrial Relations Review and Report, 2 August 1988; TUC (1984, p. 426); *BIFU Report*, November 1983; 'Successes over YTS', *Dawn*, September 1986.
26. The IRSF raised the issue at the 1984 Congress, but as a matter of equity rather than efficiency. 'True, the allowances are not good enough. But are we really talking about a wage and the rate for the job? Because the scheme we have devised is in fact not a job, it is training. Therefore if you are under training you are paid at a different rate from the people who are working 100 per cent full time on the job. Therefore there is no real justification for arguing that there should be total equality of pay rates' (TUC, 1985, p. 482).
27. The TUC leadership deflected what little pressure there was to produce an overall assessment of YTS. Although instructed in 1983 to 'report to the 1984 Congress on the scheme', the General Council responded evasively to an enquiry made about the document, claiming that a review had been conducted and the results included in a joint TUC–Labour Party document (TUC, 1985, p. 483).
28. The factual sobriety of TUC annual reviews, reminiscent of public documents from an earlier period, contrasted sharply in the 1980s with the propagandist orientation of government documents on training.
29. BIFU's prediction to 1983 Congress that a YTS boycott's 'knock-on effect will lead to depressed wages and conditions of service for all workers' assumed somewhat implausibly that indirect substitution would prove strong (TUC, 1984, p. 427).
30. Further evidence is available from responses to YTS within unions. Leaders opposed boycotts more frequently than members and conference delegates, consistent with the greater interest of the former in attracting young members and increasing the size of the union, as well as the greater threat of substitution to the latter. The more democratic the union, therefore, the less the orientation to youth interests appears generally to have been, *ceteris paribus*.
31. A NALGO speaker to 1987 Congress said 'YTS is going to be made compulsory . . . that was unacceptable a few years ago. Is it going to be acceptable now?' (TUC, 1988, p. 509)
32. The same requirement – that there be clear achievements for union regulation – applies to another defensive argument for TUC strategy, that which depicts political campaigns as ineffective relative to negotiation. To the extent that negotiation itself achieves little, its superiority over political opposition dwindles and may even be reversed.
33. The victory of rejectionism in NUPE after 'heated debate' was also promoted by employer moves to introduce YTS into patient care (*NUPE Journal*, 1988, no.6). Annual conferences where conflict over adult training schemes was associated with increased opposition to YTS included NALGO (1987, 1988), TASS (1987), USDAW (1988, 1989), UCATT (1988), BIFU (1988), IPCS (1987) and TGWU (1989). The IPCS conference saw the first anti-YTS motion in the union's history, calling for payment of the rate for the job to all trainees. The IPCS Executive, claiming that such a policy would kill YTS, secured the motion's remission (*IPCS Bulletin*, June 1987).

Bibliography

AANEEN (1985) 'Over de nieuwe werknemer', *AbvaKabo-Bulletin*, 24 October, pp. 17–27.

ADAMS, L. (1985) 'Changing employment patterns of organized workers', *Monthly Labor Review*, 108, pp. 25–31.

ADAMSKI, W. and GROOTINGS, P. (eds) (1989) *Youth, Education and Work in Europe* (London: Routledge).

AFL-CIO (1988) American Federation of Labor–Congress of Industrial Organizations, *The Economy: Domestic Issues, Employment and Training, Trade* (Washington, D.C.: AFL–CIO).

AKERLOF, G. A, and MAIN, B. G. (1981) 'An experience-weighted measure of employment and unemployment durations', *American Economic Review*, 71, pp. 1003–11.

AKKERMANS, M. (1985) *Beleidsradicalisering en ledendruk. Een studie over de Industriebond-NVV in de periode 1968–1975* (Nijmegen: ITS).

AKKERMANS, T. (1986) 'Vakbeweging: de aantrekkingskracht voor niet-leden en leden', in Nelissen, N., Geurts, J. and de Wit, H. (eds) *Het verkennen van beleidsproblemen* (Kerckebosch: Zeist).

AKKERMANS, T. and GROOTINGS, P. (1978) 'From corporatism to polarisation: elements of the development of Dutch industrial relations', in Crouch, C. and Pizzorno, A. (eds) *The Resurgence of Class Conflict in Western Europe* (London: Macmillan).

AKKERMANS, T. and HÖVELS, B. (1987) 'Young workers and trade unions: a comparison with women and workers in general', *Economia e Lavoro*, 21, pp. 119–23.

AKKERMANS, T. and NOBELEN, P. W. M. (eds) (1983) *Corporatisme en Verzorgingsstaat* (Leiden/Antwerp: Stenfert Kroese).

ALBEDA, W. and TEN HOVE, W.E. (1986) *Neocorporatisme. Evolutie van een Gedachte, Verandering van een Patroon* (Kampen: Kok).

AMAT, F. and GEHIN, J.P. (1987) 'Accès des jeunes à l'emploi et mobilité des actifs: les emplois d'exécution', *Formation Emploi*, 18, pp. 37–47.

AMMASSARI, G.P. (1986) 'Sindacato e nuove relazioni industriali', *Sociologia del Lavoro*, 26/27, pp. 263–79.

AMS (1986a) Arbetsmarknadsstyrelsen 'Uppföljning av ungdomar i ungdoms-lag', *Meddelande från utredningsinstitutet*, 6.

AMS (1986b) Arbetsmarknadsstyrelsen 'Sammansättningen av gruppen arbetslösa 20–24åringar', *Meddelande fron utredningsinstitutet*, 5.

ARONOWITZ, S. (1973) *False Promises: The Shaping of American Working Class Consciousness* (New York: McGraw-Hill).

ASHTON, D. N. (1986) *Unemployment under Capitalism* (Brighton: Wheatsheaf).

274

ASHTON, D. N. and MAGUIRE, M. J. (1986) *Young Adults in the Labour Market*, Research Paper 55 (London: Department of Employment).

ASHTON, D. N., MAGUIRE, M. J. and GARLAND, V. (1982) *Youth in the Labour Market*, Research Paper 34 (London: Department of Employment).

ATKINSON, A. B. and MICKLEWRIGHT, J. (1989) 'Turning the screw: benefits for the unemployed, 1979–88', in Atkinson, A. B., *Poverty and Social Security* (Hemel Hempstead: Harvester Wheatsheaf).

ATKINSON, J. (1987) 'Flexibility or fragmentation? The United Kingdom labour market in the eighties', *Labour and Society*, 12, pp. 87–105.

AUTORENGEMEINSCHAFT (1987) 'Zur Arbeitsmarktentwicklung 1987/ 88: Entwicklungstendenzen und Strukturen', *Mitteilungen aus der Arbeitsmarkt- und Berufsforschung*, 3, pp. 265–73.

AZARIADIS, C. (1981) 'Implicit contracts and related topics: a survey', in Hornstein, Z., Grice, J. and Webb, A. (eds) *The Economics of the Labour Market* (London: HMSO).

BAETHGE, M., HANTSCHE, B., PELULL, W. and VOSKAMP, U. (1988) *Jugend: Arbeit und Identität. Lebensperspektiven und Interessenorientierungen von Jugendlichen* (Opladen: Leske und Budrich).

BAILY, M. N., CRANSTON, A., LEVITAN, S., MANGUM, G., LITOW, S. and AMLUNG, S. (1984) *Jobs for the Future: Strategies in a New Framework* (Washington, D.C.: Center for National Policy).

BANKS, M. H. and ULLAH, P. (1987) *Youth Unemployment: Social and Psychological Perspectives*, Research Paper no. 61 (London: Department of Employment).

BAUSSANO, A. (1988) *La Transizione dalla Scuola al Lavoro: Lavoro e Politiche Regionale* (Milan: F.Angeli).

BEAN, C., LAYARD, R. and NICKELL, S. (1986) 'The rise in unemployment: a multi-country study', *Economica*, 53, pp. S1–S23.

BECKER, G.S. (1975) *Human Capital*, 2nd edition (Chicago: University of Chicago Press).

BECKER, H.A. (1985) 'Generaties,' *Hollands Maandblad*, 4, pp. 14–25.

BECKER, H.A. (1987) 'Generaties en sociale dynamiek', *Sociologisch Jaarboek*, pp. 112–29.

BEGG, I.G., BLAKE, A.P., DEAKIN, B.M. and PRATTEN, C.F. (1990) 'YTS and the Labour Market', Final Report to Training Agency, Department of Applied Economics, University of Cambridge.

BEN-PORATH, Y. (1967) 'The production of human capital and the life-cycle of earnings', *Journal of Political Economy*, 75, pp. 352–65.

BENN, C. and FAIRLEY, J. (1986) *Challenging the MSC* (London: Pluto).

BERG, I. (1970) *Education and Jobs: the Great Training Robbery* (New York: Praeger).

BIBB (1990) Bundesinstitut für Berufsansbildung, 'Ausbildungsvergütungen im Jahr 1989', *Berufsbildung in Wissenschaft und Praxis*, 3, pp. 33–4.

BINMORE, K. and DASGUPTA, P. (1986) *The Economics of Bargaining* (Oxford: Basil Blackwell).

BLANCHARD, O. and SUMMERS, L. (1988) 'Hysteresis and the European unemployment problem', in Cross, R. (ed.) *Unemployment, Hysteresis and the Natural Rate Hypothesis* (Oxford: Basil Blackwell).

BLK (1987) Bund-Länder-Kommission für Bildungsplanung und Forschungs-förderung, 'Künftige Perspektiven von Absolventen der beruflichen Bildung im Beschäftigungssystem', *Materialien zur Bildungsplanung*, Heft 15 (Bonn: BLK).

BMBW (1987a) Bundesministerium für Bildung und Wissenschaft, *Grund- und Strukturdaten 1987/88* (Bonn: BMBW).

BMBW (1987b) Bundesministerium für Bildung und Wissenschaft, *Berufsbildungsbericht 1987* (Bonn: BMBW).

BOWLES, S., GORDON, D. and WEISSKOPF, T. (1983) *Beyond the Waste Land* (New York: Doubleday).

BOYER, R. (1979) 'Wage formation in historical perspective', *Cambridge Journal of Economics*, 3, pp. 99–118.

BOYER, R. (ed.) (1988) *The Search for Labour Market Flexibility: the European Economies in Transition* (Oxford: Clarendon Press).

BRADSHAW, J., LAWTON, D. and COOKE, K. (1987) 'Income and expenditure of teenagers and their families', *Youth and Policy*, 19, pp. 15–19.

BRAY, R.A. (1911) *Boy Labour and Apprenticeship* (London: Constable).

BRINKMANN, C. (1987) 'Unemployment in the Federal Republic of Germany: recent empirical evidence', in Pedersen, P.J. and Lund, R. (eds) *Unemployment: Theory, Policy and Structure* (Berlin: Walter de Gruyter).

BROSNAN, P. and WILKINSON, F. (1988) 'A national minimum wage and economic efficiency', *Contributions to Political Economy*, 7, pp. 1–48.

BROWN, C. (1982) 'Dead end jobs and youth unemployment', in Freeman and Wise (eds).

BROWN, W. (1972) 'A consideration of custom and practice', *British Journal of Industrial Relations*, 10, pp. 42–61.

BROWN, W. (1989) 'Managing remuneration', in Sisson, K. (ed.), *Personnel Management in Britain* (Oxford: Basil Blackwell).

BRUNETTA, R., and DAL CO, M. (eds) (1987) *Report '87: Labour and Employment Policies in Italy* (Rome: Ministro del Lavoro e della Previdenza Sociale).

BRUNHES, B. (1989) 'Labour flexibility in enterprises: a comparison of firms in four European countries', in OECD (1989a).

BRUSCO, S. and GARONNA, P. (1984) 'P.M.E.: Segmentation du marché du travail et relations sociales en Italie', in Greffe, X. (ed.), *Les P.M.E., Créent-Elles des Emplois?* (Paris: Economica).

BRUSCO, S. and SABEL, C. (1981) 'Artisan production and economic growth', in Wilkinson, F. (ed.) *Dynamics of Labour Market Segmentation* (London: Academic Press).

BUDD, A., LEVINE, P. and SMITH, P. (1988) 'Unemployment, vacancies and the long-term unemployed', *Economic Journal*, 98, pp. 1071–91.

BUITELAAR, W.L. (ed.) (1988) *Technology and Work. Labour Studies in England, Germany and the Netherlands* (Aldershot: Gower).

BULGARELLI, A., GIOVINE, M., PENNISI, G. (1989) *Valutare l'Investimento Formazione* (Rome: ISFOL).

BUNDESANSTALT FÜR ARBEIT (1978) *Employment Policy in Germany. Challenges and Concepts for the 1980s* (Nürnberg: Bundesanstalt für Arbeit).

BUNDESANSTALT FÜR ARBEIT (various years) *Amtliche Nachrichten der Bundesanstalt für Arbeit*, various issues, 1975–87.

BUSHELL, R. (1986) 'Evaluation of the Young Workers' Scheme', *Employment Gazette*, 94, pp. 145–52.
BUTTLER, F. (1987) 'Labour market flexibility by deregulation: the case of the Federal Republic of Germany', *Labour and Society*, 12, pp. 19–36.
CALMFORS, L. and DRIFFIL, J. (1988) 'Bargaining structure, corporatism and macroeconomic performance', *Economic Policy*, 6, pp. 14–61.
CAMERLYNCK, G.H. and LYON-CAEN, G. (1983) *Droit du Travail*, 11th edition (Paris: Dalloz).
CAMPBELL, A. and WARNER, M. (1991) 'Training strategies and microelectronics in the engineering industries of the UK and West Germany', in Ryan (ed.).
CAMPINOS-DUBERNET, M. and GRANDO, J.-M. (1988) 'Formation professionnelle ouvrière: trois modèles Européens', *Formation Emploi*, 22, pp. 5–29.
CANGEMI, J.P., CLARK, L. and HARRYMAN, M.E. (1976) 'Differences between pro-union and pro-company employees', *Personnel Journal*, 55, pp. 451–53.
CAPDEVILLE, Y. and GRAPIN, P. (1975) 'L'insertion professionnelle à la sortie du système scolaire: quelques exemples sur la période récente', *Economie et Statistique*, 81/2, pp. 57–72.
CAREY, M. (1985) *How Workers Get Their Training*, Bulletin 2226, Bureau of Labour Statistics, US Department of Labor (Washington, D.C.: GPO).
CARRUTH, A. and OSWALD, A. (1987) 'On union preferences and labour market models: insiders and outsiders', *Economic Journal*, 97, pp. 431–45.
CARTER, D. (1986) 'The Community Programme: MSC strategies for the long-term unemployed', Workers' Educational Association, *Studies for Trade Unionists*, 12, no 46 (London: WEA).
CASEY, B. (1986) 'The dual apprenticeship system and the recruitment and retention of young persons in West Germany', *British Journal of Industrial Relations*, 24, pp. 63–82.
CASSELS, J. (1990) *Britain's Real Skills Shortage* (London: Policy Studies Institute).
CBI (1989) Confederation of British Industry, *Towards a Skills Revolution* (London: CBI).
CEC (1966) Commission of the European Communities, *Apprentices in the Netherlands*, Social Policy Series, number 35, 1966–7.
CEC (1990) Commission of the European Communities, *Employment in Europe 1990* (Luxembourg: Office for Official Publications of the European Communities).
CEDEFOP (1984) European Centre for the Development of Vocational Training, *Vocational Training Systems in the Member States of the European Community* (Berlin: CEDEFOP).
CEDEFOP (1987) *The Role of the Social Partners in Vocational Training in Italy* (Berlin: CEDEFOP).
CELLA, G.P. and TREU, T. (1982) *Relazioni Industriale* (Bologna: Il Mulino).
COATES, D. (1980) *Labour in Power?* (London: Longman).
COEFFIC, N. (1987) 'Le devenir des jeunes sortis de l'école', *Données Sociales 1987*, pp. 120–6 (Paris: INSEE).

COLEMAN, J. (1961) *The Adolescent Society* (New York: Glencoe Free Press).

COMBES, M-C. (1988) 'L'apprentissage en France', CEREQ, Document de Travail 33, March (Paris: CEREQ).

COOKE, K. (1985) 'Problems of income support for young people', *Youth and Policy*, 15, pp. 5–19.

COSTRELL, R. M., DUGUAY, G. E. and TREYZ, G. I. (1986) 'Labour substitution and complementarity among age–sex groups', *Applied Economics*, 18, pp. 777–91.

CREGAN, C. and JOHNSTON, S. (1990) 'An industrial relations approach to the free rider problem: young people and trade union membership in the UK', *British Journal of Industrial Relations*, 28, pp. 84–104.

CRONE, F. (1986) 'Does cutting youth wages help young workers to find jobs?', *Social Europe*, Supplement on Youth Pay and Employers' Recruitment Practices for Young People in the Community (Luxembourg: EEC).

CROUCH, C. and PIZZORNO, A. (1977) *Conflitti in Europa: Lotte di Classe, Sindicati e Stato dopo il '68* (Milan: Etas Libri).

CROUCHER, R. (1982) *Engineers at War* (Manchester: Merlin).

CUSACK, S. and ROLL, J. (1985) *Families Rent Apart* (London: Child Poverty Action Group).

DE GRAAF, J. and PAAUWE, J. (1984) *Jongeren over Werk, Werkloosheid en Vakbeweging* (Utrecht: CNV).

D'IRIBARNE, A. (1982) 'Vocational education and training and the new technologies: the key role of the enterprise', CERI mimeo CW/82.02 (Paris: OECD).

DEAKIN, B. M. and PRATTEN, C. F. (1987) 'Economic effects of YTS', *Employment Gazette*, 95, pp. 491–7.

DEARLE, N. A. (1914) *Industrial Training* (London: King and Son).

DEFREITAS, G., MARSDEN, D. and RYAN, P. (1990) 'Youth employment patterns in segmented labour markets in the US and Europe', mimeo, Department of Economics, Hofstra University, New York.

DEG (1980) 'Shipbuilding, engineering and chemicals earnings in June 1980', *Department of Employment Gazette*, 88, pp. 1081–8.

DEG (1986) 'The Wages Act 1986', *Employment Gazette*, 94, pp. 369–72.

DEG (1988) 'Ethnic origins and the labour market', *Employment Gazette*, 96, pp. 633–46.

DEG (1989) 'Education and labour market status of young people', *Employment Gazette*, 95, pp. 459–65.

DENISON, E. F. (1967) *Why Growth Rates Differ* (Washington, D.C.: Brookings).

DICKENS, W. and LEONARD, J. (1985) 'Accounting for the decline in union membership, 1950–1980', *Industrial and Labor Relations Review*, 38, pp. 323–34.

DICKENS, W. T. and KATZ, L. F. (1987) 'Inter-industry wage differences and industry characteristics', in Lang and Leonard (eds).

DILNOT, A. W. and MORRIS, C. N. (1984) 'Private costs and benefits of unemployment: measuring replacement rates', in Greenhalgh, C., Layard, R. and Oswald, A. J. (eds) *The Causes of Unemployment* (Oxford: OUP).

DOERINGER, P. B. and PIORE, M. (1971) *Internal Labour Markets and Manpower Analysis* (Lexington, Massachusetts: D.C.Heath).
DOERINGER, P. B. and PIORE, M. J. (1975) 'Unemployment and the "dual labour market"', *The Public Interest*, 38, pp. 67–79.
DOUGHERTY, C. (1987) 'The German dual system: a heretical view', *European Journal of Education*, 22, pp. 195–9.
ECKAUS, R. S. (1964) 'Economic criteria for education and training', *Review of Economics and Statistics*, 64, pp. 181–9.
EDWARDS, R. C., GARONNA, P. and TODTLING, F. (1986) *Unions in Crisis and Beyond* (Dover, Massachusetts: Auburn House).
EDWARDS, R. C. and PODGURSKY, M. (1986) 'The unravelling accord: American unions in crisis', in Edwards, Garonna and Todtling (eds).
EHRENBERG, R. G. and SMITH, R. S. (1987) *Modern Labour Economics: Theory and Public Policy*, 3rd edition (Glenview, Illinois: Scott Foresman).
ELBAUM, B. (1988) 'Why apprenticeship persisted in Britain but not in the United States', paper presented to the Economic History Association Annual Meetings, Detroit, September.
ELIASSON, G. (1987) 'The knowledge base of an industrial economy', in Eliasson, G. and Ryan, P., 'The human factor in economic and technological change', Educational Monograph no. 3 (Paris: OECD).
ELLWOOD, D. T. (1982) 'Teenage unemployment: permanent scars or temporary blemishes?', in Freeman and Wise (eds).
ELSINGA, E. (1984) 'De politieke representativiteit van politieke participatie', *Beleid en Maatschappij*, 6, pp. 173–81.
ERBES-SEGUIN, S. (1986) 'Rapporti collettivi, controlli economico e sindacati nella Francia contemporanea', *Sociologia del Lavoro*, 26/27, pp. 281–93.
EUROSTAT (1972) Statistical Office of the European Communities, *Survey of the Structure of Earnings in Industry* (Luxembourg: EEC).
EUROSTAT (1981) *Labour Force Survey Results 1979* (Luxembourg: Statistical Office of the European Communities).
EUROSTAT (1986) *Survey of Labour Costs in Industry, 1984* (Luxembourg: Statistical Office of the European Communities).
EVERSLEY, J. (1986) 'Trade union responses to the MSC', in Benn and Fairley (eds).
EYRAUD, F, MARSDEN, D. W, and SILVESTRE, J. J. (1990) 'Occupational and internal labour markets in Britain and France', *International Labour Review*, 129, pp. 501–18.
FELDSTEIN, M. and ELLWOOD, D. T. (1982) 'Teenage unemployment: what is the problem?', in Freeman and Wise (eds).
FELLING, A. and PETERS, J. (1986) 'Conservatism: a multidimensional concept', *The Netherlands Journal of Sociology*, 22, pp. 36–60.
FELLING, A., PETERS, J. and SCHREUDER, O. (1983) *Burgerlijk en Onburgerlijk Nederland. Een Nationaal Onderzoek naar Waardenorientaties op de Drempel van de Jaren Tachtig* (Deventer: Van Loghum Slaterus).
FELLING, A., PETERS, J. and SCHREUDER, O. (1987) *Religion in Dutch Society 85. Documentation of a National Survey on Religious and Secular Attitudes in 1985* (Amsterdam: Steinmetz Archive).

FGA (1982) Fondazione Giovanni Agnelli, *La Formazione Professionale in Italia*, 2 volumes (Bologna: Il Mulino).

FINEGOLD, D. (1990) 'The changing economic context and its relationship with education and training', paper presented to Conference on US and UK Education and Training Reform, University of Warwick, June.

FINEGOLD, D. (1991) 'Institutional prerequisites for a high skill equilibrium', in Ryan (ed).

FINEGOLD, D. and SOSKICE, D. (1988) 'The failure of training in Britain: analysis and prescription', *Oxford Review of Economic Policy*, 4, pp. 21–53.

FINN, D. (1987) *Training without Jobs* (London: Macmillan).

FLANAGAN, R. J. (1987) 'Efficiency and Equality in Swedish Labor Markets' in Bosworth, B. P. and Rivlin, A. M. (eds) *The Swedish Economy* (Washington: Brookings Institution).

FLANDERS, A. (1964) *The Fawley Productivity Agreements* (London: Faber).

FLECK, J. (1983) 'Robotics in manufacturing organisations', in Winch, G. (ed.) *Information Technology in Manufacturing Processes* (London: Rossendale).

FOX, A. (1974) *Beyond Contract* (London: Society Today and Tomorrow).

FREEMAN, R. B. (1979) 'The effects of demographic factors on age-earnings profiles', *Journal of Human Resources*, 14, pp. 289–318.

FREEMAN, R. B. (1988a) 'Labour market institutions and economic performance', *Economic Policy*, 6, pp. 63–80.

FREEMAN, R. B. (1988b) 'Contraction and expansion: the divergence of private sector and public sector unionism in the United States', *Economic Perspectives*, 2, pp. 63–88.

FREEMAN, R. B. and HOLZER, H. (eds) (1986) *The Black Youth Employment Crisis* (Chicago/NBER: University of Chicago).

FREEMAN, R. B. and MEDOFF, J. L. (1982) 'The youth labour market problem in the United States: an overview', in Freeman and Wise (eds).

FREEMAN, R. B. and WISE, D. A. (eds) (1982) *The Youth Labour Market Problem: its Nature, Causes and Consequences* (Chicago/NBER: University of Chicago).

FREY, L. (1988) 'The impact of labour policy measures', in Ministero del Lavoro, *Report '88: Labour and Employment Policies in Italy* (Rome: Istituto Poligrafico e Zecca dello Stato).

FYFE, A. (1989) *Child Labour* (Cambridge: Polity Press).

GAMBETTA, D. (ed.) (1988) *Trust: Making and Breaking Cooperative Relations* (Oxford: Basil Blackwell).

GARONNA, P. (1980a) 'Modelling the labour adjustment process: an approach to segmentation', *Economic Notes* (Siena), 9, pp. 14–38.

GARONNA, P. (1980b) 'The theory and practice of employment policy in Italy in the seventies', in Buttler, F., Gerlach, K. and Sengenberger, W. (eds) *Job Creation and Job Maintenance – Experiences from Western Countries in the '70s* (Paderborn: SAMF).

GARONNA, P. (1986) 'Youth unemployment, labour market deregulation and union strategies in Italy', *British Journal of Industrial Relations*, 24, pp. 43–62.

GARONNA, P. (1989) 'Valutazione e benefici della formazione professionale', mimeo, June (Rome: ISFOL).

GARONNA P., and PISANI, E. (1986) 'Italian unions in transition: the crisis of political unionism', in Edwards et al. (eds).

GARONNA P, and RYAN, P. (1986) 'Youth labour, industrial relations and deregulation in advanced economies', *Economia e Lavoro*, 20, pp. 3–19.

GARONNA, P. and RYAN, P. (1989) 'Le travail des jeunes, les relations professionnelles et les politiques sociales dans les économies avancées', *Formation Emploi*, 25, pp. 78–90.

GB DE (1974) Department of Employment, *Unqualified, Untrained and Unemployed*, Report of Working Party set up by National Youth Employment Council (London: HMSO).

GB DE (1981) Department of Employment, *A New Training Initiative: a Programme for Action*, Cmnd 8455 (London: HMSO).

GB DE (1983) *1983 New Earnings Survey* (London: Department of Employment).

GB DE (1985) 'A survey of Youth Training Scheme providers', *Employment Gazette*, 93, pp. 307–12.

GB DE (1987) 'Education and labour market status of young people', *Employment Gazette*, 95, pp. 459–65.

GB DE (1988) Department of Employment, *Employment for the 1990s*, Cm 540 (London: HMSO).

GB DE (1989) 'Education and labour market status of young people', *Employment Gazette*, 97, pp. 262–3.

GB DE (1990) '1989 Labour Force Survey: preliminary results', *Employment Gazette*, 98, pp. 199–212.

GB DE EMO (1968) 'Earnings and hours in October 1968', *Employment and Productivity Gazette*, 76, pp. 106–18.

GB DE EMO (1973) Great Britain, Department of Employment, 'Earnings and hours of manual workers in October 1972', *Department of Employment Gazette*, 81, pp. 148–57.

GB DES (1985) Department of Education and Science, *The Development of Higher Education into the 1990s*, Cmnd 9524 (London: HMSO).

GB DES (1988) Department of Education and Science, *Top-up Loans for Students*, Cm 520 (London: HMSO).

GB MSC (1977) *Young People and Work* (Sheffield: Manpower Services Commission).

GB MSC (1982a) 'Review of fourth year of special programmes', *Special Programme News*, Special Issue, October (Sheffield: Manpower Services Commission).

GB MSC (1982b) *Labour Market Quarterly Report*, September (Sheffield: Manpower Services Commission).

GB MSC (1982c) *Youth Task Group Report* (Sheffield: Manpower Services Commission).

GB MSC (1984) *MSC Annual Report 1983/84* (Sheffield: Manpower Services Commission).

GB MSC (1987) *Labour Market Quarterly Report*, February (Sheffield: Manpower Services Commission).

GB MSC/NEDO (1985) Manpower Services Commission/National Economic Development Office, *A Challenge to Complacency: Changing Attitudes to Training* (Sheffield, MSC).

GB NEDO (1986) *Changing Working Patterns: How Companies achieve Flexibility to Meet New Needs* (London: National Economic Development Office).

GB NEDO (1988) National Economic Development Office, *Young People and the Labour Market* (London: NEDO).

GB NEDO/MSC (1984) National Economic Development Office/Manpower Services Commission, *Competence and Competition* (London: NEDO).

GB NEDO/TA (1989) National Economic Development Office/Training Agency, *Defusing the Demographic Timebomb* (London: NEDO).

GB OPCS (1986) *Labour Force Survey 1983 and 1984*, Office of Population Censuses and Surveys (London: HMSO).

GB TA (1989a) *Training in Britain: a Study of Funding, Activity and Attitudes*, Main Report (Sheffield: Training Agency).

GB TA (1989b) *YTS Progress Report 1987/88* (Sheffield: Training Agency).

GB TA (1990) *Labour Market Quarterly Report*, May (Sheffield: Training Agency).

GB TC (1988) *Annual Report 1987/88* (Sheffield: Training Commission).

GERME, J. F. (1986) 'Employment policies and the entry of young people into the labour market in France', *British Journal of Industrial Relations*, 24, pp. 29–42.

GEUL, A., NOBELEN, P. W. AND SLOMP, H. (1985) 'The future of tripartism in the low countries', in Ten Hove, M. D. (ed.), *Institutional Arrangements in a Changing Welfare State* (Maastricht: Presses Universitaires Européennes) .

GINTIS, H. (1970) 'New working class and revolutionary youth', *Socialist Revolution*, 1, pp. 26–47.

GMBATU (1985) *Report of the 2nd Congress 1984* (Esher, Surrey: General, Municipal, Boilermakers and Allied Trades Union).

GODSCHALK, J. J. (1986) *Werkloosheid en Normvervaging* (Amersfoort/ Leuven: ACCO).

GOLDFIELD, M. (1987) *The Decline of Organized Labor in the United States* (Chicago: University of Chicago Press).

GOLLAN, J. (1937) *Youth in British Industry* (London: Gollancz).

GORDON, D. M., EDWARDS, R. C. and REICH, M. (1982) *Segmented Work, Divided Workers* (Cambridge: CUP).

GORDON, R. J. (1973) 'The welfare cost of higher unemployment', *Brookings Papers on Economic Activity*, 1, pp. 133–95.

GRANT FOUNDATION (1988) William T. Grant Foundation Commission on Work, Family and Citizenship, *The Forgotten Half: Non-College Youth in America* (Washington, D.C.: William T. Grant Foundation).

GRANT, J. and HAMERMESH, D. S. (1981) 'Labour market competition among youths, white women and others', *Review of Economics and Statistics*, 63, pp. 354–60.

GRIFFIN, T. (1984) 'Technological change and craft control in the newspaper industry: an international comparison', *Cambridge Journal of Economics*, 8, pp. 41–61.

GROSS, M. (1990) 'Labour market segmentation: the role of product market and industry structure in determining labour market outcomes', unpublished Ph.D. dissertation, University of Cambridge.

GUFFENS, T. (1985) 'Mensen met een handicap en hun emancipatie', in Nelissen et al. (eds), pp. 389–430.

HAKIM, C. (1979) *Occupational Segregation*, Research Paper number 9 (London: Department of Employment).

HAKIM, C. (1990) 'Core and periphery in employers' workforce strategies: evidence from the 1987 ELUS Survey', *Work, Employment and Society*, 4, pp. 157–88.

HALL, R. E. (1982), 'The importance of lifetime jobs in the US economy', *American Economic Review*, 72, pp.716–24.

HAMERMESH, D. S. (1985) 'Substitution between different categories of labour, relative wages and youth unemployment', *OECD Economic Studies*, 5, pp. 57–85.

HART, P. E. (1988) *Youth Unemployment in Great Britain* (Cambridge: CUP).

HECKMAN, J. and BORJAS, G. (1980) 'Does unemployment cause future unemployment?', *Economica*, 47, pp. 247–83.

HILLS, S. M. and REUBENS, B. G. (1983) 'Youth employment in the United States', in Reubens (ed.).

HUGHES, J. J. and BRINKLEY, I. (1979) 'Attitudes and expectations of Skillcentre trainees towards trade unions and trade union membership', *British Journal of Industrial Relations*, 17, pp. 64–9.

HUTCHINSON, G., BARR, N. and DROBNY, A. (1984) 'The employment of young people in a segmented labour market: the case of Great Britain', *Applied Economics*, 16, pp. 187–204.

IDS (1983) Incomes Data Services, *IDS Report 393*, January (London: IDS).

IDS (1987) Incomes Data Services, *Young Workers' Pay*, Study 383 (London: IDS).

IMS (1982) Institute of Manpower Studies, 'Evaluation of Apprentice Support Awards' (Brighton: University of Sussex).

INGLEHART, R. (1977) *The Silent Revolution* (Princeton: Princeton University Press).

INGLEHART, R. (1979) 'Value priorities and socioeconomic change', in Barnes, S. H. and Kaase, M. (eds), *Political Action: Mass Participation in Five Western Democracies* (Beverly Hills: Sage).

ISFOL (1984) *I Contratti di Formazione-Lavoro* (Rome: ISFOL).

ISFOL (1987) *Rapporto sulla Forazione Professionale in Italia* (Milan: F.Angeli).

ISFOL (1988a) 'La formazione nella contrattazione aziendale', *Quaderni di Formazione Isfol*, August (Milan: F.Angeli).

ISFOL (1988b) 'La formazione per i nuovi imprenditori', *Quaderni di Formazione Isfol*, April (Milan: F.Angeli).

ISFOL (1989) *Percorsi Giovanili di Studio e di Lavoro* (Milan: F.Angeli).

JACKMAN, R. (1987) *A Job Guarantee for Long-Term Unemployed People* (London: Employment Institute).

JACKMAN, R. and LAYARD, R. (1988) 'Does long-term unemployment reduce a person's chance of a job? A time-series test', Discussion Paper 309, Centre for Labour Economics, London School of Economics.

JACKSON, M.P. and HANBY, V.J.B. (1982) *British Work Creation Programmes* (Aldershot: Gower).

JAHODA, M. (1982) *Employment and Unemployment: a Social-Psychological Analysis* (Cambridge: CUP).

JARVIS, V. AND PRAIS, S. (1989) 'Two nations of shopkeepers: training for retailing in France and Britain', *National Institute Economic Review*, 128, pp. 58–73.

JOHNSON, G. E. and LAYARD, R. (1986) 'The natural rate of unemployment: explanation and policy', in Ashenfelter, O. and Layard, R. (eds) *Handbook of Labour Economics*, Volume 2 (Amsterdam: North Holland).

JOHNSTON, W. and PACKER, A. (1987) *Workforce 2000* (Indianopolis: Hudson Institute).

JONES, I. S. (1985) 'Skill formation and pay relativities', in Worswick (ed.).

JONES I. S. (1986) 'Apprentice training costs in British manufacturing establishments: some new evidence', *British Journal of Industrial Relations*, 24, pp. 333–62.

JONGEREN EN DE VAKBOND (1986) 'Motieven van werkende en werkloze jongeren om al dan niet lid van AbvaKabo te worden; verwachtingen ten aanzien van het bondslidmaatschap', Zoetermeer, AbvaKabo-jongerensecretariaat, July.

JUNANKAR, P. N. (ed.) (1987) *From School to Unemployment? The Labour Market for Young People* (London: Macmillan).

JUNANKAR, P. N. and NEALE, A. (1987) 'Relative wages and the youth labour market', in Junankar (ed.).

KAUFMAN, R. (1984) 'On wage stickiness in Britain's competitive sector', *British Journal of Industrial Relations*, 22, pp. 101–12.

KEELING, F. (1914) *Child Labour in the United Kingdom* (London: King and Son).

KEEP, E. (1986) 'Designing the stable door: a study of how the Youth Training Scheme was planned', Warwick Paper on Industrial Relations no. 8, Industrial Relations Research Unit, University of Warwick.

KEEP, E. (1991) 'The grass looked greener: some thoughts on the influence of comparative vocational training research on the UK policy debate', in Ryan (ed.).

KEEP, E. and MAYHEW, K. (1988) 'The assessment: education, training and economic performance', *Oxford Review of Economic Policy*, 4.3, pp. i–xv.

KERN, H. and SCHUMANN, M. (1984) *Das Ende der Arbeitsteilung?* (München: Beck).

KOEPKE, G. (1987) 'De positie en structuur van de vakbeweging in West-europese landen, en de ontwikkelingen hierin. Inleiding omtrent het internationale perspectief voor de studieconferentie van de Bouw en Houtbond FNV', Amersfoort, November.

KOHLER, H. and REYHER, L. (1988) *Arbeitszeit und Arbeitsvolumen in der Bundesrepublik Deutschland 1960–1986. Datenlage – Struktur – Entwicklung.* Band 123 (Nürnberg: Beiträge zur Arbeitsmarkt- und Berufsforschung).

KOMMENTAR TILL VERKSTADSAVTALET (1987) *87 års utgåva* (Katrineholm: Verkstädernas Förlag).

KRANENBURG, M. (1985) 'De vakbeweging in een technologische samenleving; is er nog een toekomst voor de FNV?', in *NRC-Handelsblad*, 11 September.

KRUEGER, A. and SUMMERS, L. H. (1987) 'Reflections on the inter-industry wage structure', in Lang and Leonard (eds).

KÜHL, J. (1987) 'Labour policy in the Federal Republic of Germany: challenges and concepts', *Labour*, 1, no.3, pp. 25–56.

LANG, K. and LEONARD, J. S. (eds) (1987) *Unemployment and the Structure of Labour Markets* (Oxford: Basil Blackwell).

LAYARD, R. and NICKELL, S. (1987) 'The labour market', in Dornbusch, R. and Layard, R. (eds) *The Performance of the British Economy* (Oxford: OUP).

LAZEAR, E. (1981) 'Agency, earnings profiles and hour restrictions', *American Economic Review*, 71, pp. 606–20.

LECHER, W. (1987) 'Deregulierung der Arbeitsbeziehungen. gesellschaftliche und gewerkschaftliche Entwicklungen in Grossbritannien, den USA, Japan und Frankreich', *Soziale Welt*, 38, pp. 148–65.

LEE, D. (1979) 'Craft unions and the force of tradition: the case of apprenticeship', *British Journal of Industrial Relations*, 17, pp. 34–49.

LEE, D., MARSDEN, D., RICKMAN, P. and DUNCOMBE, J. (1990) *Scheming for Youth: a Study of YTS in the Enterprise Culture* (Milton Keynes: Open University Press).

LEVITAN, S. and MANGUM, G. (1984) 'A quarter century of employment and training policy', in Baily et al.

LINDBECK, A. and SNOWER, D. (1988) 'Cooperation, harassment and involuntary unemployment: an insider–outsider approach', *American Economic Review*, 78, pp. 167–88.

LINDLEY, R. M. (1983) 'Active manpower policy', in Bain, G. S. (ed.) *Industrial Relations in Britain* (Oxford: Basil Blackwell).

LINDLEY, R. M. (1991) 'Interactions in the markets for education, training and labour: a European perspective on intermediate skills', in Ryan (ed.).

LO-STATISTIK (1986) *Medlemmar, Organisation, Avtal och Ekonomi för LO och Anslutna Foerbund* (Stockholm: Landsorganisationen i Sverige).

LUCAS, R. E. and RAPPING, L. (1970) 'Real wages, employment and inflation', in Phelps, E. S. (ed.) *Microfoundations of Employment and Inflation Theory* (New York: Norton).

LYNCH, L. and RICHARDSON, R. (1982) 'Unemployment of young workers in Britain', *British Journal of Industrial Relations*, 20, pp. 362–71.

MACKAY, D. I, BODDY, D., BRACK, J., DIACK, J. A. and JONES, N. (1971) *Labour Markets Under Different Employment Conditions* (London: George Allen and Unwin).

McNABB, R. and RYAN, P. (1989) 'Segmented labour markets', in Tzannatos, Z. and Sapsford, D. (eds) *Current Issues in Labour Economics* (London: Macmillan).

McRAE, S. (1987) *Young and Jobless: the Social and Personal Consequences of Long-Term Youth Unemployment* (London: Policy Studies Institute).

MAIN, B. G. M. (1981) 'The length of employment and unemployment in Great Britain', *Scottish Journal of Political Economy*, 28, pp.146–64.

MAIN, B. G. M. (1982) 'The length of a job in Great Britain', *Economica*, 49, pp. 325–33.

MAIN, B. G. M. (1987) 'Earnings, expected earnings and unemployment amongst school-leavers', in Junankar (ed.).

MAIWALD, H. (1985) 'Aktuelle Probleme des Kampfes der gewerkschaftsbewegung in den USA', in *Wissenschaftliche Zeitschrift der Paedagogischen Hochschule Karl Liebknecht Potsdam*, 29, pp. 623–30.

MAKSYMIW, W., EATON, J. and GILL, C. (1990) *The British Trade Union Directory* (Harlow: Longman).

MARECHAL, P. and VINEY, X. (1983) 'Les premiers emplois de la vie active des jeunes sortis en 1975 des classes terminales de CAP et BEP', *Formation Emploi*, 2, pp. 19–34.

MARIANI, I. F. (1986) 'Youth pay and employers' recruiting practices: the Italian experience', *Social Europe*, Supplement on Youth Pay and Employers' Recruitment Practices for Young People in the Community (Luxembourg: EEC).

MARKLUND, S. (1982) *Skolsverige 1950–1975, Del 3* (Stockholm: Liber).

MARSDEN, D. W. (1981) 'Pay differentials in Britain, West Germany, France and Italy', *Employment Gazette*, 89, pp. 309–18.

MARSDEN, D. W. (1985) 'Youth pay in Britain compared with France and FR Germany', *British Journal of Industrial Relations*, 23, pp. 399–414.

MARSDEN, D. W. (1986a) *The End of Economic Man? Custom and Competition in the Labour Market* (Brighton: Wheatsheaf).

MARSDEN, D. W. (1986b) 'Youth pay and employers' recruitment practices for young workers in Western Europe', *Social Europe*, Supplement, pp. 3–25.

MARSDEN, D. W. (1987a) 'Youth pay in some OECD countries since 1966,' in Junankar (ed.).

MARSDEN, D. W. (1987b) 'Collective bargaining and industrial adjustment in Britain, France, Italy and West Germany', in Duchene, F., and Shepherd, G. (eds) *Managing Industrial Change in Western Europe* (London: Frances Pinter).

MARSDEN, D. W. (1988) 'Short-run wage flexibility and labour market adaptation in Western Europe', *Labour*, 2, pp. 31–54.

MARSDEN, D. W. (1990a) 'Institutions and labour mobility: occupational and internal labour markets in Britain, France, Italy and West Germany', in Brunetta, R. and Dell'Aringa, C. (eds) *Labour Relations and Economic Performance* (London: Macmillan).

MARSDEN, D. W., (1990b) 'United Kingdom', in Sengenberger, W., Loveman, G. and Piore, M. J. (eds) *The Reemergence of Small Enterprises: Industrial Restructuring in Industrial Countries* (Geneva: International Labour Office).

MARSDEN, D. W. and RYAN, P. (1986) 'Where do young workers work? The distribution of youth employment by industry in various European economies', *British Journal of Industrial Relations*, 24, pp. 83–102.

MARSDEN, D. W. and RYAN, P. (1988a) 'Youth labour market structures and the quality of youth employment in major EEC economies', Report to Joseph Rowntree Memorial Trust, York, August.

MARSDEN, D. W. and RYAN, P. (1988b) 'Apprenticeship and labour market structure: UK youth employment and training within comparative context', paper presented to OECD Symposium on Innovations in Apprenticeship and Training, Paris, November.

MARSDEN, D. W. and RYAN, P. (1989a) 'Statistical tests for the universality of youth employment mechanisms in segmented labour markets', *International Review of Applied Economics*, 3, pp 148–69.

MARSDEN, D. W. and RYAN, P. (1989b) 'Employment and training of young people: have the government misunderstood the labour market?', in Harrison, A. and Gretton, J. (eds) *Education and Training UK 1989: an Economic, Social and Policy Audit* (Newbury, Berkshire: Policy Journals).

MARSDEN, D. W. and RYAN, P. (1990a) 'The transferability of skills and the mobility of skilled workers in the European Community', in Garonna, P. and Edwards, R.C. (eds) *The Forgotten Link: Labour's Stake in International Economic Cooperation* (Rome: Peritaca).

MARSDEN, D. W. and RYAN, P. (1990b) 'Institutional aspects of youth employment and training policy in Britain', *British Journal of Industrial Relations*, 28, pp. 351–70.

MARSDEN, D. W. and RYAN, P. (1991) 'Initial training, labour market structure and public policy: intermediate skills in British and German industry', in Ryan (ed.).

MARTIN, J. and ROBERTS, C. (1984) *Women and Employment: a Lifetime Perspective*, Department of Employment/OPCS (London: HMSO).

MATTHEWS, K. (1989) 'UK skills shortage: short-term problem or long-term crisis?', *Quarterly Economic Bulletin*, 10, pp. 28–32.

MAURICE, M., SELLIER, F. and SILVESTRE, J. J. (1984) 'The search for a societal effect in the production of hierarchy: a comparison of France and Germany', in Osterman (ed.).

MAURICE, M., SELLIER, F., and SILVESTRE, J.J. (1986) *The Social Foundations of Industrial Power* (Cambridge, Mass: MIT Press).

MERRILEES, W. J. and WILSON, R. A. (1979) 'Disequilibrium in the labour market for young people in Great Britain', Discussion paper 10, Manpower Research Group (Coventry: University of Warwick).

METCALF, D. and RICHARDS, J. (1983) 'Youth unemployment in Great Britain', in Reubens (ed.).

MEULDERS, D. and WILKIN, L. (1987) 'Labour market flexibility: a critical introduction to the analysis of a concept', *Labour and Society*, 12, pp. 3–18.

MILLER, A. R., TREIMAN, D. J., CAIN, P. S. and ROOS, P. A. (1980) *Work, Jobs and Occupations* (Washington, D.C.: National Academy Press).

MINISTERO DEL LAVORO (1988) *Report '88: Labour and Employment Policies in Italy*, Ministero del Lavoro e della Previdenza Soziale (Rome: Istituto Poligrafico e Zecca dello Stato).

MINISTERO DEL LAVORO (1989) *Piano per l'Occupazione e per la Formazione Professionale da Realizzarsi con il Contributo del Fondo Sociale Europeo: Misure a Favore della Disoccupazione Giovanile e di Lunga Durata* (Rome: Isfol).

MIT TASKFORCE ON PRODUCTIVITY (1989) *Made in America* (Cambridge, Mass.: MIT Press).

MOKKEN, R. J. (1971) *A Theory and Procedure of Scale Analysis* (Den Haag: Mouton).

MOON, J. and RICHARDSON, J.J. (1985) *Unemployment in the UK* (Aldershot: Gower).

MOUY, P. (1983) 'La formation professionnelle initiale des ouvriers et l'évolution du travail industriel', *Formation Emploi*, 1, pp. 52–70.

MPR (1978) Mathematica Policy Research, 'Evaluation of the Economic Impact of the Job Corps Program', Special Report (Princeton, N.J.: Mathematica Policy Research, Inc.).

MURPHY, M. (1990) 'Unemployment among young people: social and psychological causes and consequences', *Youth and Policy*, 29, pp. 11–19.

NAPOLI, M. (1984) *Occupazione e Politica del Lavoro in Italia* (Milan: Vita e Pensiero).

NELISSEN, N., AKKERMANS, T. AND DE WIT, H. (eds) (1985) *Het Verkennen van Sociale Problemen* (Zeist: Kerckebosch).

NIE, N.H. (1983) *SPSSX User's Guide* (New York: McGraw-Hill).

NOLL, I., BEICHT, U., BOELL, G., MALCHER, W. and WIEDERHOLD-FRITZ, S. (1983) *Nettokosten der betrieblichen Berufsausbildung*, Schriften zur Berufsbildungsforschung, Bundesinstitut fur Berufsausbildung (Berlin: Beuth Verlag).

NOMISMA (1988) *Metodi e Problemi di Valutazione di Interventi Integrati a Carattere Territoriale Finalizzati alla Promozione dello Sviluppo Tecnologico* (Bologna: NOMISMA).

NUPE (1983) *Report of 56th National Conference* (London: National Union of Public Employees).

NUPE (1984) *Report of 57th National Conference* (London: National Union of Public Employees).

NUPE (1985) *Report of 58th National Conference* (London: National Union of Public Employees).

OECD (1979) *Policies for Apprenticeship* (Paris: OECD).

OECD (1980a) *Youth Unemployment: the Causes and Consequences* (Paris: OECD).

OECD (1980b) 'Review of youth employment policies: Federal Republic of Germany', mimeo (Paris: OECD).

OECD (1984a) *OECD Employment Outlook* (Paris: OECD).

OECD (1984b) *New Policies for the Young* (Paris: OECD).

OECD (1985) *Social Expenditure 1960–1900: Problems of Growth and Control* (Paris: OECD).

OECD (1986a) *Labour Market Flexibility*, Dahrendorf Report (Paris: OECD).

OECD (1986b) *Flexibility in the Labour Market: the Current Debate* (Paris: OECD).

OECD (1988a) *OECD Employment Outlook 1988* (Paris: OECD).

OECD (1988b) *Economic Survey: the Netherlands* (Paris: OECD).

OECD (1988c) *New Technologies in the 1990s: a Socioeconomic Strategy* (Paris: OECD).

OECD (1989a) *Labour Market Flexibility: Trends in Enterprises* (Paris: OECD).

OECD (1989b) *Labour Force Statistics 1966–86* (Paris: OECD).

OPPENHEIM, C. (1990) *Holes in the Safety Net: Falling Standards for People in Poverty* (London: Child Poverty Action Group).

OSTERMAN, P. (1980) *Getting Started: the Youth Labour Market* (Cambridge, Mass.: MIT Press).

OSTERMAN, P. (1982a) 'Employment structures within firms', *British Journal of Industrial Relations*, 20, pp. 349–61.

OSTERMAN, P. (1982b) 'Comment', in Freeman and Wise (eds).

OSTERMAN, P. (ed.) (1984) *Internal Labour Markets* (Cambridge, Mass.: MIT Press).

OSTERMAN, P. (1988) *Employment Futures: Reorganization, Dislocation and Public Policy* (New York: Oxford University Press).

OSWALD, A. (1985) 'The economic theory of trade unions: an introductory survey', *Scandinavian Journal of Economics*, 87, pp. 160–93.

PAAUWE, J. (1987) 'Trends of Trade Union Membership in The Netherlands', paper presented at the European Conference on Industrial Relations in Europe, Brussels, Management Centre Europe, 25–26 November.

PAYNE, J. (1989) 'Trade union membership and activism among young people in Great Britain', *British Journal of Industrial Relations*, 27, pp. 111–32.

PEMBERTON, J. (1988) 'A managerial model of the trade union', *Economic Journal*, 98, pp. 755–70.

PIORE, M. J. (1972) 'Notes for a theory of labor market stratification', Working Paper, Department of Economics, MIT.

PIORE, M. J. (1987) 'Historical perspectives and the interpretation of unemployment', *Journal of Economic Literature*, 25, pp. 1834–50.

PIORE, M. J. and SABEL, C. (1984) *The Second Industrial Divide: Possibilities for Prosperity* (New York: Basic Books).

POHL, R., and SOLEILHAVOUP, J. (1981) 'Entrées des jeunes et mobilité des moins jeunes', *Economie et Statistique*, 134, pp. 85–108.

POLITICHE DEL LAVORO (1987) Special issue on Vocational Training in the Regional Experience, *Politiche del Lavoro*, 5.

POND, C. (1983) 'Wages Councils, the unorganised and the low paid', in Bain, G. (ed.) *Industrial Relations in Britain* (Oxford: Basil Blackwell).

PRAIS, S. J. (1981) *Productivity and Industrial Structure* (Cambridge: CUP).

PRAIS, S. J., JARVIS, V. and WAGNER, K. (1991) 'Productivity and vocational skills in services in Britain and Germany: hotels', in Ryan (ed.).

RAFFE, D. (1984) 'Youth unemployment and the MSC', in McCrone, D. (ed.) *Scottish Government Yearbook 1984* (Edinburgh: Unit for Study of Government in Scotland).

RAFFE, D. (1987a) 'The Youth Training Scheme: an analysis of its strategy and development', *British Journal of Education and Work*, 1, pp. 1–31.

RAFFE, D. (1987b) 'Small expectations: the first year of the Youth Training Scheme', in Junankar (ed.).

RAFFE, D. (1988) 'Going with the grain: youth training in transition', in Brown, S. and Wake, R. (eds) *Education and Training: What Role for Research?* (Edinburgh: Scottish Council for Research in Education).

RAFFE, D. (1990) 'The transition from YTS to work: content, context and the external labour market', in Wallace, C. and Cross, M. (eds) *Youth in Transition: the Sociology of Youth and Youth Policy* (Lewes: Falmer).

RAGGATT, P. (1988) 'Quality control in the dual system of West Germany', *Oxford Review of Education*, 14, pp. 163–86.

RAINBIRD, H. (1988) 'Trade union perspectives on YTS: the dimension of wages and conditions of employment', *British Journal of Education and Work*, 2, pp. 29–47.

RAJAN, A. (1987) 'The Young Workers' Scheme: a Preliminary Assessment', in Junankar (ed.).

REES, A. (1986) 'An essay on youth joblessness', *Journal of Economic Literature*, 24, pp. 613–28.

REUBENS, B. G. (1981) 'Lessons from foreign apprenticeship systems', in Briggs, V. and Foltman, F. (eds), *Apprenticeship Research: Emerging Findings and Future Trends* (Ithaca, N.Y.: New York State School of Industrial and Labour Relations).

REUBENS, B. G. (ed.) (1983) *Youth at Work: an International Survey* (Totowa, New Jersey: Rowman & Allanheld).

REUBENS, B. G. and HARRISON, J. A. C. (1983) 'Occupational dissimilarity by age and sex', in Reubens (ed.).

REYNAERTS, W. and NAGELKERKE, A. (1986) *Arbeidsverhoudingen, Theorie en Praktijk*, Deel 1, 2nd druk (Leiden/Antwerp: Stenfert Kroese).

RICE, P. (1986) 'Juvenile unemployment, relative wages and social security in Great Britain', *Economic Journal*, 96, pp. 352–74.

ROBERTS, K., DENCH, S. and RICHARDSON, D. (1987) *The Changing Structure of Youth Labour Markets*, Research Paper 59 (London: Department of Employment).

ROBINSON, D., (ed.) (1970) *Local Labour Markets and Wage Structures* (London: Gower).

ROSE, R. (1991) 'Prospective evaluation through comparative analysis: youth training in a time-space perspective', in Ryan (ed.).

ROSENBERG, S. (1989a) 'Labour market restructuring in Europe and the US: the search for flexibility', in Rosenberg, S. (ed.).

ROSENBERG, S. (1989b) 'From segmentation to flexibility', *Labour and Society*, 14, pp. 363–407.

ROSENBERG, S. (ed.) (1989c) *The State and the Labour Market* (New York: Plenum).

ROTTENBERG, S. (1961) 'The irrelevance of union apprentice/journeyman ratios', *Journal of Business*, 34, pp. 384–6.

ROWTHORN, R. (1989) 'Corporatism and labour market performance', Discussion Paper 93 (Helsinki: Labour Institute for Economic Research).

RUBERY, J. (ed.) (1988) *Women and Recession* (London: Routledge).

RUBERY, J. (1989) 'Labour market flexibility in Britain', in Green, F. (ed.) *The Restructuring of the UK Economy* (Hemel Hempstead: Harvester Wheatsheaf).

RUBERY, J., TARLING, R. and WILKINSON, F. (1987) 'Flexibility, marketing and the organisation of production', *Labour and Society*, 12, pp. 131–51.

RUSSELL, R. and PARKES, D. (1984) *Career Development Education in the Federal Republic of Germany*, Studies in Vocational Eucation and Training in the FRG, number 10.

RYAN, P. (1977) 'Job Training', unpublished Ph.D. thesis, Harvard University.

RYAN, P. (1981) 'Segmentation, duality and the internal labour market', in

Wilkinson, F. (ed.) *The Dynamics of Labour Market Segmentation* (London: Academic Press).

RYAN, P. (1983) 'Youth labour, trade unionism and state policy in contemporary Britain', paper presented to Fifth conference of the International Working Party on Labour Market Segmentation, Aix-en-Provence, July.

RYAN, P. (1984a) 'Job training, employment practices and the large enterprise: the case of costly transferable skills', in Osterman (ed.).

RYAN, P. (1984b) 'The New Training Initiative after two years', *Lloyds Bank Review*, 152, pp. 31–45.

RYAN, P. (1984c) 'Do trade unions raise the pay of young workers?', paper presented to Conference on the Young Persons' Labour Market, Institute for Employment Research, University of Warwick.

RYAN, P. (1986) 'Apprentices, employment and industrial disputes in engineering in the 1920s', paper presented to Workshop on Child Labour and Apprenticeship, University of Essex, May.

RYAN, P. (1987a) 'Trade unionism and the pay of young workers', in Junankar (ed.).

RYAN, P. (1987b) 'New technology and human resources', in Elaisson, G. and Ryan, P., 'The human factor in economic and technological change', Educational Monograph no. 3 (Paris: OECD).

RYAN, P. (1988) 'The prospects for higher education in the information age', Information Society Studies Working Paper Series, Institute for Research on Public Policy, Toronto.

RYAN, P. (1989) 'Youth interventions, job substitution and trade union policy in Great Britain, 1976–86', in Rosenberg, S. (ed.).

RYAN, P. (1990) 'Job training, individual opportunity and low pay' in Bowen, A. and Mayhew, K. (eds), *Improving Incentives for the Low Paid* (London: Macmillan).

RYAN, P. (ed.) (1991a) *International Comparisons of Vocational Education and Training for Intermediate Skills* (Lewes: Falmer).

RYAN, P. (1991b) 'Patterns of response to YTS in the British trade union movement, 1983–8', mimeo, University of Cambridge.

SAF (1984) 'Ungdomsplatser – en positiv nödlösning' (Malmö: SAF).

SAUNDERS, C. and MARSDEN, D. W. (1981) *Pay Inequalities in the European Communities* (London: Butterworths).

SB (1988) Statistisches Bundesamt, *Tariflöhne Oktober 1987 und Tarifgehälter Oktober 1987* (Wiesbaden: Kohlhammer).

SCHOBER, K. (1983) 'Youth employment in West Germany', in Reubens (ed.).

SCHOBER, K. (1984) 'The Educational System, Vocational Training and Youth Unemployment in West Germany', *Compare*, 14, no. 2, pp. 129–44.

SCHOBER, K. (1986a) 'Aktuelle trends auf dem teilarbeitsmarkt für jugendliche', *Mitteilungen aus der Arbeitsmarkt- und Berufsforschung*, 19, no. 3, pp. 365–70.

SCHOBER, K. (1986b) 'Die Massnahmen der Bundesanstalt für Arbeit im Spannungsfeld zwischen Bildungssystem und Arbeitsmarkt', *Recht der Jugend und des Bildungswesens*, no. 1, pp. 2–24.

SCHOBER, K. (1988) 'Ausbildungs- und Beschäftigungssituation Jugendlicher', in Breuer, K. H. (ed.) *Jarhbuch für Jugendsozialarbeit* (Köln: Die Heimstatt).
SCHOBER-BRINKMANN, K. (1986) 'The crisis of youth employment and training in West Germany: public intervention and the response of employers and trade unions', *Economia et Lavoro*, 4, pp. 117–27.
SELLIN, B. (1983) 'The development of alternance training for young people in the European Community', *Vocational Training*, 12, pp. 73–83.
SENKER, P. (1986) 'The Technical and Vocational Education Initiative and economic performance in the UK: an initial assessment', *Journal of Education Policy*, 1, pp. 293–303.
SHAPIRO, C. and STIGLITZ, J. E. (1984) 'Equilibrium unemployment as a worker discipline device', *American Economic Review*, 74, pp. 433–44.
SIEBERT, W. S. (1985) 'Wage fixing loses 230,000 youth jobs', *Economic Affairs*, 3, pp. 14–18.
SIEBERT, W. S. (1989) 'Workplace safety in Britain and the USA: the role of market forces in deterring accidents', mimeo, Department of Industrial Economics, University of Birmingham.
SIFO (1983), *Företagens erfarenheter av ungdomsplatser 1982* (Stockholm: SAF).
SLICHTER, S. (1941) *Union Policies and Industrial Management* (Washington, D.C.: Brookings Institution).
SOU (1986) Statens Offentliga Utredningar 1986:2, *En treårig yrkesutbildning* (Stockholm: SOU).
SPILSBURY, M., HOSKINS, M., ASHTON, D. N. and MAGUIRE, M. J. (1987) 'A note on the trade union membership of young adults', *British Journal of Industrial Relations*, 25, pp. 267–74.
ST JOHN-BROOKS, C. (1985) *Who Controls Training? The Rise of the Manpower Services Commission*, Fabian Tract 506 (London: Fabian Society).
STANDING, G. (1988) *Unemployment and Labour Market Flexibility: Sweden* (Geneva: ILO).
STAROBIN, P. (1989) 'GOP members pressuring Bush to deal on minimum wage', *Congressional Quarterly*, 23 September, p. 2453.
STATERA, G. (1978) *Emarginazione e Sovversione Sociale* (Rome: Il Politecnico).
STEEDMAN, H. and WAGNER, K. (1989) 'Productivity, machinery and skills: clothing manufacture in Britain and Germany', *National Institute Economic Review*, 128, pp. 40–57.
STEGMANN, H. and KRAFT, H. (1987) 'Ausbildungs- und Berufswege von 23–24-jährigen. Methode und ausgewählte Ergebnisse der Wiederholungserhebung Ende 1985', *Mitteilungen aus der Arbeitsmarkt- und Berufsforschung*, 20, no. 2, pp. 142–63.
STEGMANN, H. and KRAFT, H. (1988) 'Erwerbslosigkeit in den ersten Berufsjahren', *Mitteilungen aus der Arbeitsmarkt- und Berufsforschung*, 21, no. 1, pp. 1–15.
STERN, J. (1983) 'The relationship between unemployment, morbidity and mortality in Britain', *Population Studies*, 37, pp. 61–74.

STRAUSS, G. (1984) 'Industrial relations: time of change', *Industrial Relations*, 23, pp. 1–15.

STREECK, W. (1989) 'Skills and the limits of neoliberalism: the enterprise of the future as a place of learning', *Work, Employment and Society*, 3, pp. 89–104.

STREECK, W., HILBERT, J., VAN KEVELAER, K-H., MAIER, F. and WEBER, H. (1987) *The Role of the Social Partners in Vocational Training and Further Training in the Federal Republic of Germany* (Berlin: CEDE-FOP); a translation of *Steuerung und Regulierung der beruflichen Bildung. Die Rolle der Sozialpartner in der Ausbildung und beruflichen Weiterbildung in der Bundesrepublik Deutschland* (Berlin: Sigma).

STRIKKER, F. (1987) 'Staatliche Massnahmen gegen Jugendarbeitslosigkeit. Eine Analyse arbeitsmarkttheoretischer Konzepte und staatlicher Massnahmen am Beispiel eines Vergleichs von vier Bundesländern', unpublished dissertation, University of Bielefeld.

STUC (1983) *86th Annual Report* (Glasgow: Scottish Trades Union Congress).

STUDIENOTITIE (1986) *Ontwikkeling ledenaantal vakbeweging 1977–1985* ('s-Gravenhage: V.N.O.).

TARLING, R. (ed.) (1987) *Flexibility in Labour Markets* (London: Academic Press).

TAWNEY, R. H. (1909) 'The economics of boy labour', *Economic Journal*, 19, pp. 517–37.

TAYLOR, M. E. (1981) *Education and Work in the Federal Republic of Germany* (London: Anglo-German Foundation for the Study of Industrial Society).

TESSARING, M. (1988), 'Arbeitslosigkeit, Beschäftigung und Qualifikation. Ein Rück- und Ausblick', *Mitteilungen aus der Arbeitsmarkt- und Berufsforschung*, 21, no. 2, pp. 177–93.

THUROW, L. C. (1969) *Poverty and Discrimination* (Washington, D.C.: Brookings Institution).

THUROW, L. C. (1975) *Generating Inequality* (New York: Basic Books).

TUC (1978) *Report of 109th Annual Trades Union Congress* (London: TUC).

TUC (1982) *Youth Training: TUC Guide and Checklist for Union Negotiators* (London: TUC).

TUC (1983a) *Report of 114th Annual Trades Union Congress* (London: TUC).

TUC (1983b) *TUC Handbook on the MSC's Youth Training Scheme* (London: TUC).

TUC (1984) *Report of 115th Annual Trades Union Congress* (London: TUC).

TUC (1985) *Report of 116th Annual Trades Union Congress* (London: TUC).

TUC (1986) *Report of 117th Annual Trades Union Congress* (London: TUC).

TUC (1987) *Report of 118th Annual Trades Union Congress* (London: TUC).

TUC (1988) *Report of 119th Annual Trades Union Congress* (London: TUC).

TUC (1989a) *Report of 120th Annual Trades Union Congress* (London: TUC).

TUC (1989b) *Report of the General Council, 1989* (London: TUC).

US DOL (1964) Department of Labour, *Formal Occupational Training of Adult Workers* (Washington, D.C.: US GPO).

US DOL (1988) Department of Labour, *Apprenticeship 2000* (Washington, D.C.: Government Printing Office).

294   *Bibliography*

US DOL (1989) Department of Labour, *Investing in People* (Washington, D.C.: GPO).

US GAO (1985) General Accounting Office, *Job Training Partnership Act: Initial Implementation of Program for Disadvantaged Youth and Adults* GAO/HRD-85-4 (Washington, D.C.: GPO).

US GAO (1986) General Accounting Office, *Job Corps: Its Costs, Employment Outcomes, and Service to the Public* GAO/HRD-86-121BR (Washington, D.C.: GPO).

US GAO (1987a) General Accounting Office, *Dislocated Workers: Exemplary Local Projects Under the Job Training Partnership Act* GAO/HRD-87-70BR (Washington, D.C.: GPO).

US GAO (1987b) General Accounting Office, *Dislocated Workers: Local Programs and Outcomes Under the Job Training Partnership Act* GAO/HRD-87-41 (Washington, D.C.: GPO).

US NCEE (1983) National Commission on Excellence in Education, *A Nation at Risk* (Washington: GPO).

US PRESIDENT (various years) *Employment (or Manpower) and Training Report of the President* (Washington, D.C.: US GPO).

VAN DE VALL, M. (1967) *De Vakbeweging in de Welvaartsstaat*, 2nd druk (Meppel: Boom).

VAN DIJK, C., AKKERMANS, T. AND HÖVELS, B. (1988) *Social Partners and Vocational Education in the Netherlands* (Berlin: European Centre for the Development of Vocational Training).

VAN HAM, J.C., PAAUWE, J. and WILLIAMS, A.R.T. (1985) 'De vakbeweging in Nederland; van leden naar klanten. Een bijdrage tot discussie', in *Economisch-Statistische Berichten*, 70, pp. 468–73.

VAN RINTEL, P.J.L. (1986) 'The fight against youth unemployment in the Netherlands (plans and impact)', *Social Europe*, Supplement on Youth Pay and Employers' Recruitment Practices for Young People in the Community (Luxembourg: EEC).

VAN VOORDEN, W. (1984) 'Employers Associations in the Netherlands', in Windmuller, J.P. and Gladstone, A. (eds) *Employers Associations and Industrial Relations* (Oxford: Clarendon Press).

VISSER, D. (1984) 'De industriebond FNV vernieuwt om te overleven', *NRC-Handelsblad*, 31 October.

VISSER, J. (1984) 'Union growth and the present employment crisis in Western Europe', paper presented at the EGOS Colloquium, Amersfoort, October.

VISSER, J. (1985) 'Vakbondsgroei en vakbondsmacht in West-Europa', in *Tijdschrift voor Arbeidsvraagstukken*, 1, pp. 18–38.

WADENSJÖ, E. (1987a) 'Labour market policy and employment growth in Sweden', *Labour*, 1, no. 3, pp. 3–23.

WADENSJÖ, E. (1987b) 'The youth labor market in Sweden: changes in the 1980s', *Economia et Lavoro*, 21, no. 1, pp. 97–104.

WALSH, J. and BROWN, W. (1990) 'Regional earnings and pay flexibility', paper presented to NEDO Policy Seminar on Regional Issues, Newcastle, March.

WATTS, A.G., JAMIESON, I. and MILLER, A. (1989) 'School-based work experience: some international comparisons', *British Journal of Education and Work*, 3, pp. 33–48.

WEBB, S. and WEBB, B. (1920) *Industrial Democracy* (London: Longmans).

WELCH, F. (1979) 'Effects of cohort size on earnings: the baby boom babies' financial bust', *Journal of Political Economy*, 87, pp. S65–97.

WELLS, W. (1983) *The Relative Pay and Employment of Young People*, Research paper 42, Department of Employment (London: HMSO).

WELLS, W. (1987) 'The relative pay and employment of young people', in Junankar (ed.).

WELLS, W. (1989) 'The labour market for young and older workers', *Employment Gazette*, 97, pp. 319–31.

WEST, A. (1989) 'Beauty and the beast', *Youth and Policy*, 27, pp. 36–9.

WHITE, M. (1989) 'Motivating education and training,' *Policy Studies*, 10, pp. 29–40.

WHITE, M. and McRAE S. (1989) *Young Adults and Long-Term Unemployment* (London: Policy Studies Institute).

WHITFIELD, K. and WILSON, R. A. (1988) 'Staying on in full time education: a time-series analysis', paper presented to EMRU Study Group, Institute for Employment Research, University of Warwick.

WIAL, H. J. (1988) 'The transition from secondary to primary employment: jobs and workers in ethnic neighbourhood labour markets', unpublished doctoral dissertation, MIT, Cambridge Mass.

WILENSKY, H. L. (1981) 'Democratic corporatism, consensus, and social policy. Reflections on changing values and the "crisis" of the welfare state', in OECD, *The Welfare State in Crisis* (Paris: OECD).

WINDMULLER, J. P. (1969) *Labor Relations in the Netherlands* (Ithaca: Cornell).

WORSWICK, G. D. N. (ed.) (1985) *Education and Economic Performance* (Aldershot: Gower).

WRAY J. V. C. (1959) 'Trade unions and young workers in Great Britain', *International Labour Review*, 75, pp. 304–18.

YGNACE, N. G. (1987) 'Economic and political determinants of trade union growth in selected OECD countries', *Journal of Industrial Relations*, 29, pp. 233–42.

YOUTH AND POLICY (1990) 'Young, gifted and broke', *Youth and Policy*, 29, pp. 47–8.

ZIMMERMANN, E. (1984) *Industriepolitik und Kollektive Arbeitsbeziehungen in den Niederlanden* (Konstanz: Universität Konstanz).

Index